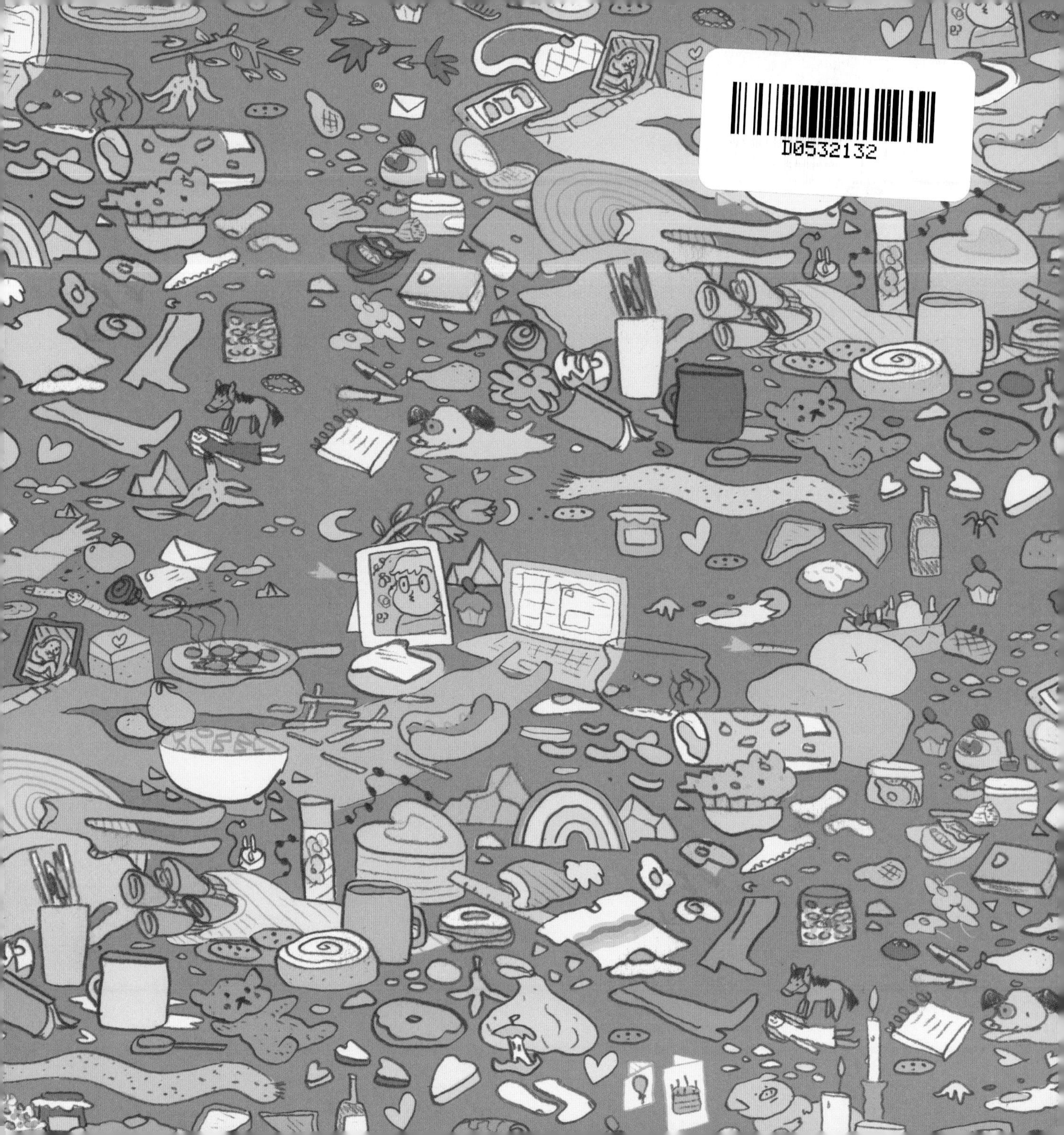

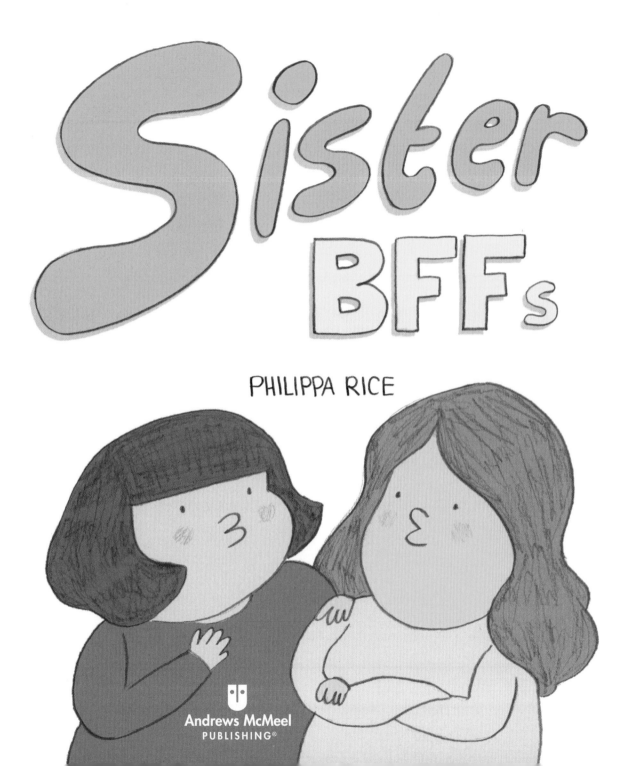

Sister
BFFs

PHILIPPA RICE

Andrews McMeel
PUBLISHING®

Also by Philippa Rice

Soppy
Our Soppy Love Story Journal

Dedicated to my older, kinder, prettier sister, Kate, who didn't have to suffer the indignity of appearing in this book.

NOT dedicated to my younger sister, Holly,

who appears on nearly every page.

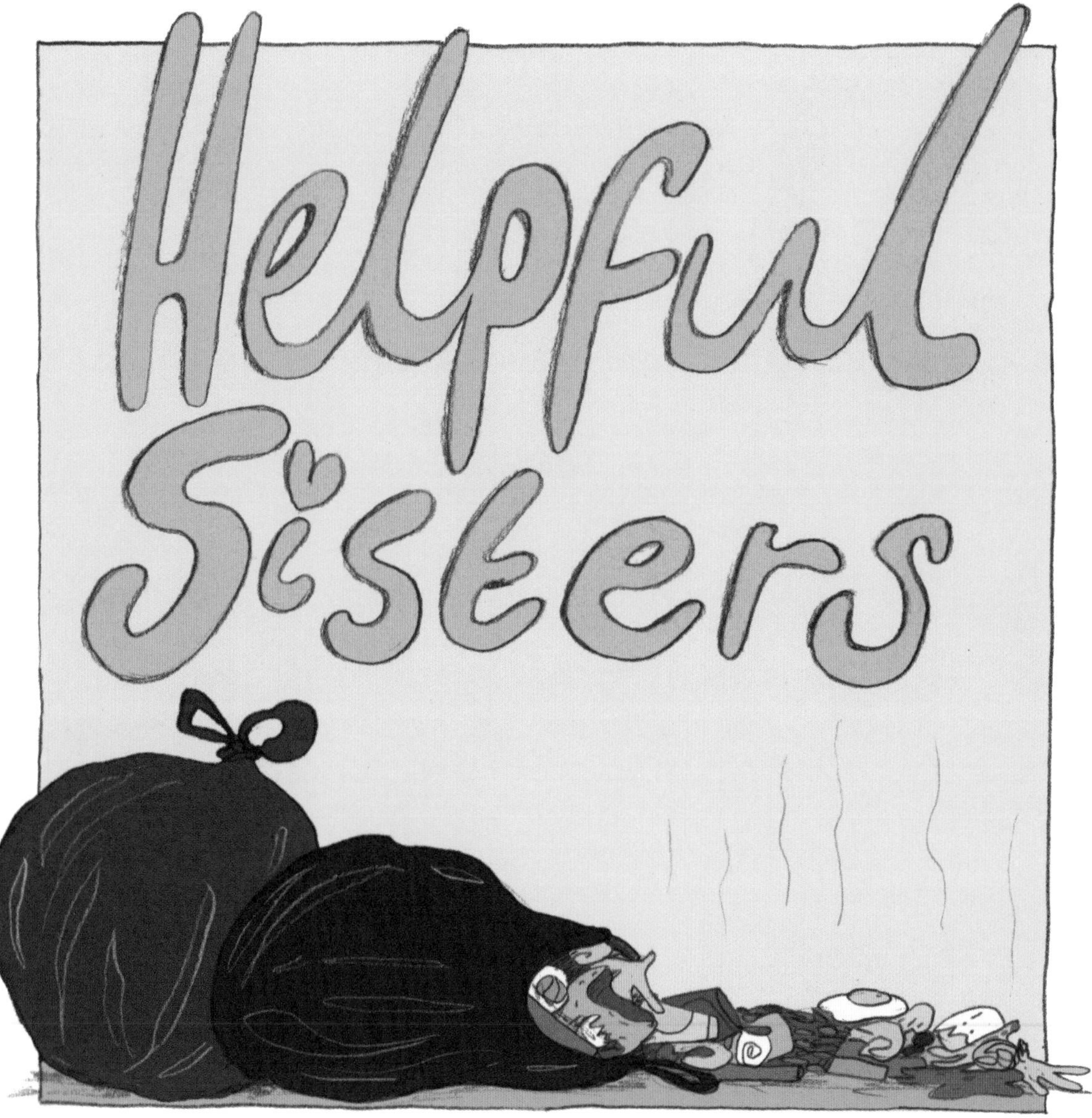
Helpful
Sisters

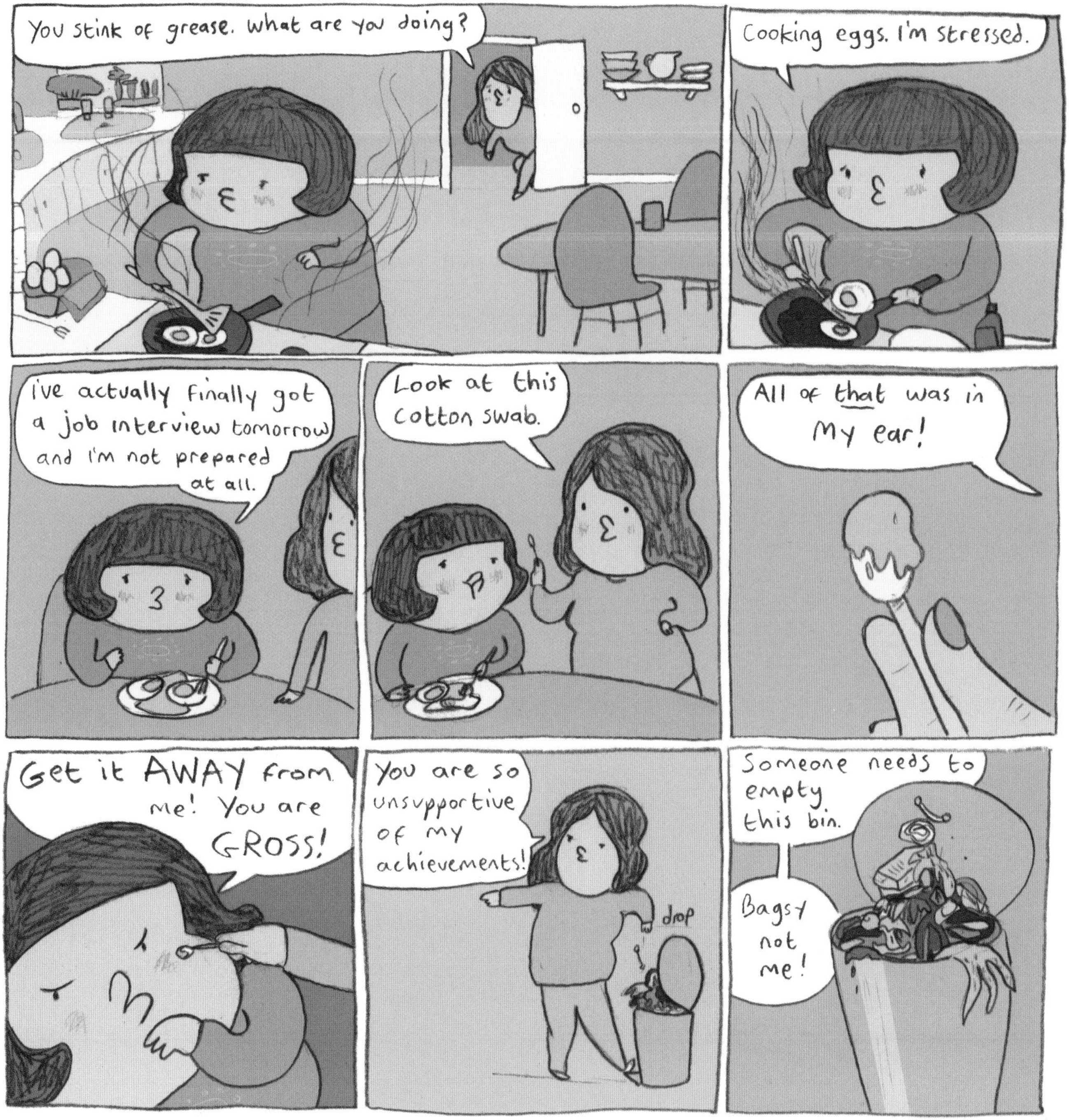
You stink of grease. What are you doing?
Cooking eggs. I'm stressed.
I've actually finally got a job interview tomorrow and I'm not prepared at all.
Look at this cotton swab.
All of that was in my ear!
Get it AWAY from me! You are GROSS!
You are so unsupportive of my achievements!
drop
Someone needs to empty this bin.
Bagsy not me!

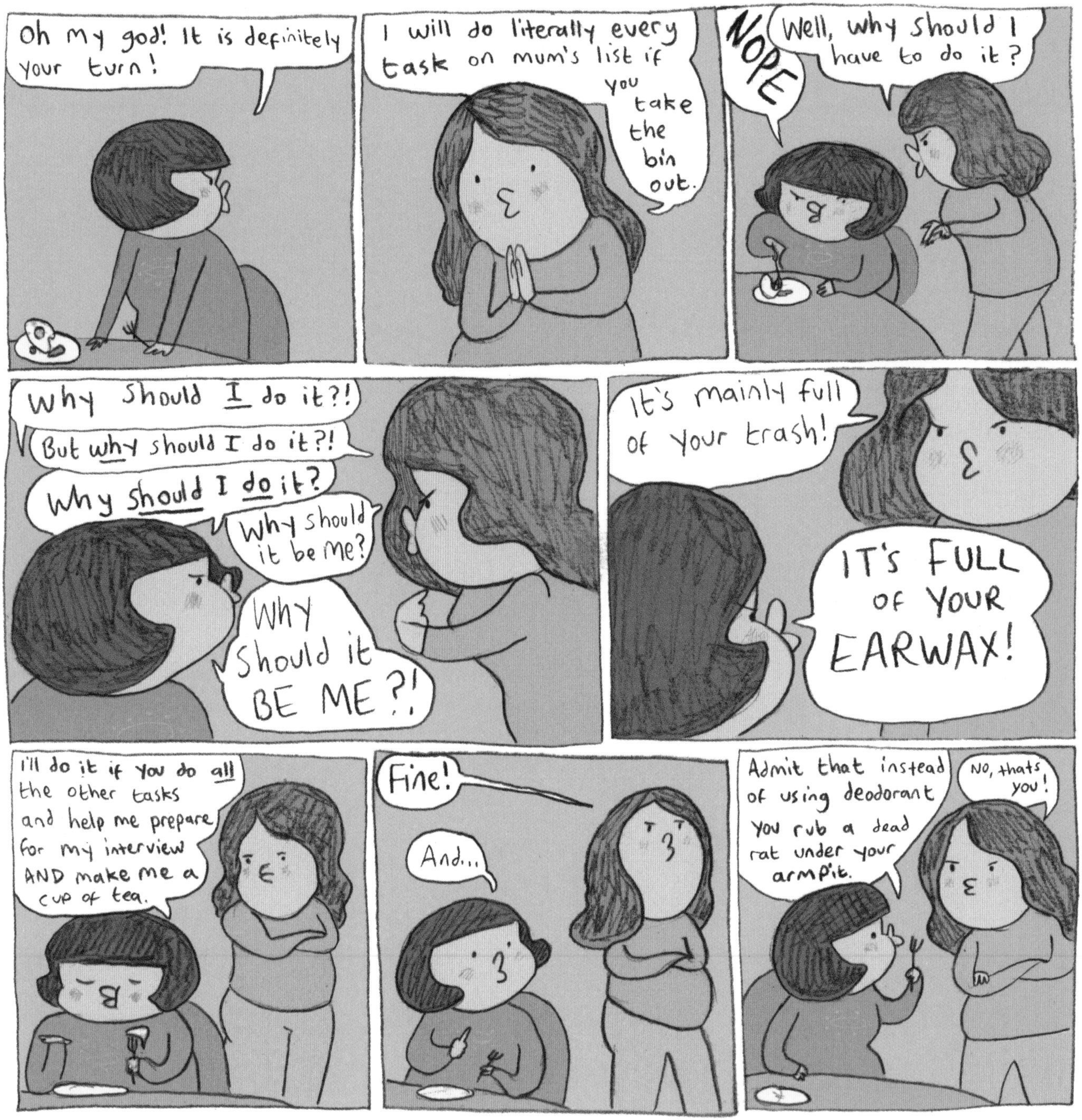
Oh my god! It is definitely your turn!
I will do literally every task on mum's list if you take the bin out.
NOPE
Well, why should I have to do it?
Why should I do it?!
But why should I do it?!
Why should I do it?
Why should it be me?
Why should it BE ME?!
It's mainly full of your trash!
IT'S FULL OF YOUR EARWAX!
I'll do it if you do all the other tasks and help me prepare for my interview AND make me a cup of tea.
Fine!
And...
Admit that instead of using deodorant you rub a dead rat under your armpit.
No, thats you!

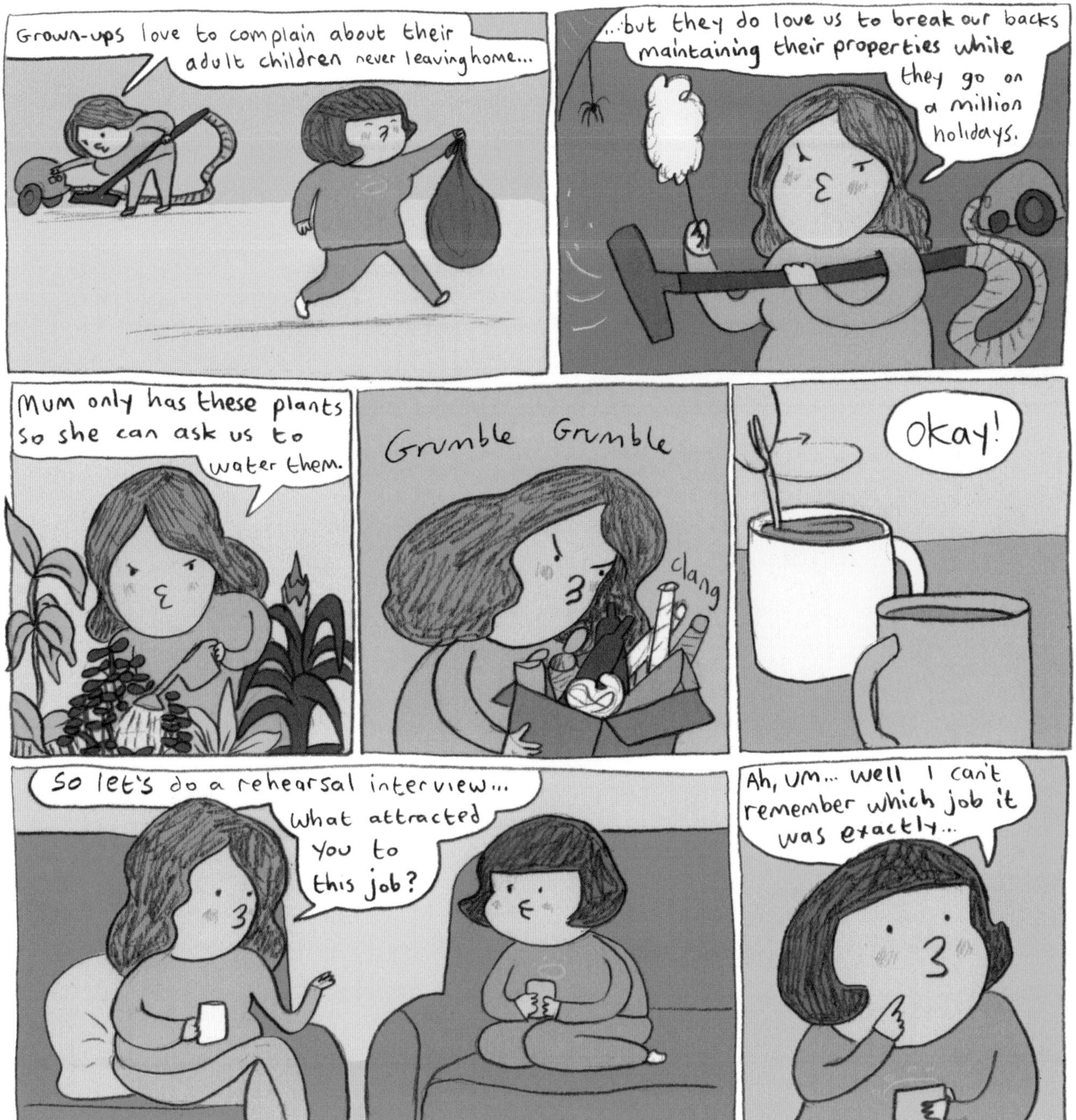
Grown-ups love to complain about their adult children never leaving home...
...but they do love us to break our backs maintaining their properties while they go on a million holidays.
Mum only has these plants so she can ask us to water them.
Grumble Grumble
clang
Okay!
So let's do a rehearsal interview... What attracted you to this job?
Ah, um... well I can't remember which job it was exactly...

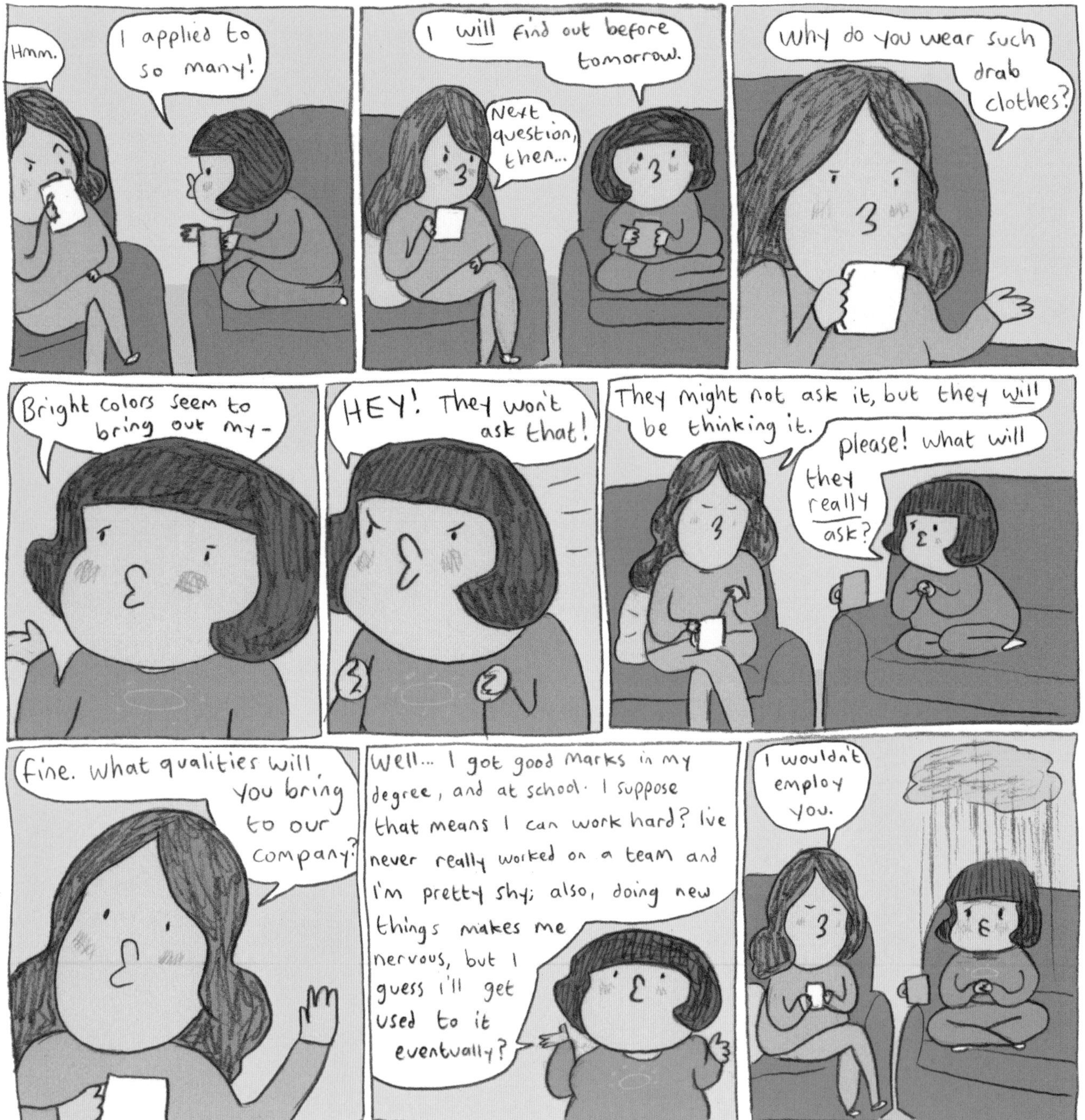
Hmm.
I applied to so many!
I will find out before tomorrow.
Next question, then...
Why do you wear such drab clothes?
Bright colors seem to bring out my-
HEY! They won't ask that!
They might not ask it, but they will be thinking it.
please! what will they really ask?
fine. what qualities will you bring to our company?
Well... I got good marks in my degree, and at school. I suppose that means I can work hard? I've never really worked on a team and I'm pretty shy; also, doing new things makes me nervous, but I guess I'll get used to it eventually?
I wouldn't employ you.

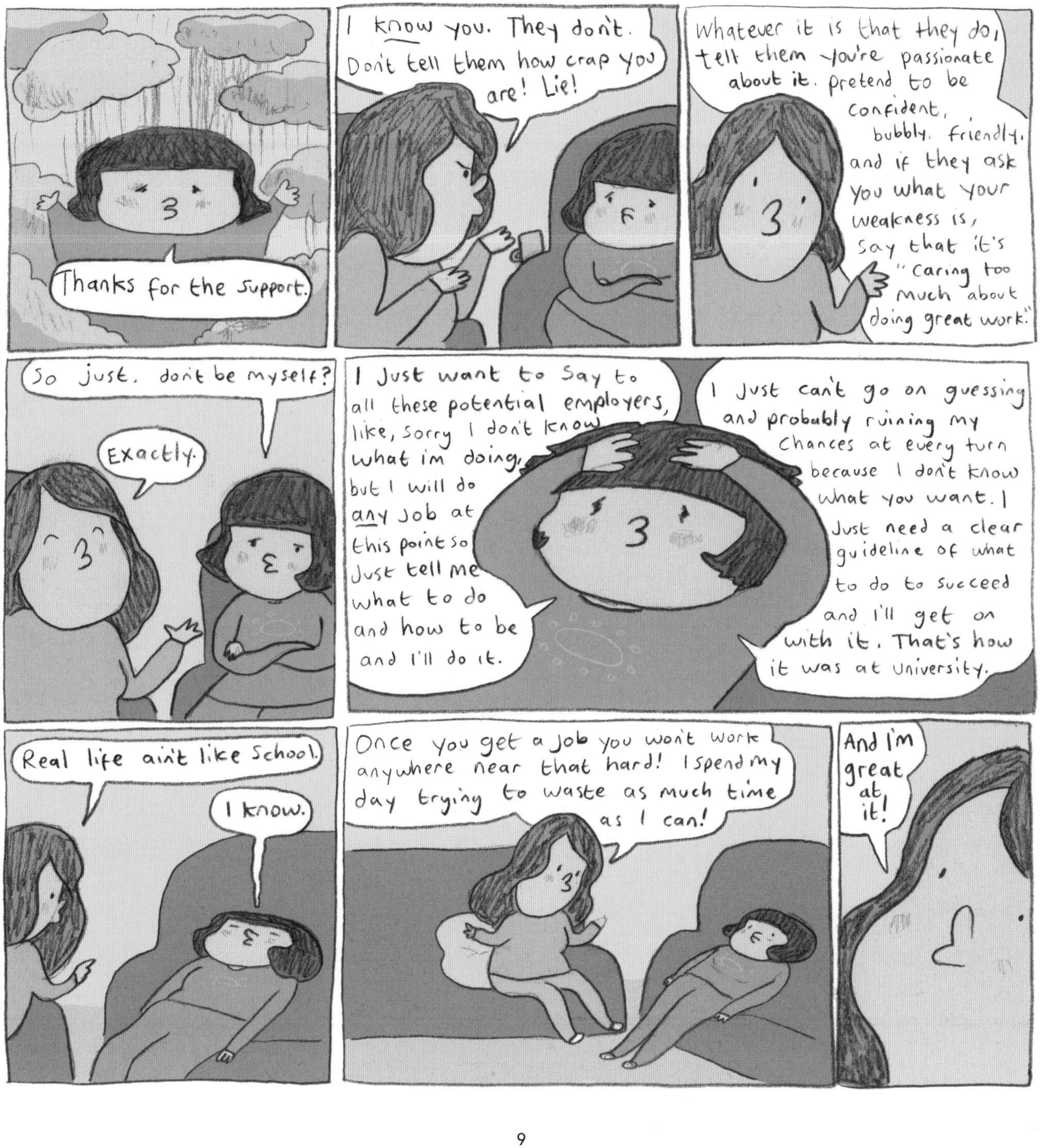
Thanks for the support.
I know you. They don't. Don't tell them how crap you are! Lie!
Whatever it is that they do, tell them you're passionate about it. pretend to be confident, bubbly, friendly, and if they ask you what your weakness is, say that it's "caring too much about doing great work."
So just, don't be myself?
Exactly.
I just want to say to all these potential employers, like, sorry I don't know what im doing, but I will do any job at this point so just tell me what to do and how to be and I'll do it.
I just can't go on guessing and probably ruining my chances at every turn because I don't know what you want. I just need a clear guideline of what to do to succeed and I'll get on with it. That's how it was at university.
Real life ain't like school.
I know.
Once you get a job you won't work anywhere near that hard! I spend my day trying to waste as much time as I can!
And I'm great at it!

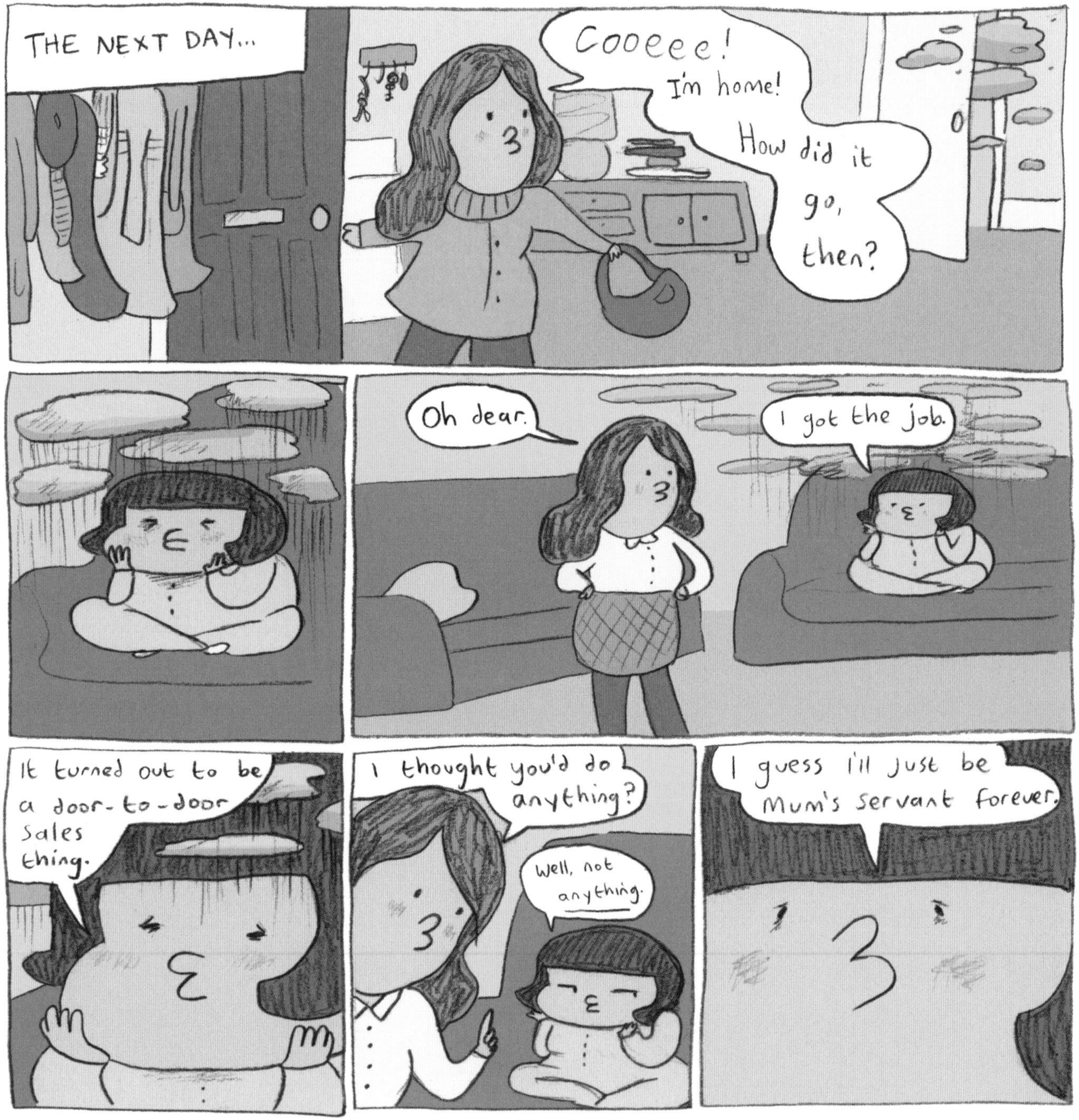
THE NEXT DAY...
Cooeee!
I'm home!
How did it go, then?
Oh dear.
I got the job.
It turned out to be a door-to-door sales thing.
I thought you'd do anything?
Well, not anything.
I guess I'll just be Mum's servant forever.

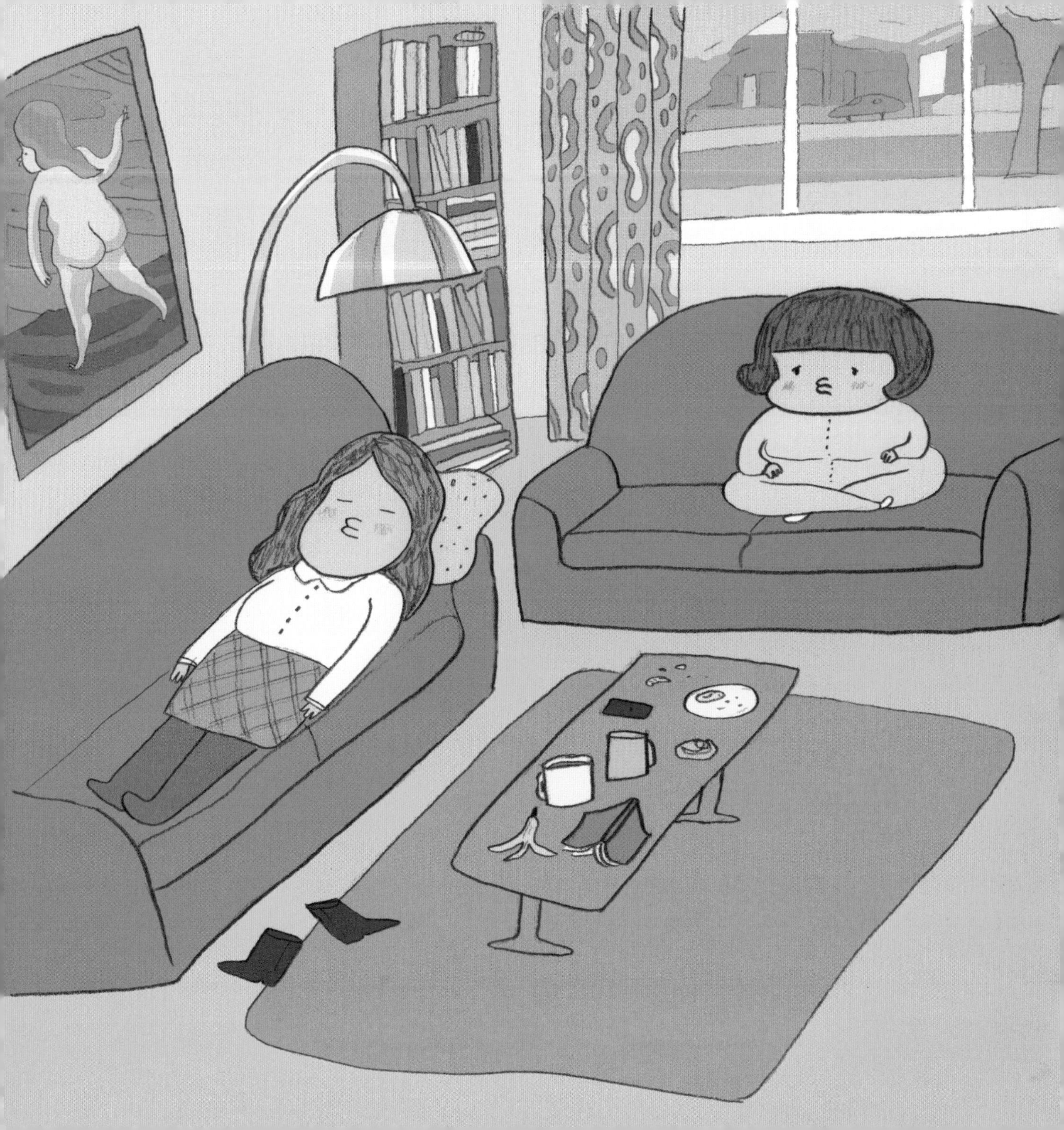

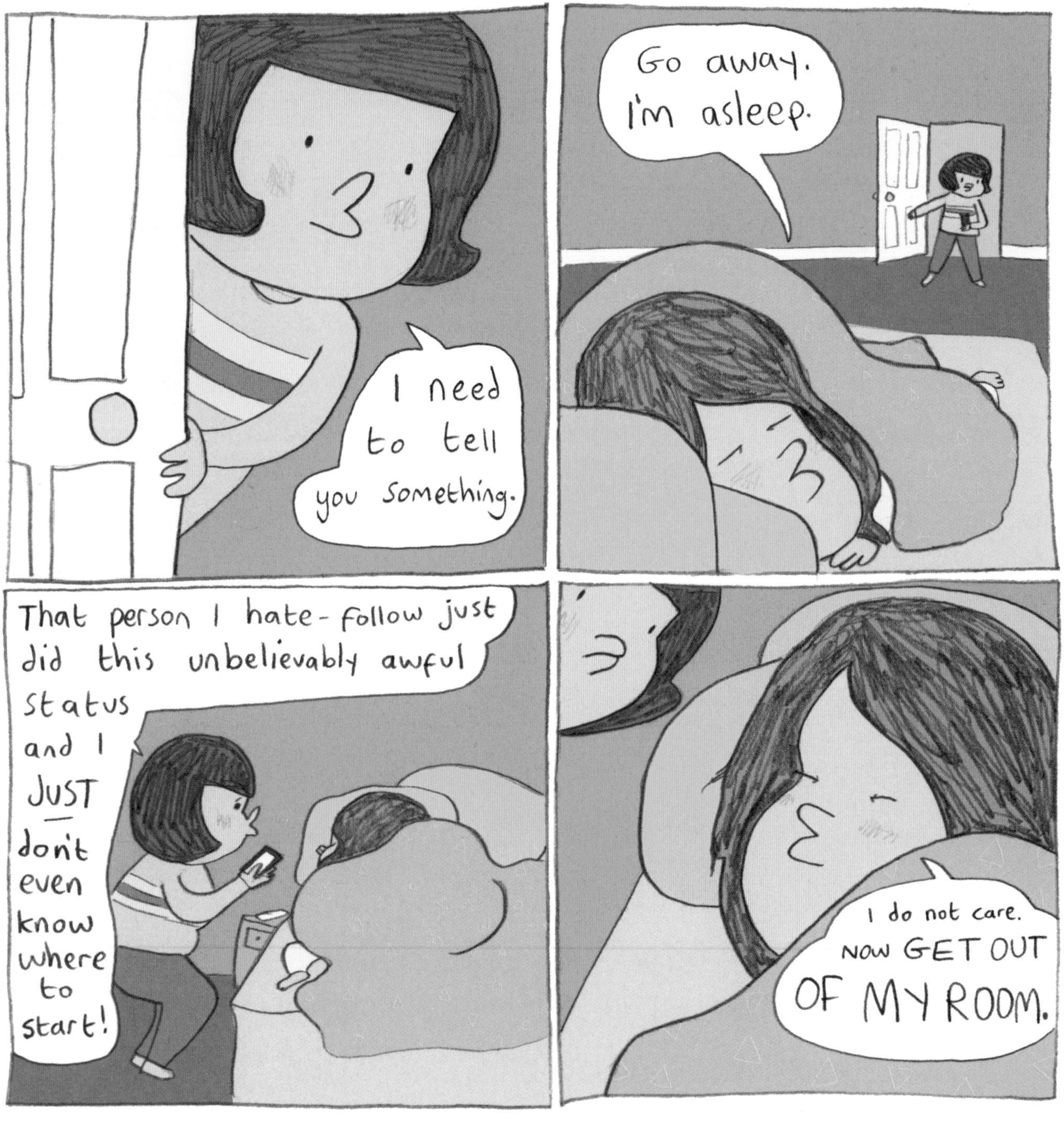
I need to tell you something.
Go away. I'm asleep.
That person I hate-follow just did this unbelievably awful status and I JUST — don't even know where to start!
I do not care. Now GET OUT OF MY ROOM.

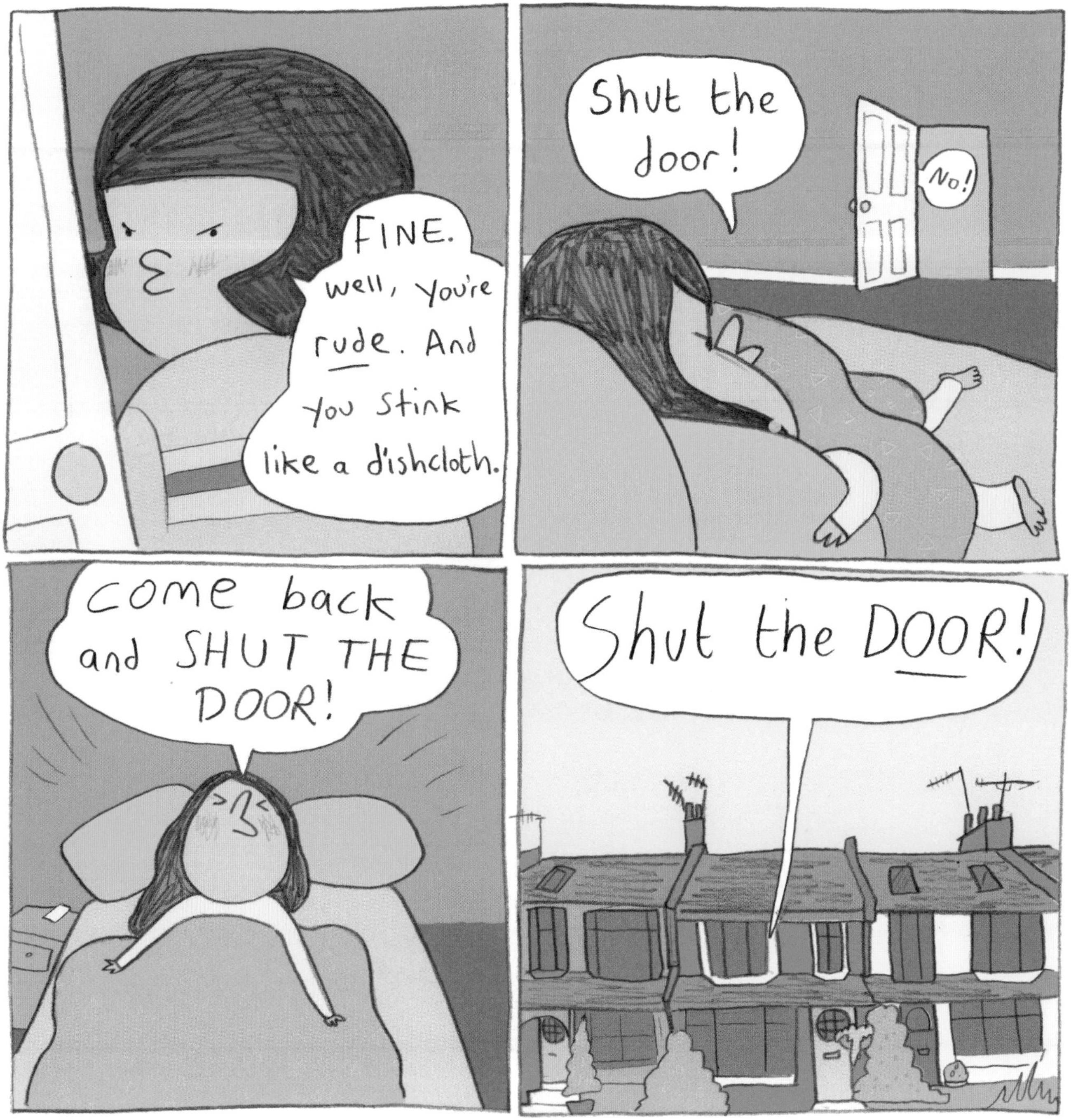
FINE.
Well, you're rude. And you stink like a dishcloth.
Shut the door!
No!
Come back and SHUT THE DOOR!
Shut the DOOR!

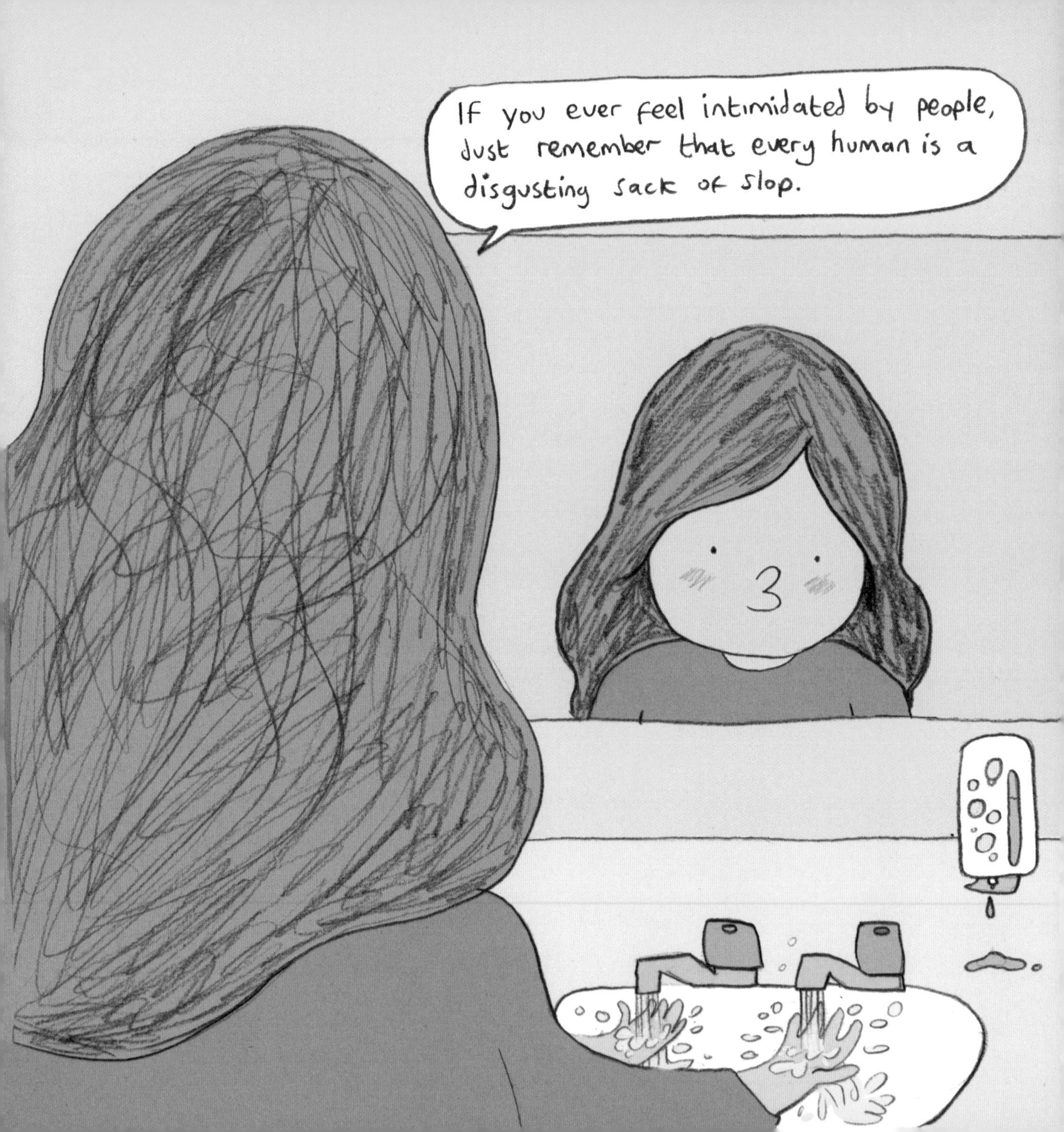
If you ever feel intimidated by people, just remember that every human is a disgusting sack of slop.

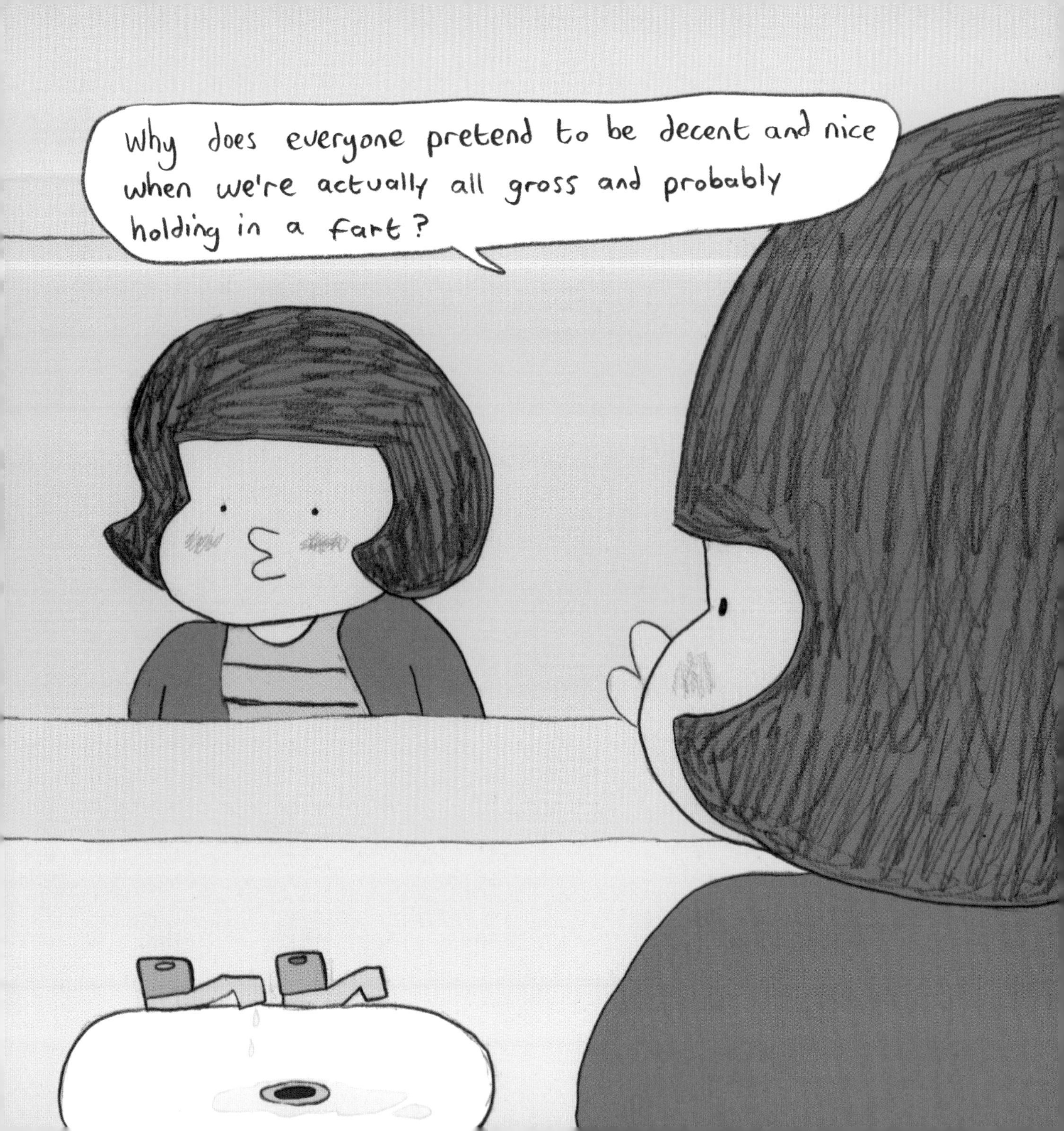
Why does everyone pretend to be decent and nice when we're actually all gross and probably holding in a fart?

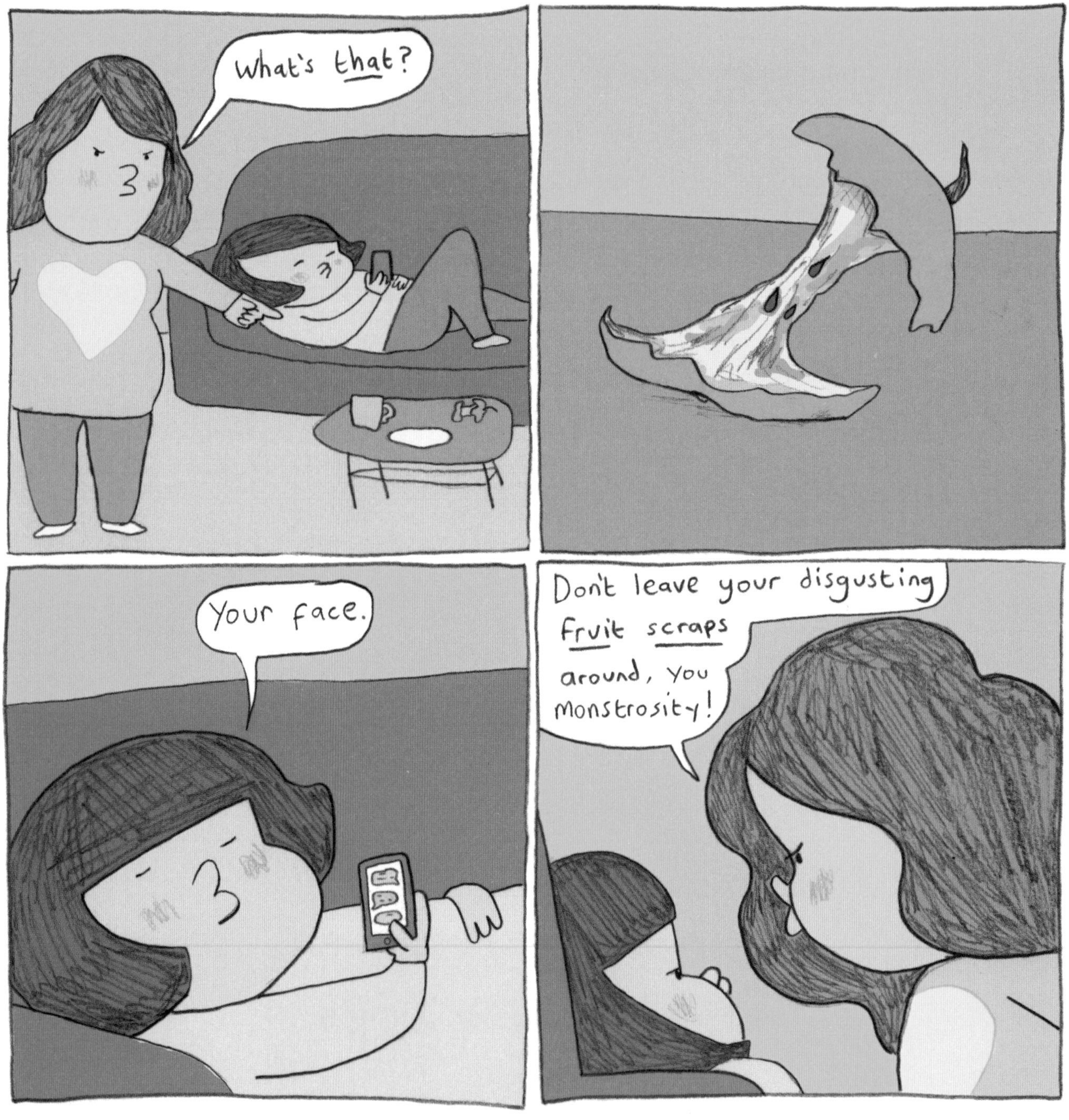
What's that?
Your face.
Don't leave your disgusting fruit scraps around, you monstrosity!

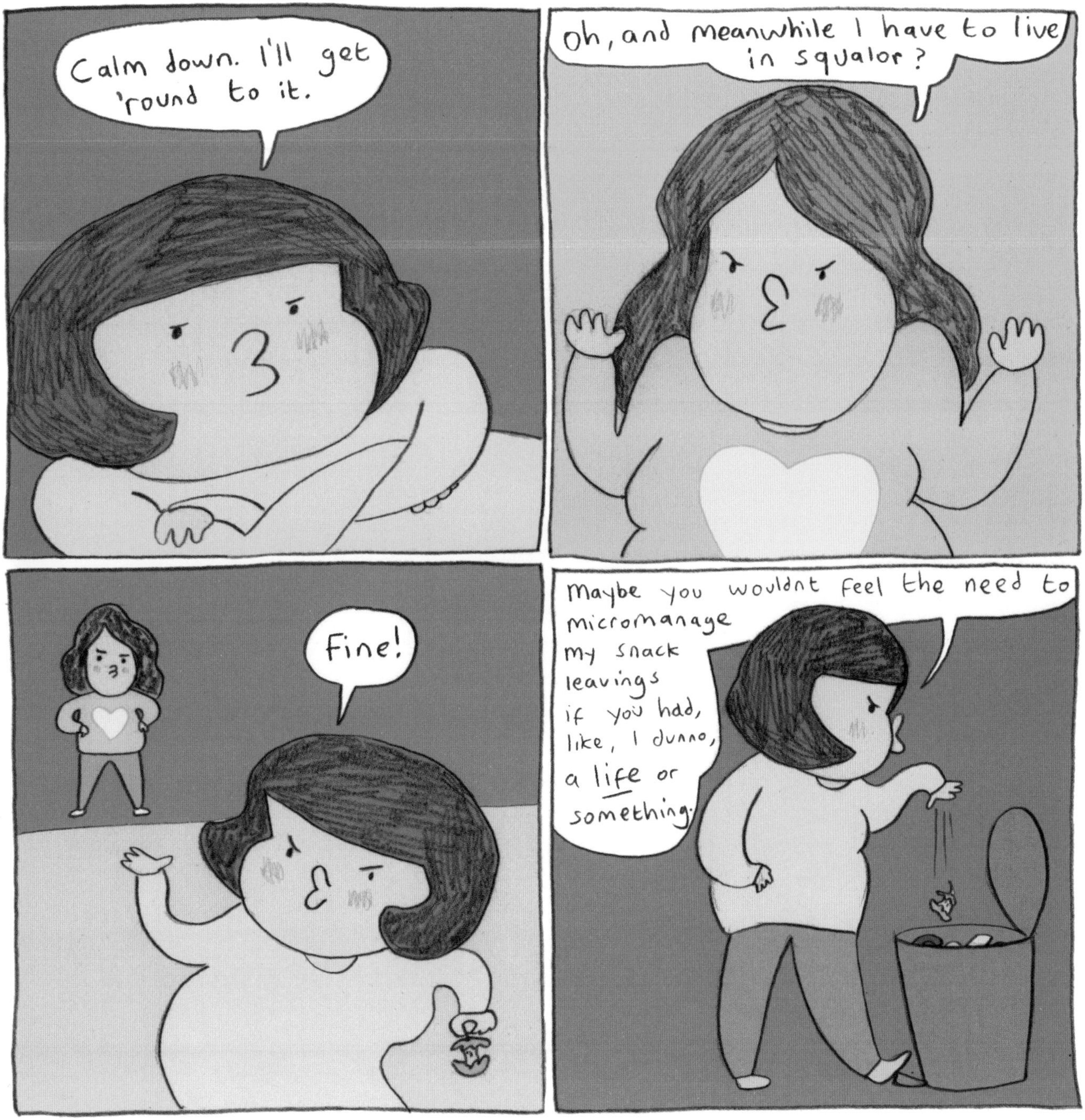
Calm down. I'll get 'round to it.
Oh, and meanwhile I have to live in squalor?
Fine!
Maybe you wouldnt feel the need to micromanage my snack leavings if you had, like, I dunno, a life or something.

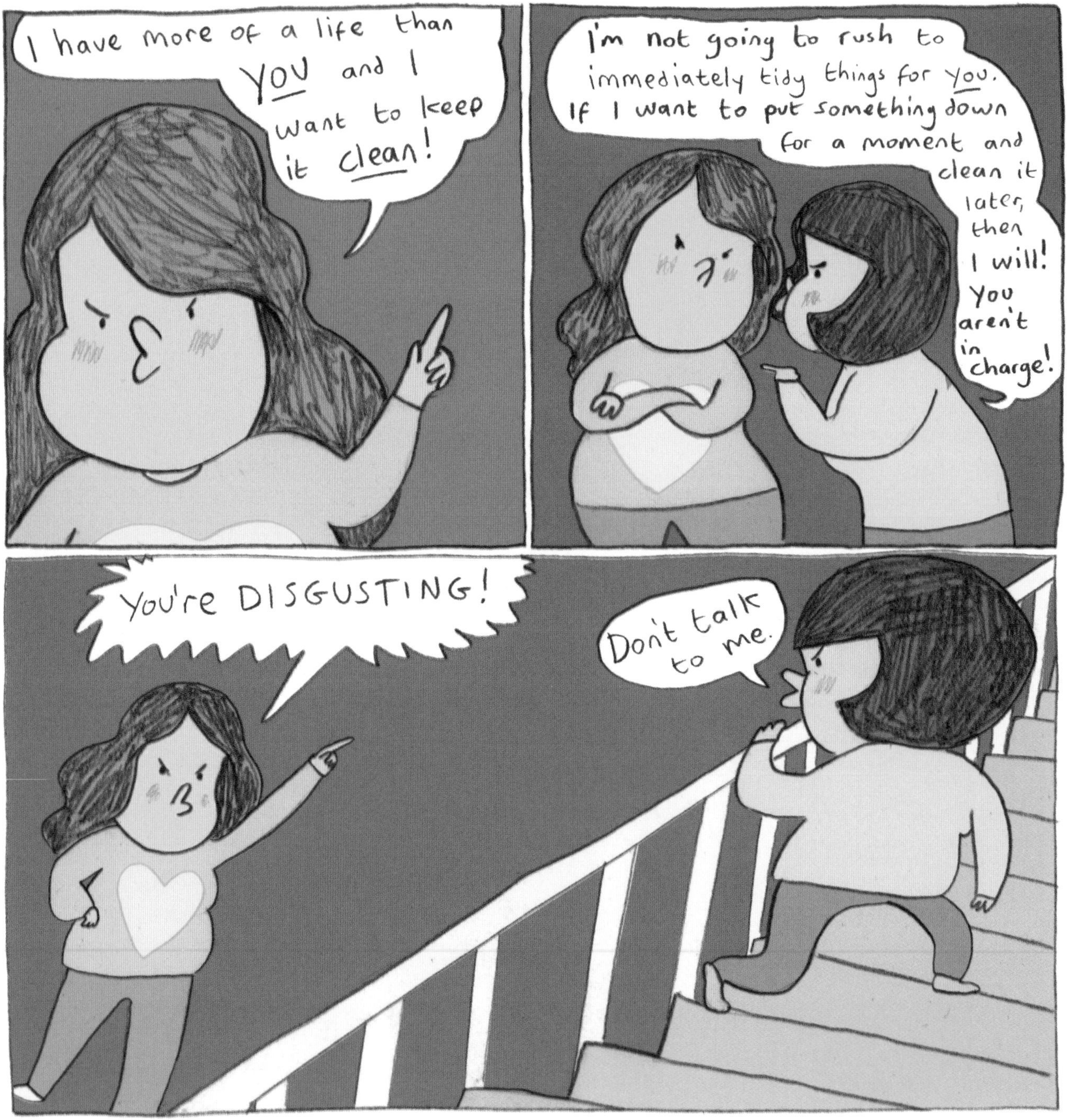
I have more of a life than YOU and I want to keep it clean!
I'm not going to rush to immediately tidy things for you. If I want to put something down for a moment and clean it later, then I will! You aren't in charge!
You're DISGUSTING!
Don't talk to me.

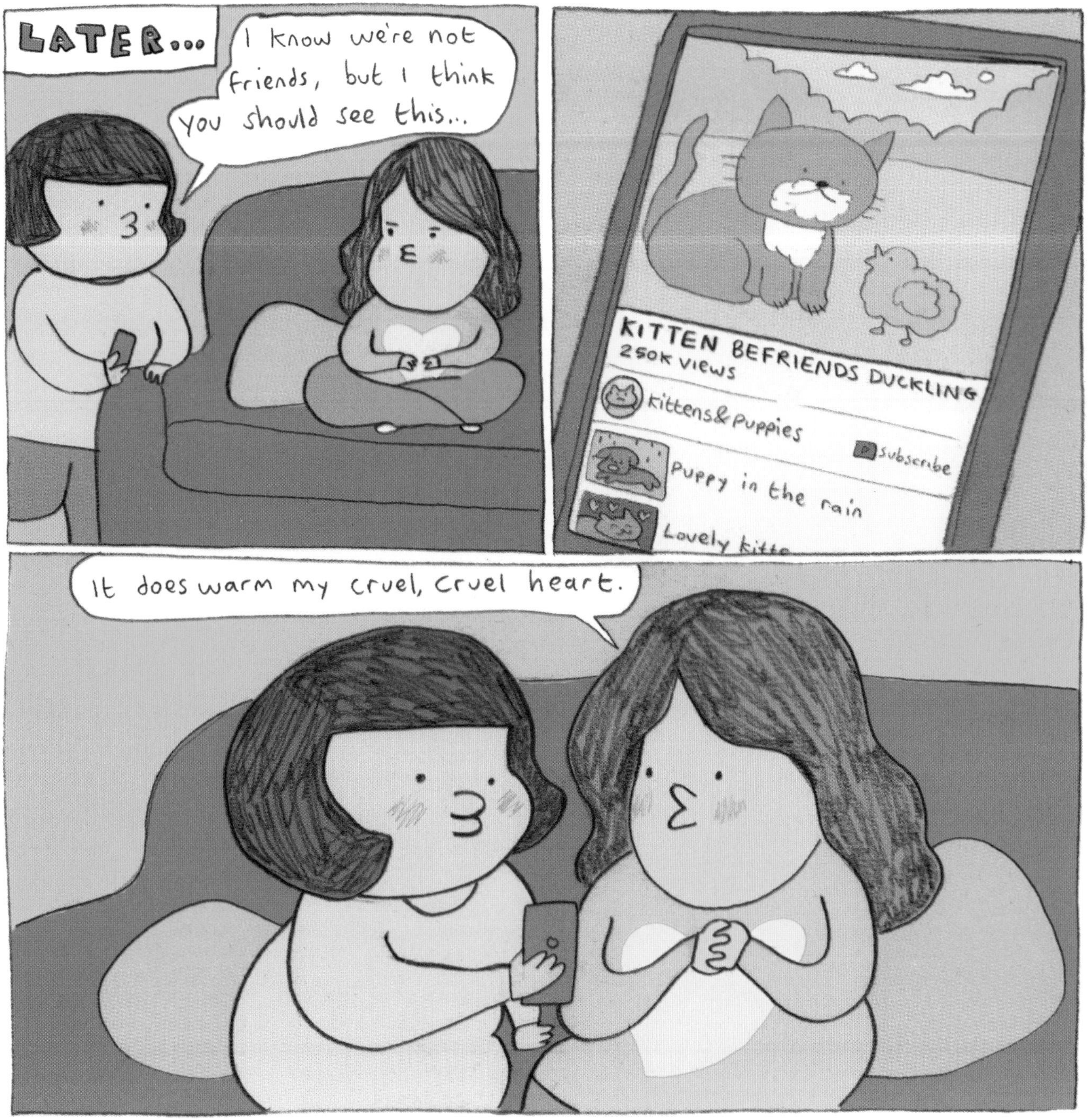
LATER...
I know we're not friends, but I think you should see this...
KITTEN BEFRIENDS DUCKLING
250K VIEWS
kittens&puppies
Subscribe
Puppy in the rain
It does warm my cruel, cruel heart.

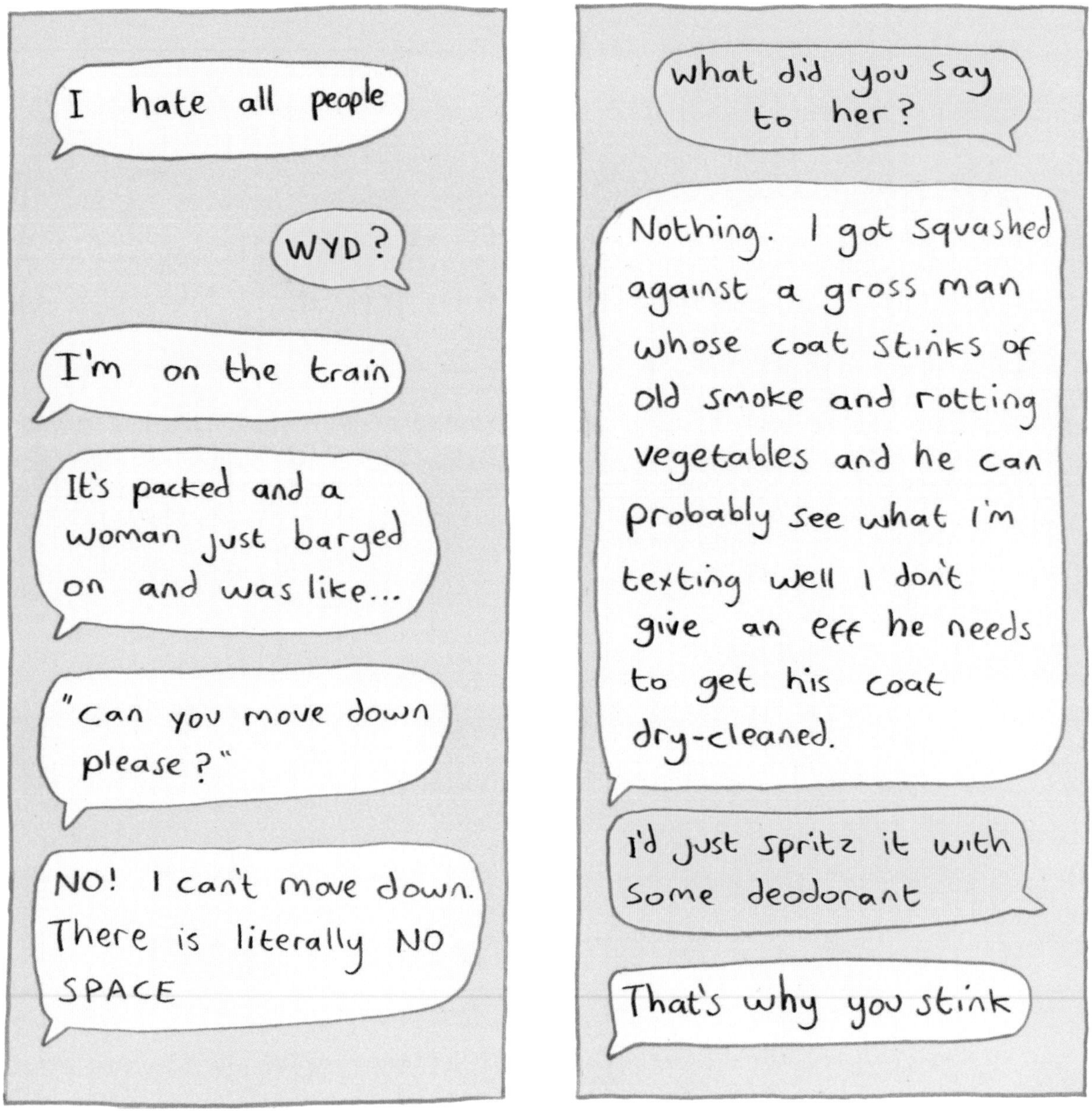
I hate all people
WYD?
I'm on the train
It's packed and a woman just barged on and was like...
"Can you move down please?"
NO! I can't move down. There is literally NO SPACE
What did you say to her?
Nothing. I got squashed against a gross man whose coat stinks of old smoke and rotting vegetables and he can probably see what I'm texting well I don't give an eff he needs to get his coat dry-cleaned.
I'd just spritz it with some deodorant
That's why you stink

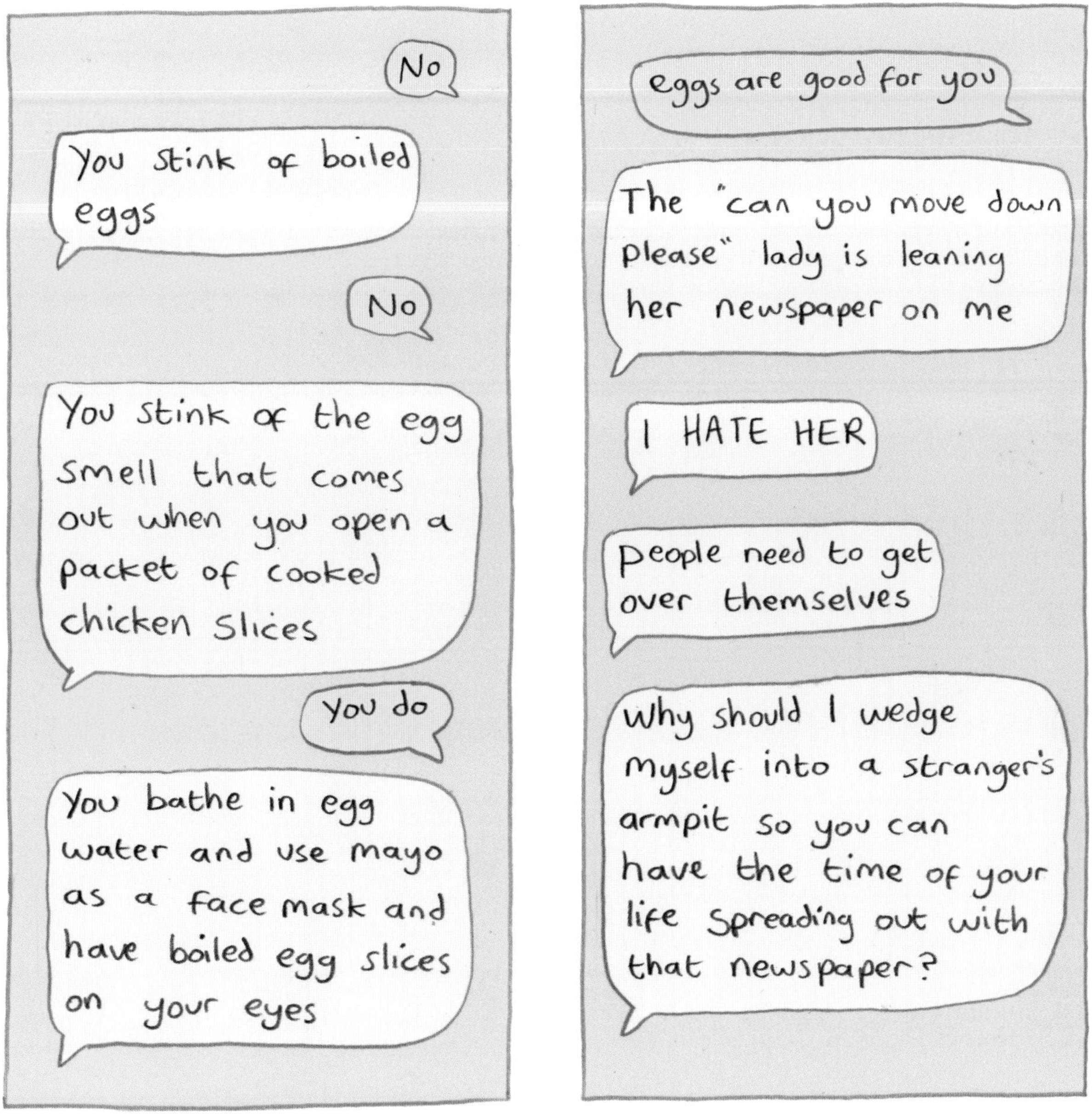
No
You stink of boiled eggs
No
You stink of the egg smell that comes out when you open a packet of cooked chicken slices
You do
You bathe in egg water and use mayo as a face mask and have boiled egg slices on your eyes
eggs are good for you
The "can you move down please" lady is leaning her newspaper on me
I HATE HER
People need to get over themselves
Why should I wedge myself into a stranger's armpit so you can have the time of your life spreading out with that newspaper?

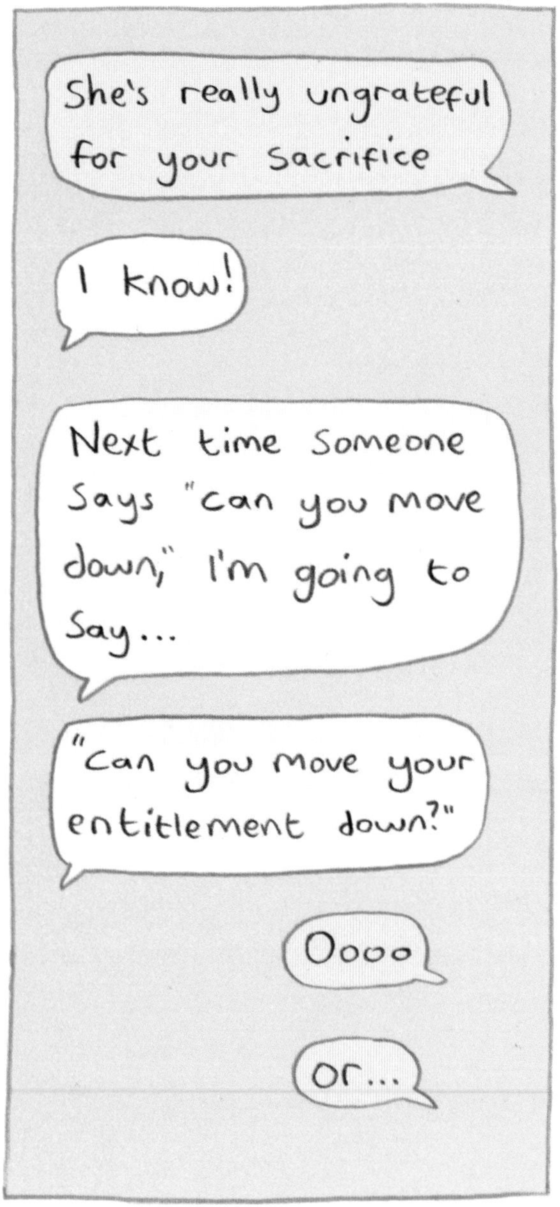
She's really ungrateful for your sacrifice
I know!
Next time someone says "can you move down," I'm going to say...
"Can you move your entitlement down?"
Oooo
or...

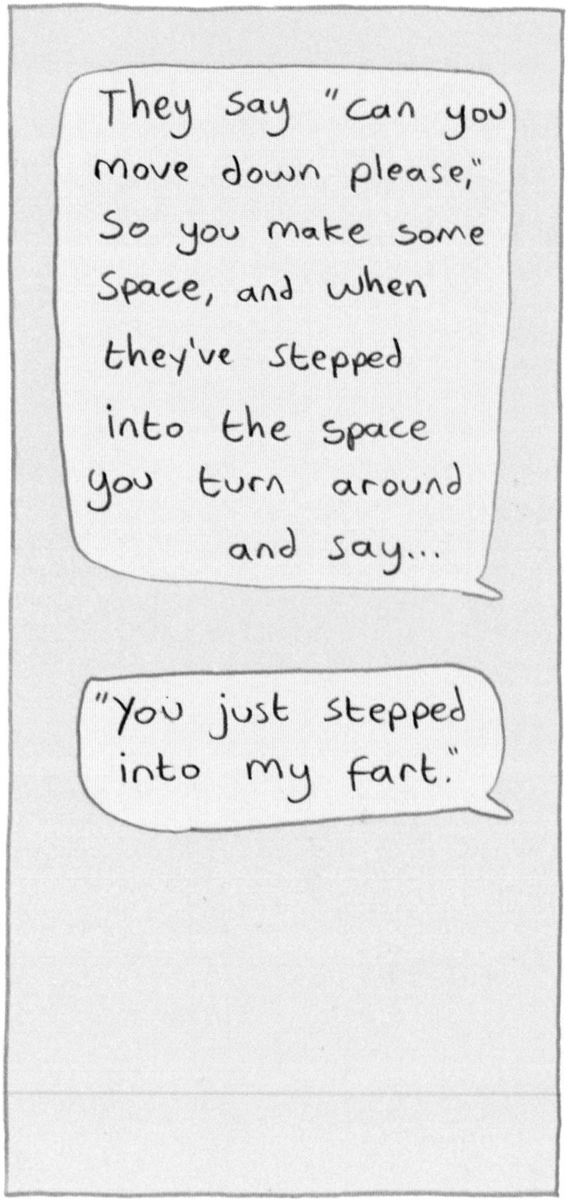
They say "can you move down please," so you make some space, and when they've stepped into the space you turn around and say...
"You just stepped into my fart."

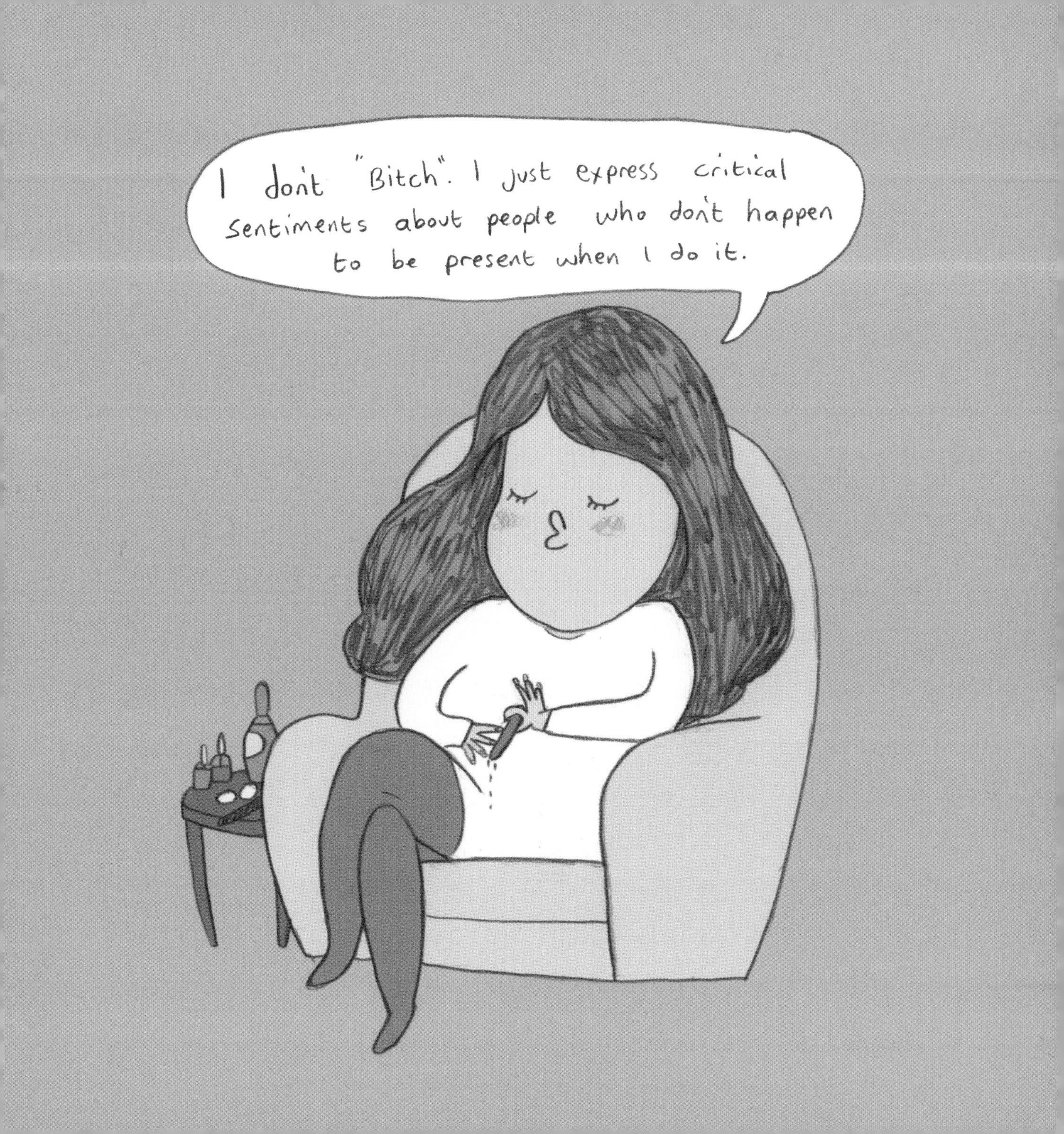
I don't "Bitch". I just express critical sentiments about people who don't happen to be present when I do it.

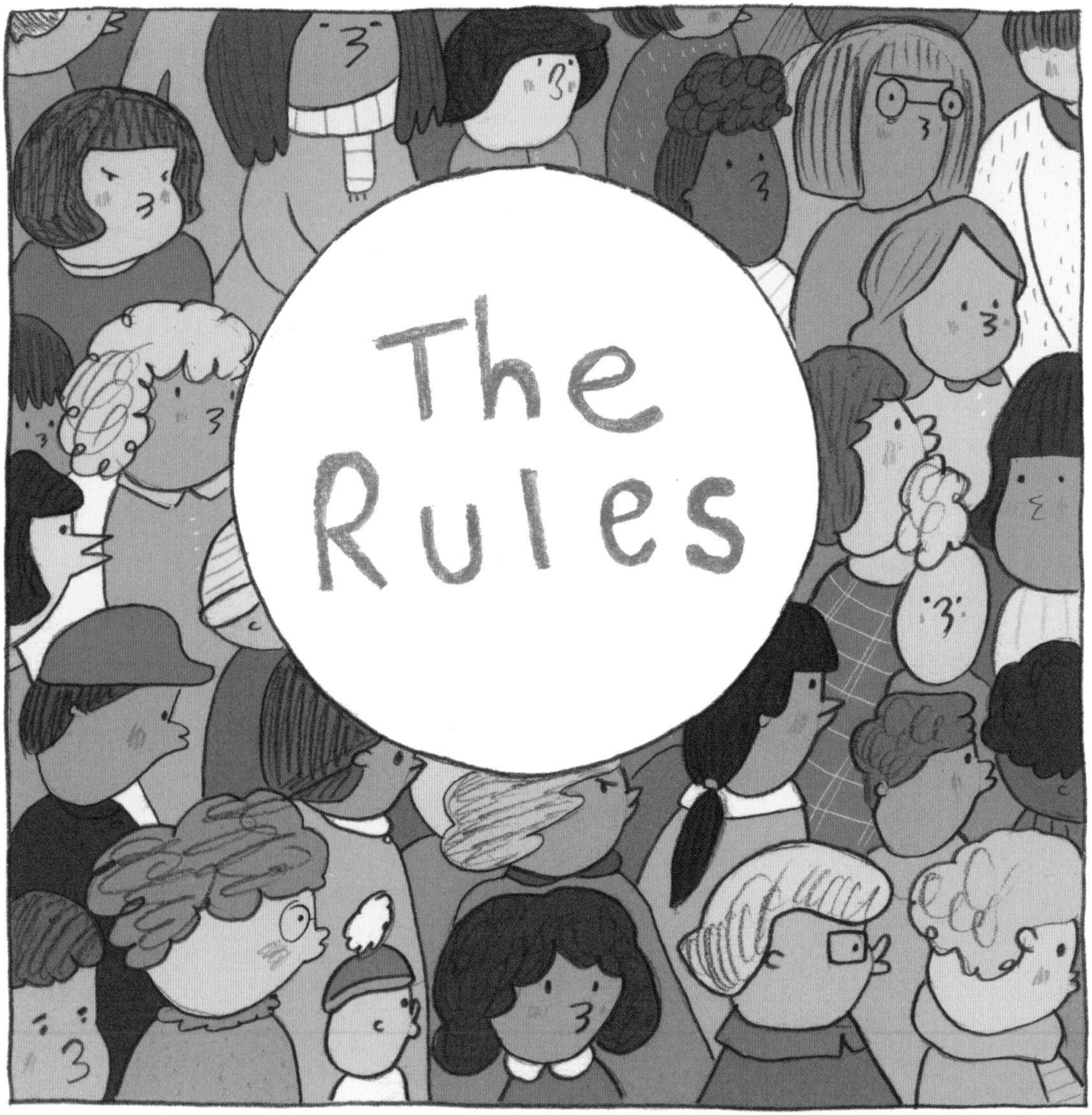
The Rules

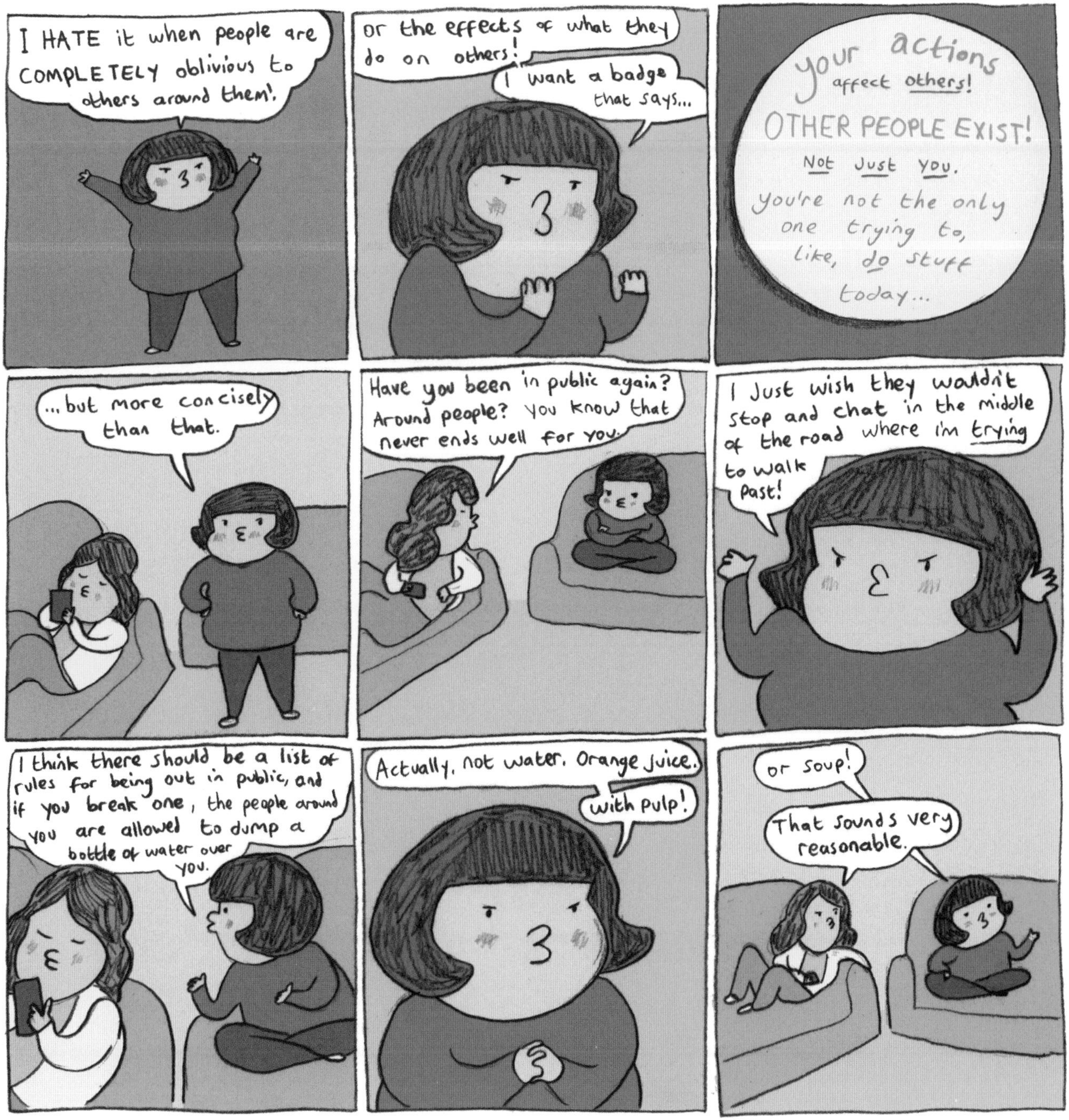
I HATE it when people are COMPLETELY oblivious to others around them!
or the effects of what they do on others!
I want a badge that says...
your actions affect others!
OTHER PEOPLE EXIST!
Not Just You.
you're not the only one trying to, like, do stuff today...
...but more concisely than that.
Have you been in public again? Around people? You know that never ends well for you.
I Just wish they wouldn't stop and chat in the middle of the road where I'm trying to walk past!
I think there should be a list of rules for being out in public, and if you break one, the people around you are allowed to dump a bottle of water over you.
Actually, not water. Orange juice.
with pulp!
or soup!
That sounds very reasonable.

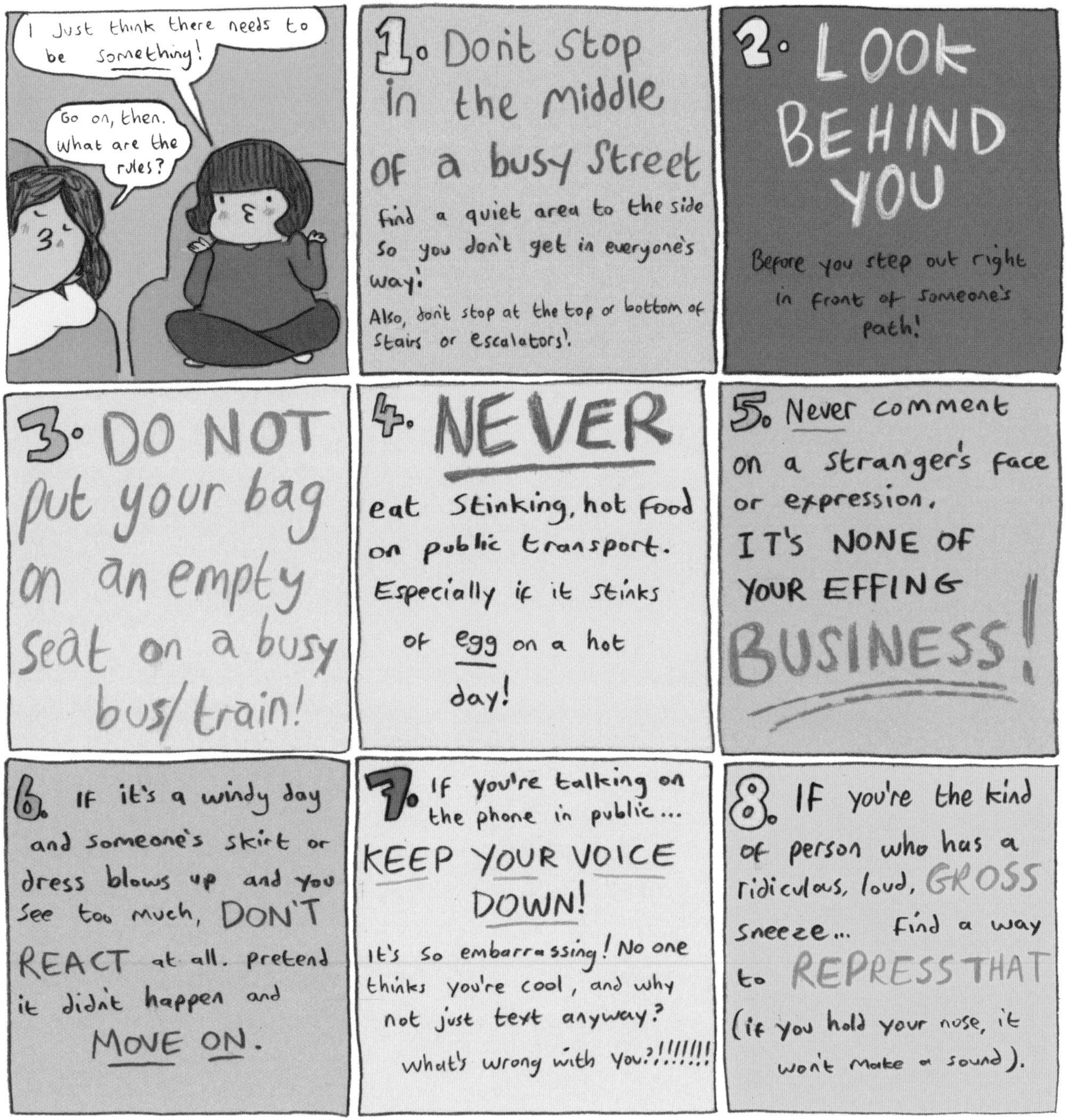
I just think there needs to be something!
Go on, then. What are the rules?
1. Don't stop in the middle of a busy street
Find a quiet area to the side so you don't get in everyone's way!
Also, don't stop at the top or bottom of stairs or escalators!
2. LOOK BEHIND YOU
Before you step out right in front of someone's path!
3. DO NOT put your bag on an empty seat on a busy bus/train!
4. NEVER
eat stinking, hot food on public transport. Especially if it stinks of egg on a hot day!
5. Never comment on a stranger's face or expression. IT'S NONE OF YOUR EFFING BUSINESS!
6. If it's a windy day and someone's skirt or dress blows up and you see too much, DON'T REACT at all. Pretend it didn't happen and MOVE ON.
7. If you're talking on the phone in public...
KEEP YOUR VOICE DOWN!
It's so embarrassing! No one thinks you're cool, and why not just text anyway?
What's wrong with you?!!!!!!!
8. If you're the kind of person who has a ridiculous, loud, GROSS sneeze... Find a way to REPRESS THAT
(if you hold your nose, it won't make a sound).

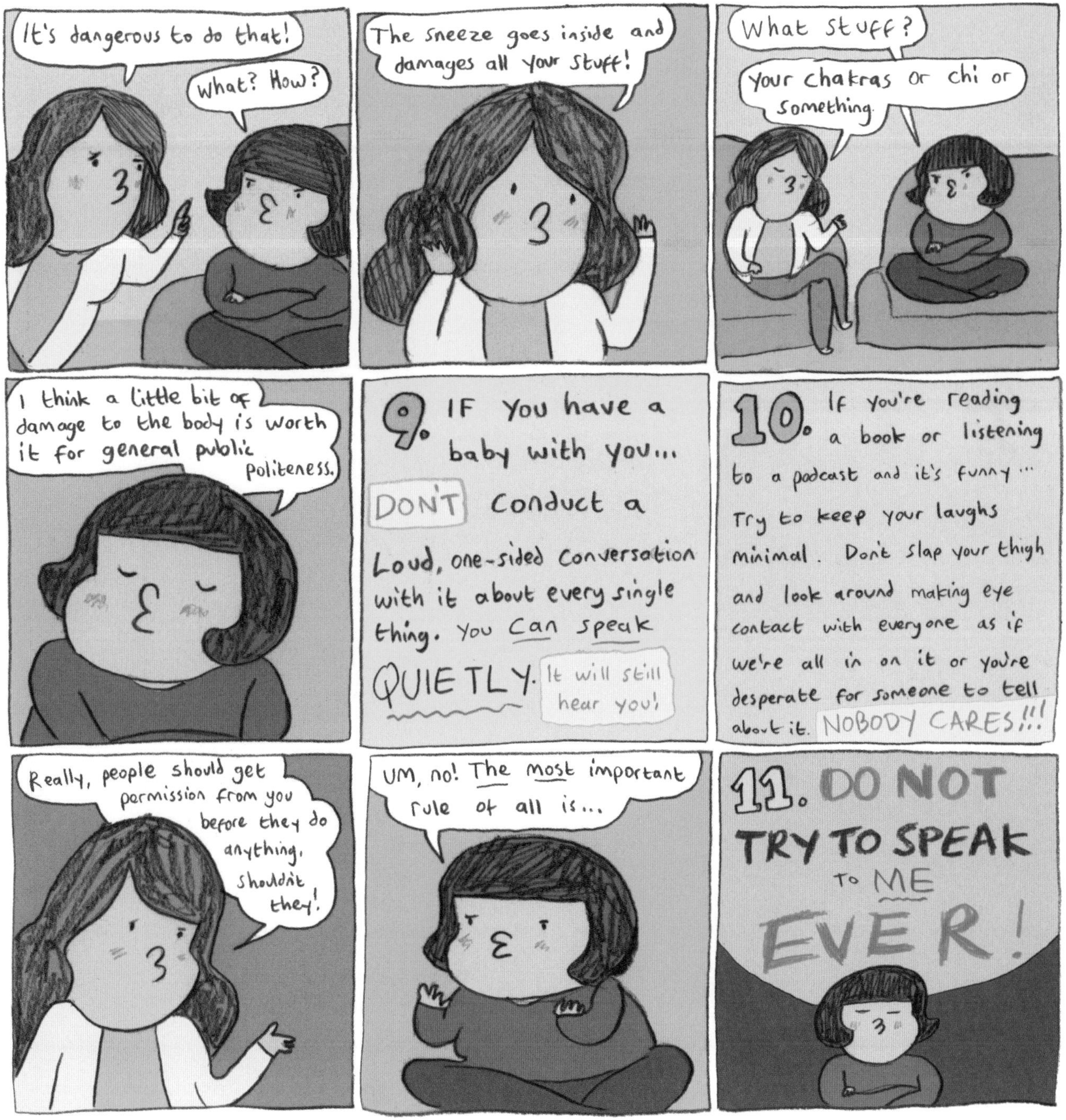
It's dangerous to do that!
What? How?
The sneeze goes inside and damages all your stuff!
What stuff?
Your chakras or chi or something.
I think a little bit of damage to the body is worth it for general public politeness.
9. If you have a baby with you... DON'T conduct a loud, one-sided conversation with it about every single thing. You can speak QUIETLY. It will still hear you!
10. If you're reading a book or listening to a podcast and it's funny... Try to keep your laughs minimal. Don't slap your thigh and look around making eye contact with everyone as if we're all in on it or you're desperate for someone to tell about it. NOBODY CARES!!!
Really, people should get permission from you before they do anything, shouldn't they!
Um, no! The most important rule of all is...
11. DO NOT TRY TO SPEAK TO ME EVER!

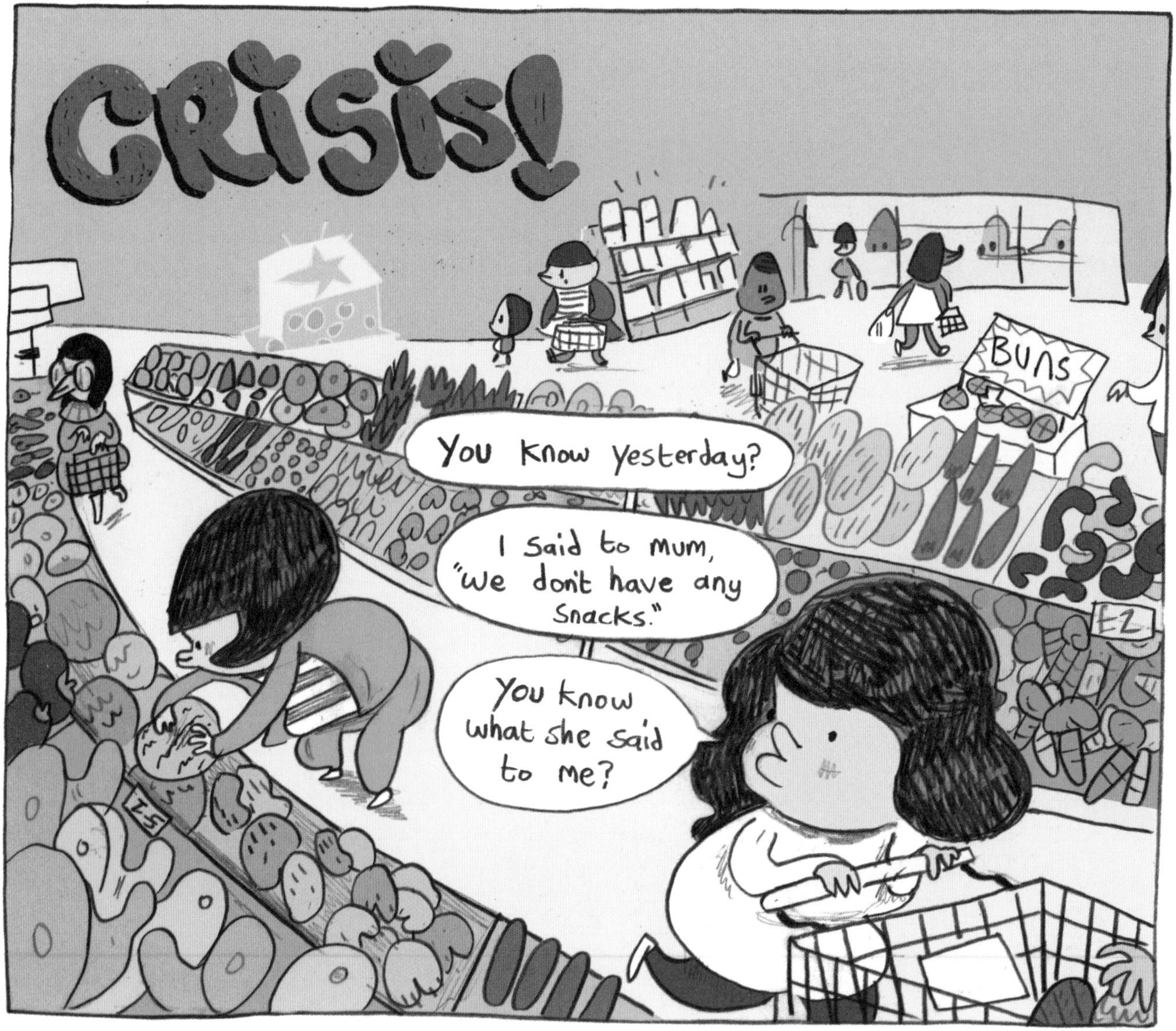
CRISIS!
BUNS
You know yesterday?
I said to mum, "We don't have any snacks."
You know what she said to me?

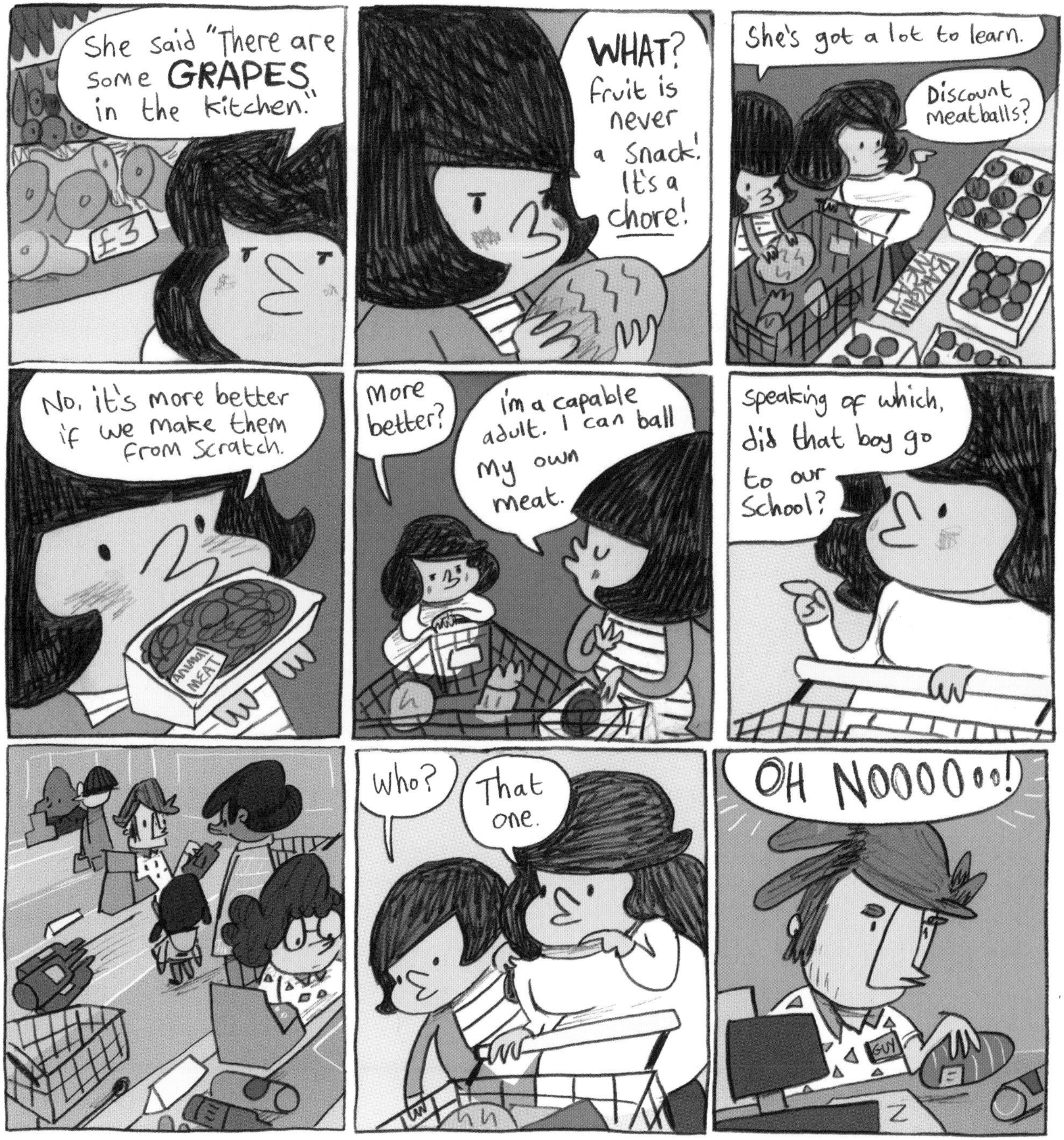
She said "There are some GRAPES in the kitchen."
£3
WHAT? fruit is never a snack! It's a chore!
She's got a lot to learn.
Discount meatballs?
No, it's more better if we make them from scratch.
Animal MEAT
More better?
I'm a capable adult. I can ball my own meat.
speaking of which, did that boy go to our school?
Who?
That one.
OH NOOOOoo!
GUY

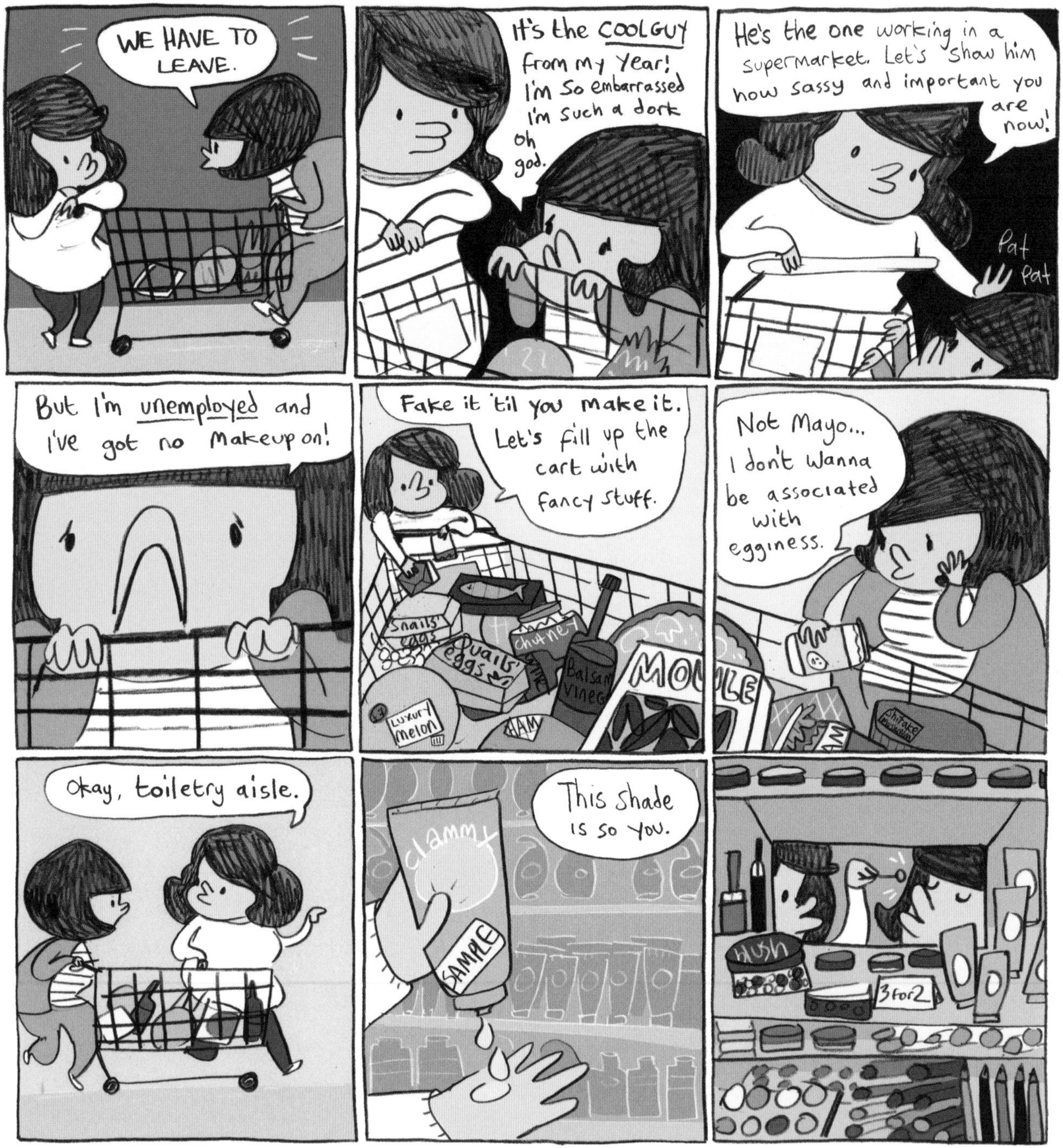
WE HAVE TO LEAVE.
It's the COOLGUY from my Year! I'm so embarrassed I'm such a dork oh god.
He's the one working in a supermarket. Let's show him how sassy and important you are now!
Pat pat
But I'm unemployed and I've got no makeup on!
Fake it 'til you make it. Let's fill up the cart with fancy stuff.
Snails' eggs
Quails' eggs
chutney
Balsam vineg
MOULE
Luxury melon
HAM
Not Mayo... I don't wanna be associated with egginess.
Okay, toiletry aisle.
This shade is so you.
clammy
SAMPLE
Hush
3for2

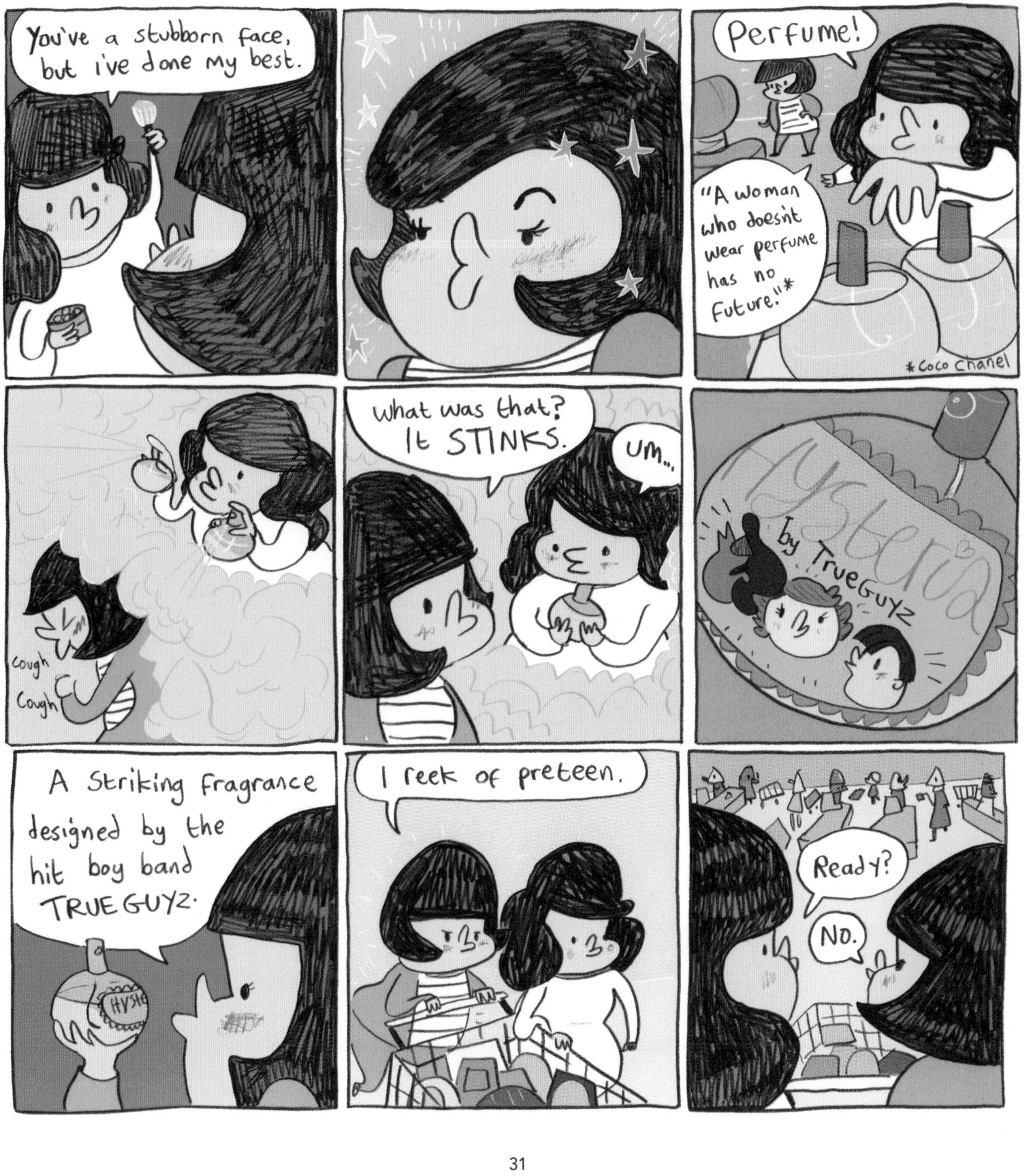
You've a stubborn face, but i've done my best.
Perfume!
"A woman who doesn't wear perfume has no future."*
*Coco Chanel
cough
cough
what was that? It STINKS.
UM...
Hysteria
by TrueGuyz
A striking fragrance designed by the hit boy band TRUE GUYZ.
I reek of preteen.
Ready?
No.

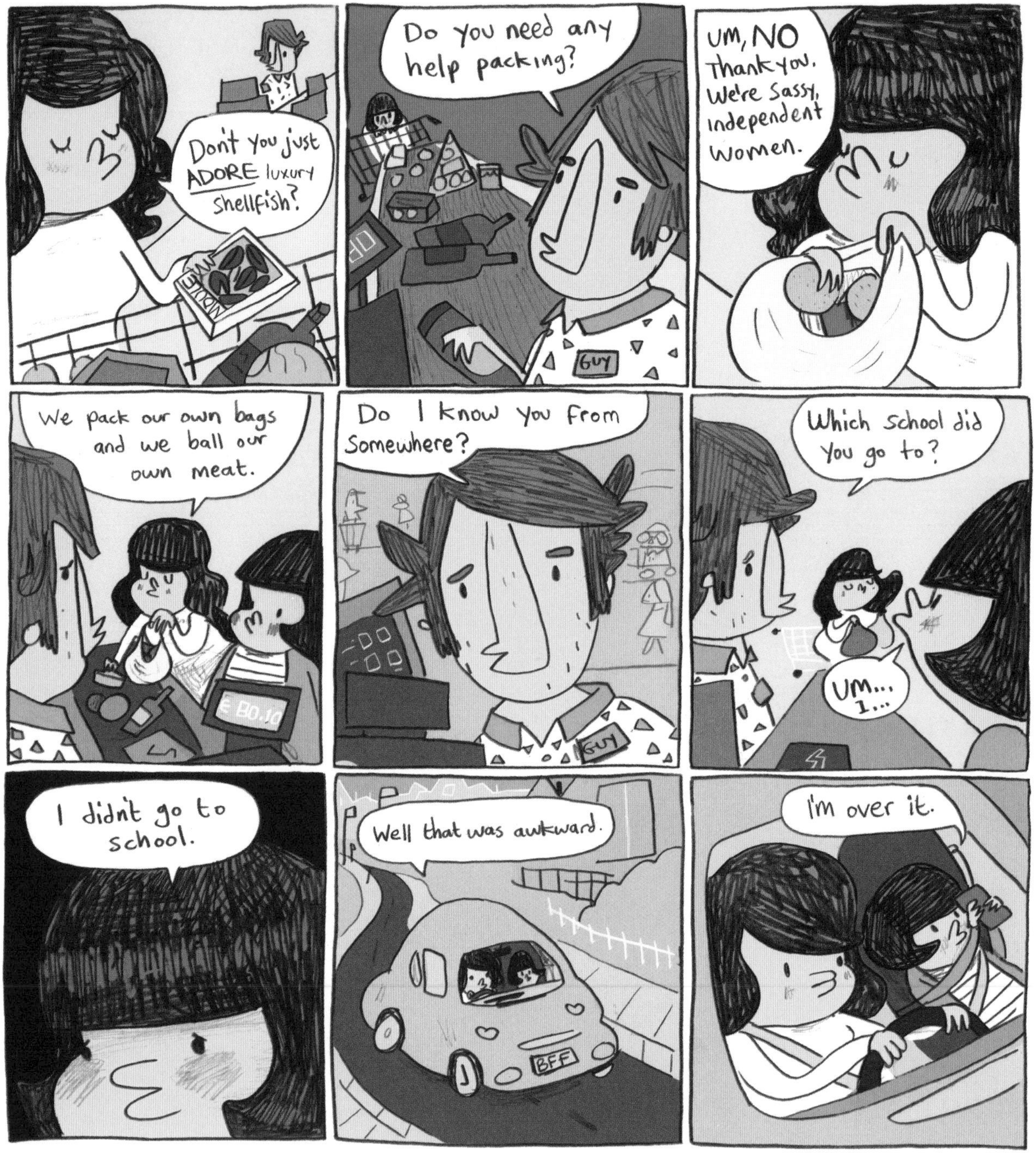
Don't you just ADORE luxury shellfish?
Do you need any help packing?
UM, NO Thank you. We're sassy, independent women.
We pack our own bags and we ball our own meat.
Do I know you from somewhere?
Which school did you go to?
UM... I...
I didn't go to school.
Well that was awkward.
BFF
I'm over it.

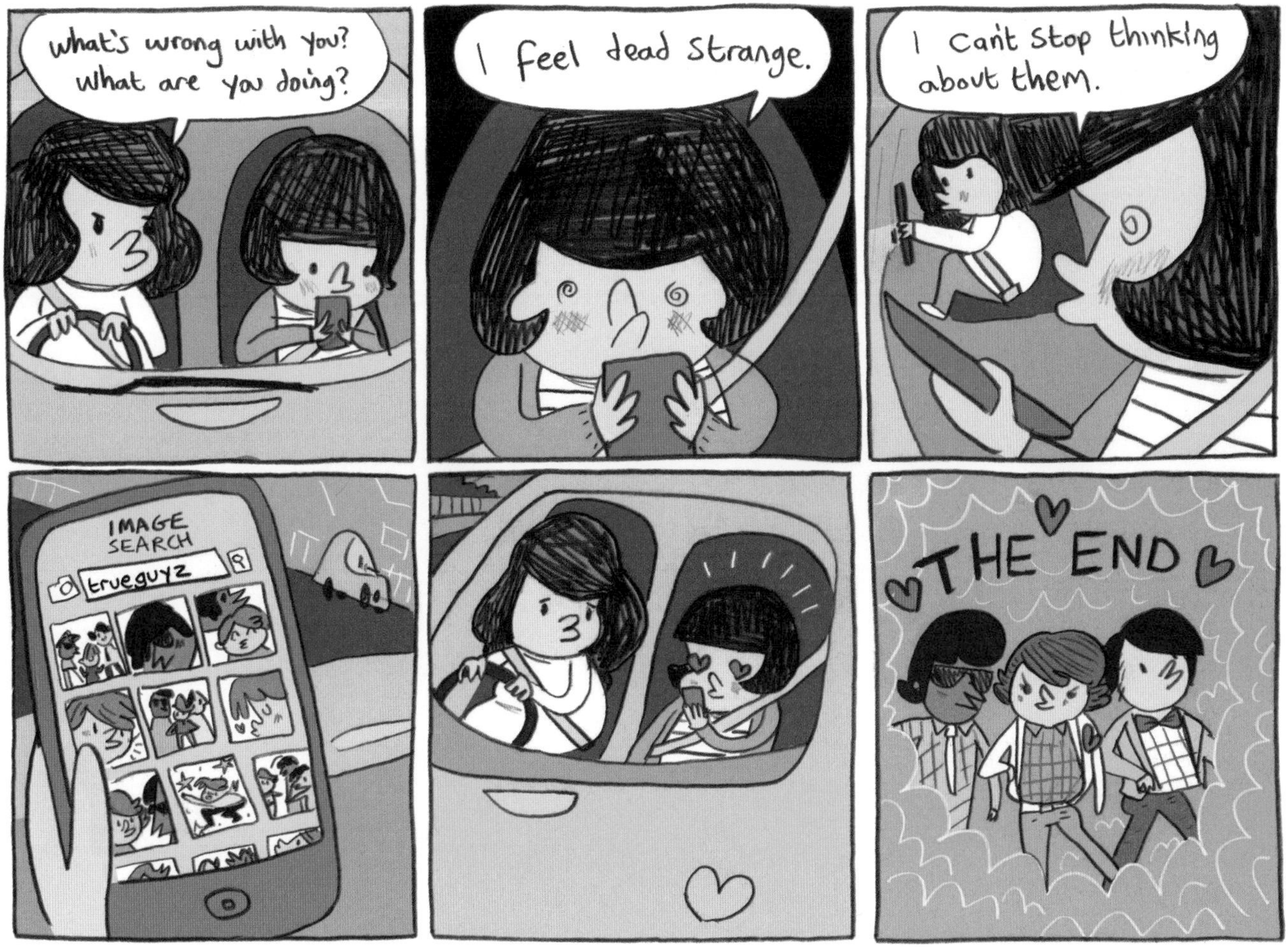
what's wrong with you? what are you doing?
I feel dead strange.
I can't stop thinking about them.
IMAGE SEARCH
trueguyz
THE END

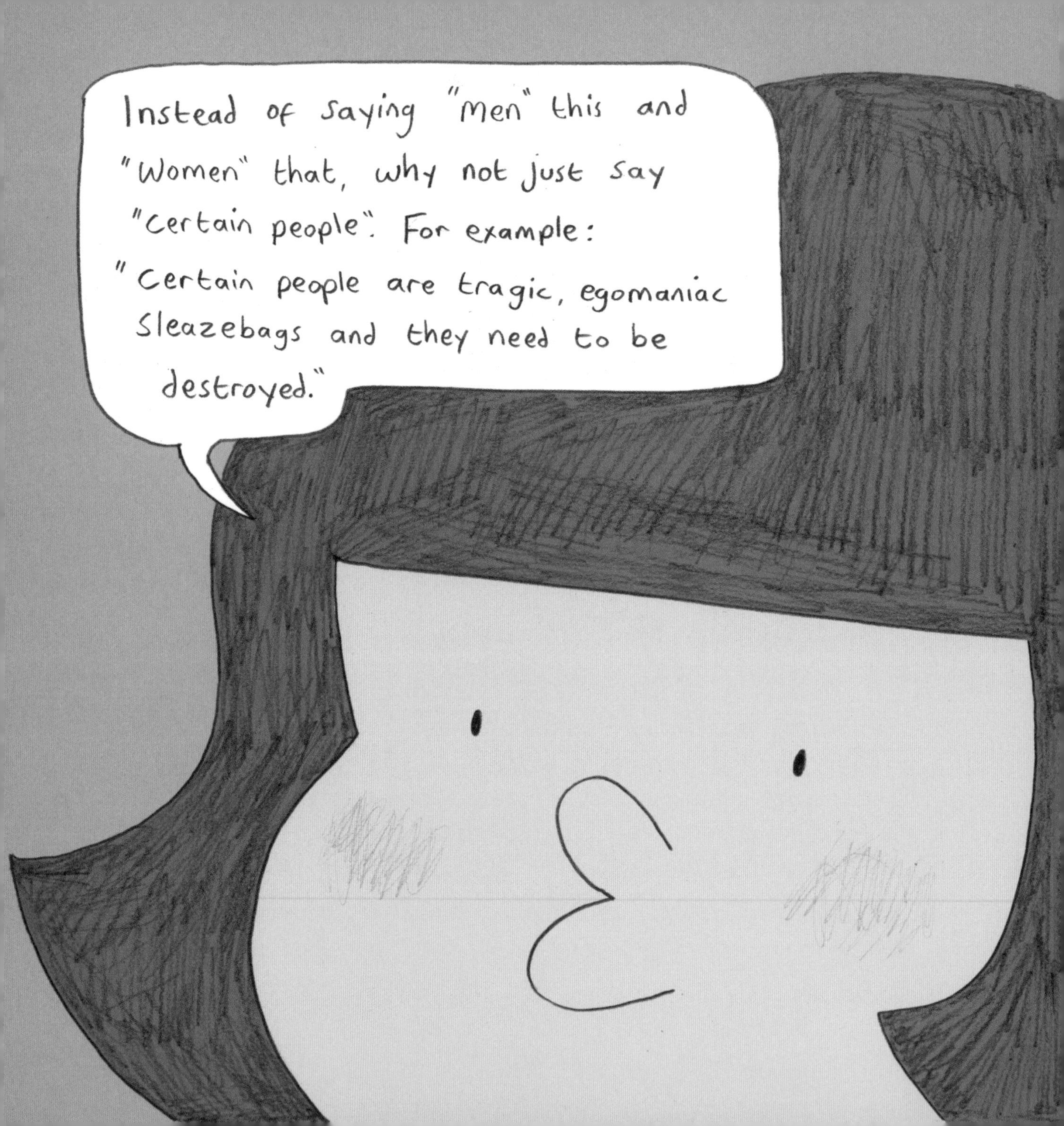
Instead of saying "men" this and "Women" that, why not just say "certain people". For example: "Certain people are tragic, egomaniac sleazebags and they need to be destroyed."

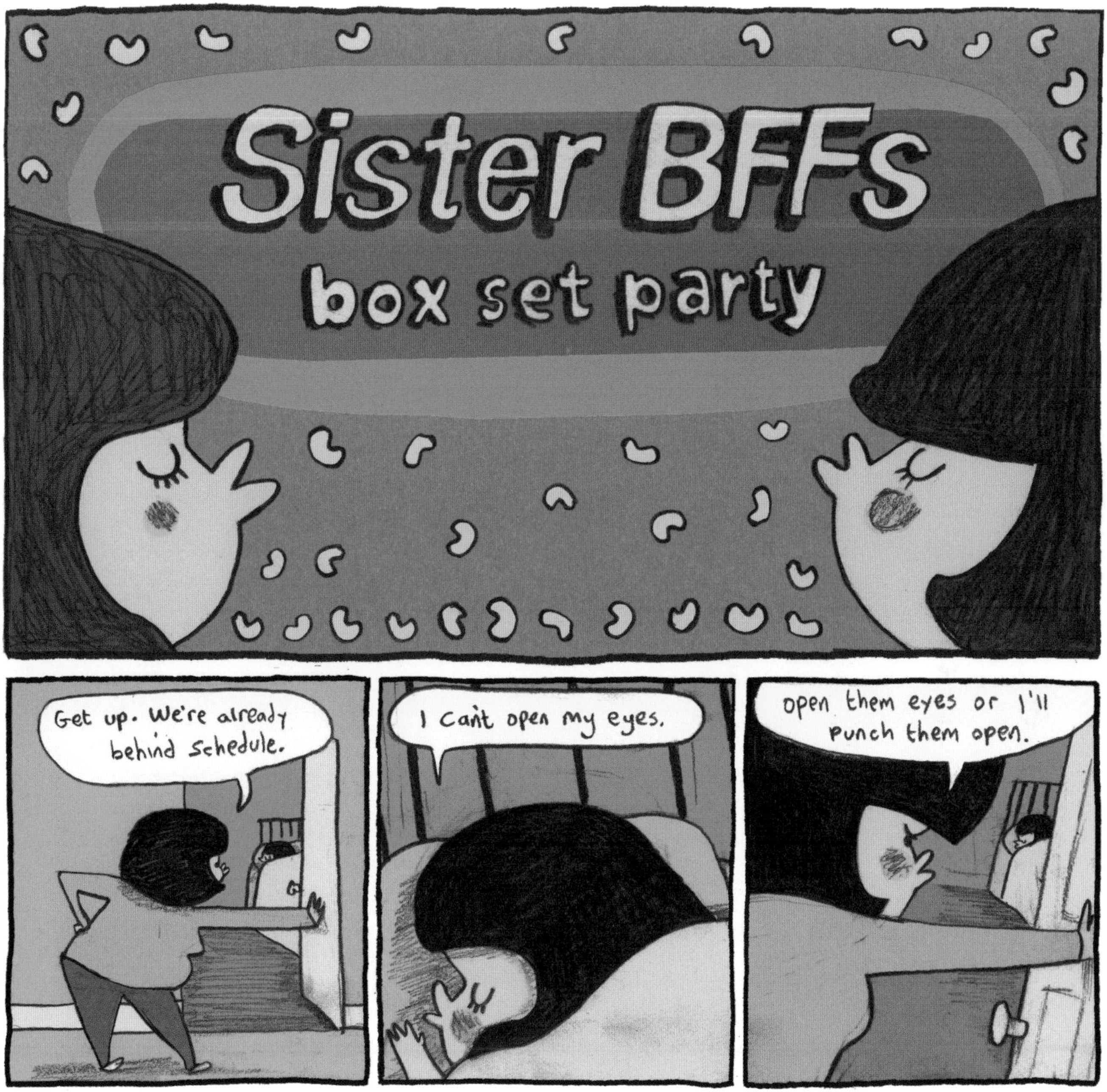
Sister BFFs
box set party
Get up. We're already behind schedule.
I can't open my eyes.
open them eyes or I'll punch them open.

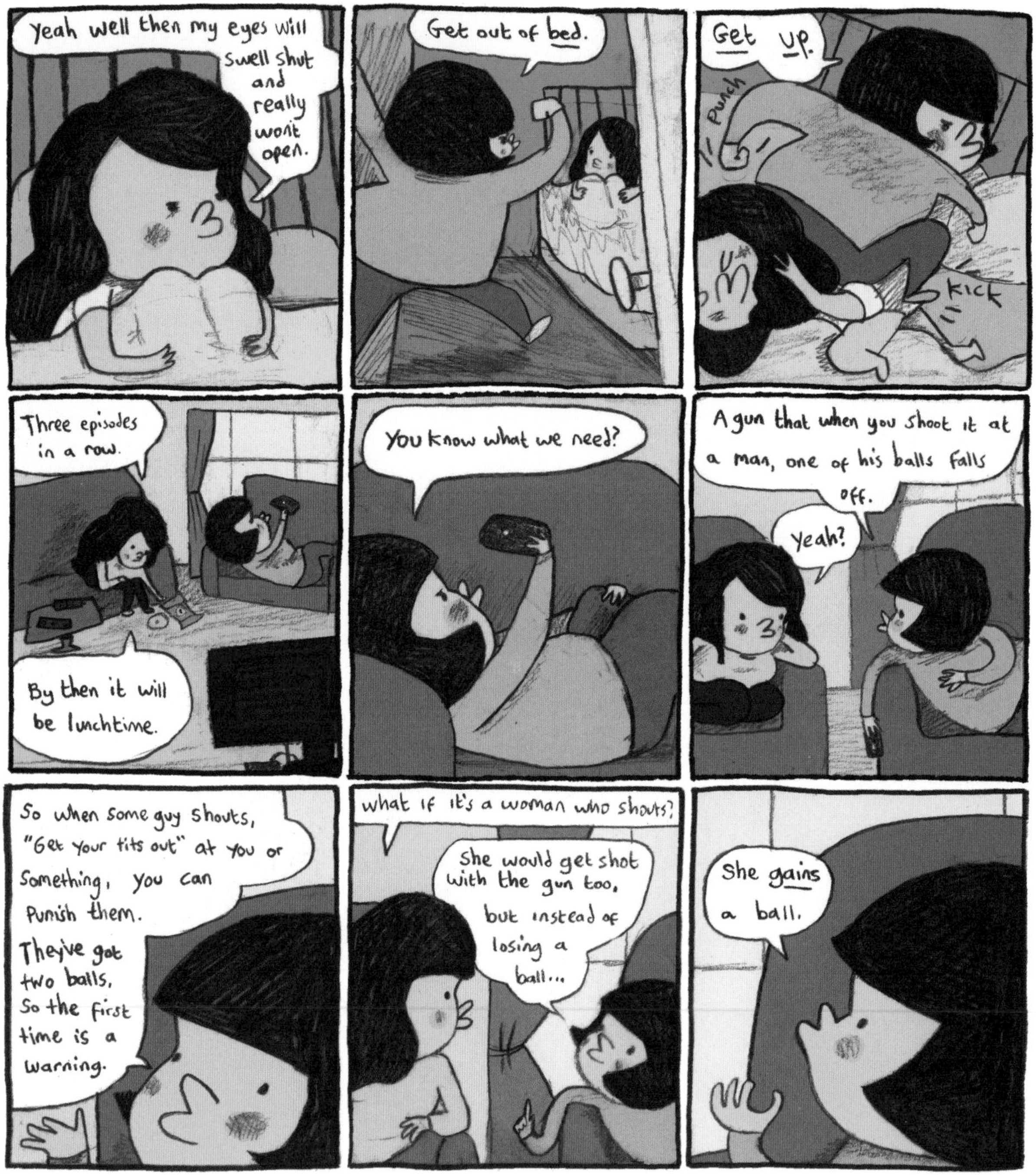
Yeah well then my eyes will swell shut and really won't open.
Get out of bed.
Get up.
Punch
Kick
Three episodes in a row.
By then it will be lunchtime.
You know what we need?
A gun that when you shoot it at a man, one of his balls falls off.
Yeah?
So when some guy shouts, "Get your tits out" at you or something, you can punish them.
They've got two balls, So the first time is a warning.
what if it's a woman who shouts?
She would get shot with the gun too, but instead of losing a ball...
She gains a ball.

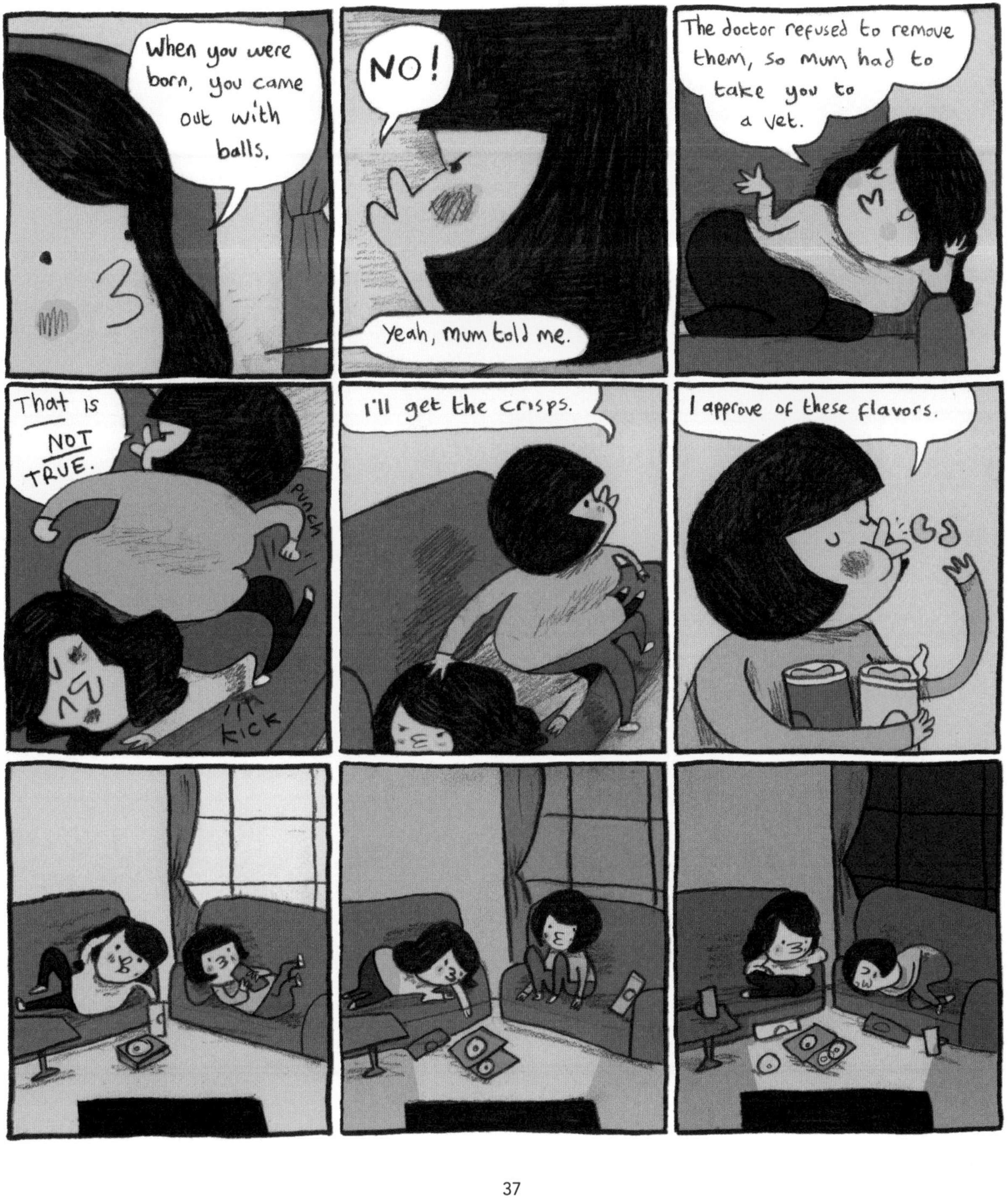
When you were born, you came out with balls.
NO!
Yeah, mum told me.
The doctor refused to remove them, so Mum had to take you to a vet.
That is NOT TRUE.
PUNCH
KICK
I'll get the crisps.
I approve of these flavors.

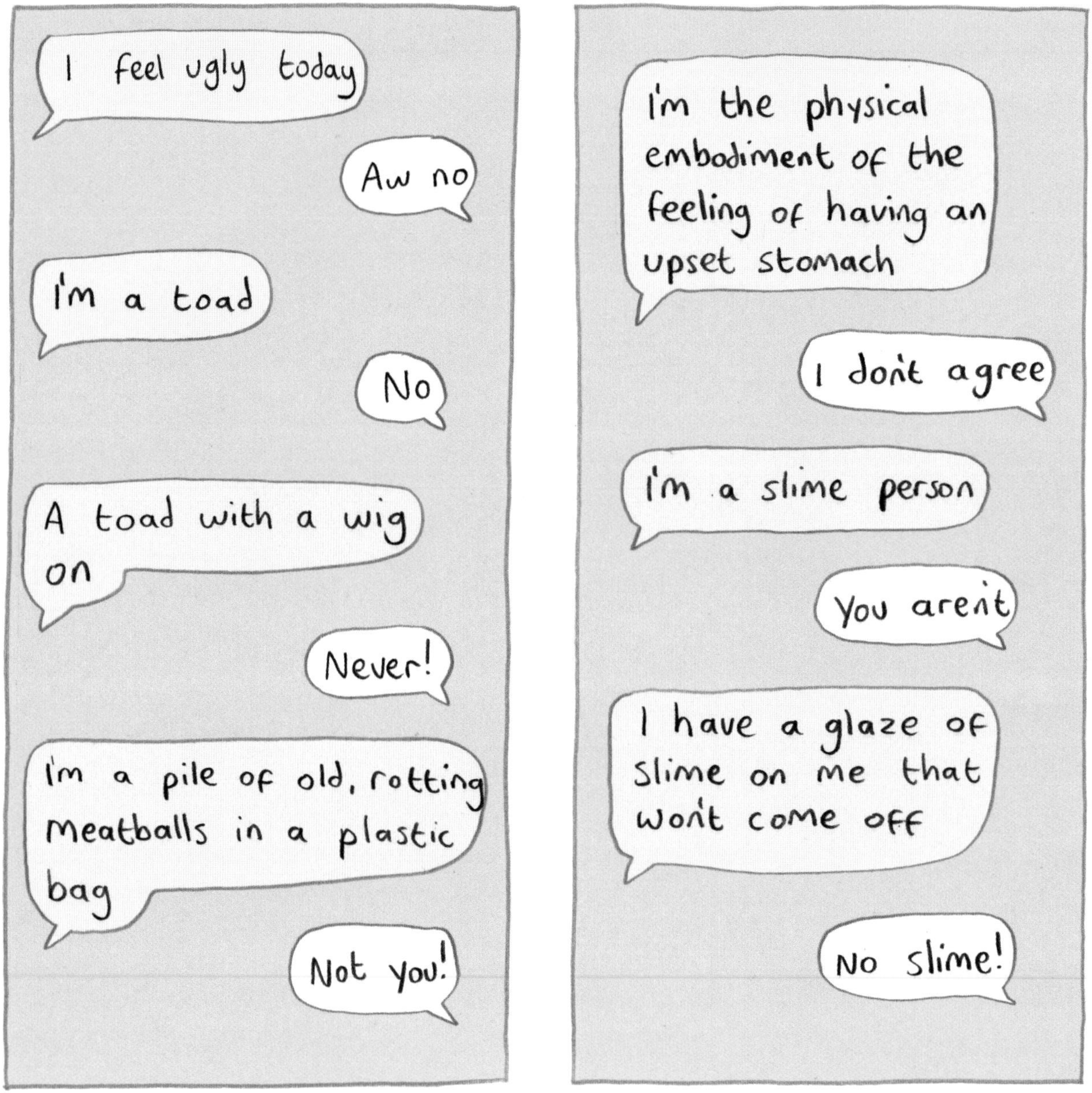
I feel ugly today
Aw no
I'm a toad
No
A toad with a wig on
Never!
I'm a pile of old, rotting meatballs in a plastic bag
Not you!
I'm the physical embodiment of the feeling of having an upset stomach
I don't agree
I'm a slime person
You aren't
I have a glaze of slime on me that won't come off
No slime!

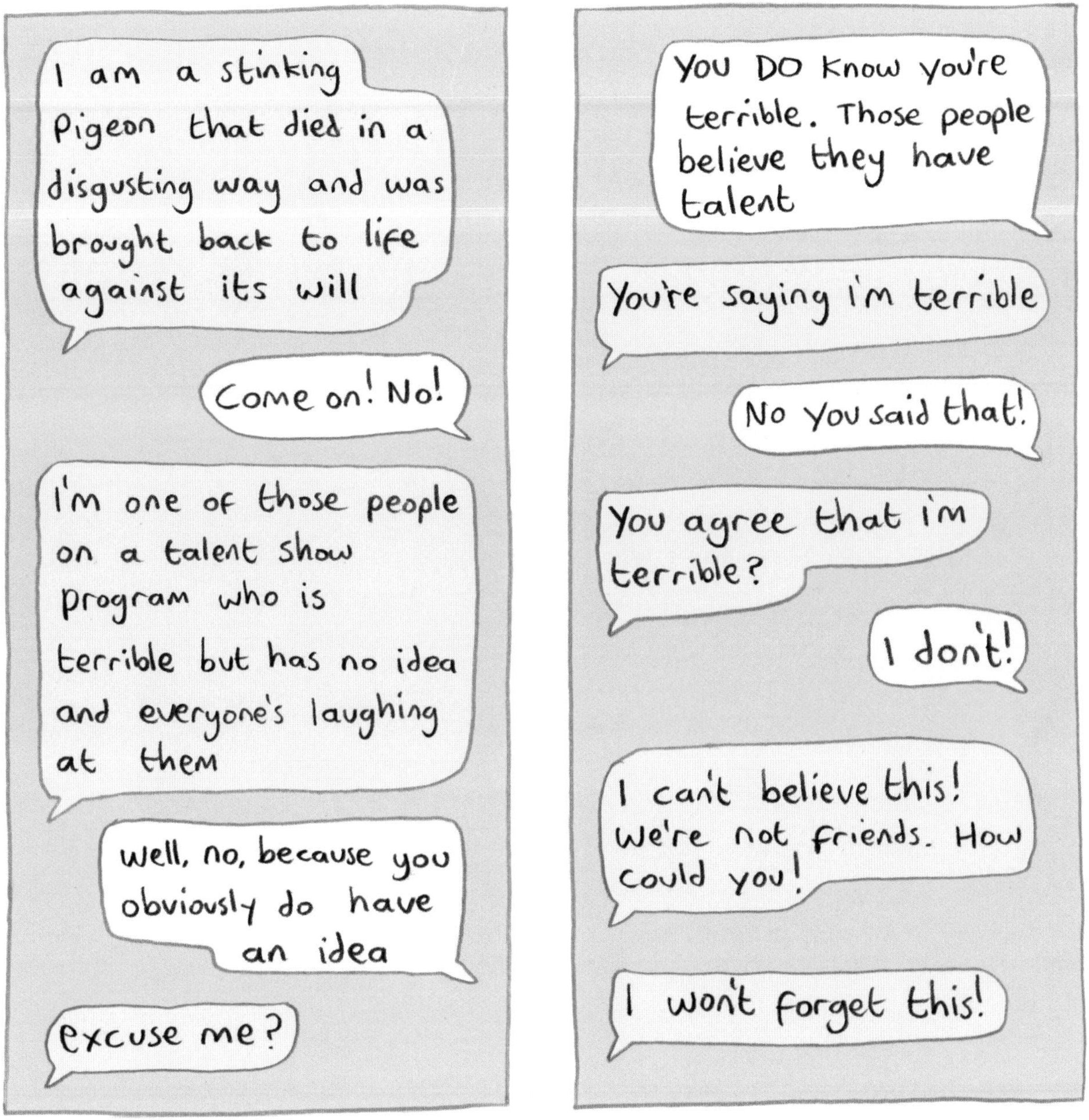
I am a stinking pigeon that died in a disgusting way and was brought back to life against its will
Come on! No!
I'm one of those people on a talent show program who is terrible but has no idea and everyone's laughing at them
Well, no, because you obviously do have an idea
excuse me?
YOU DO know you're terrible. Those people believe they have talent
You're saying i'm terrible
No You said that!
You agree that i'm terrible?
I don't!
I can't believe this! We're not friends. How could you!
I won't forget this!

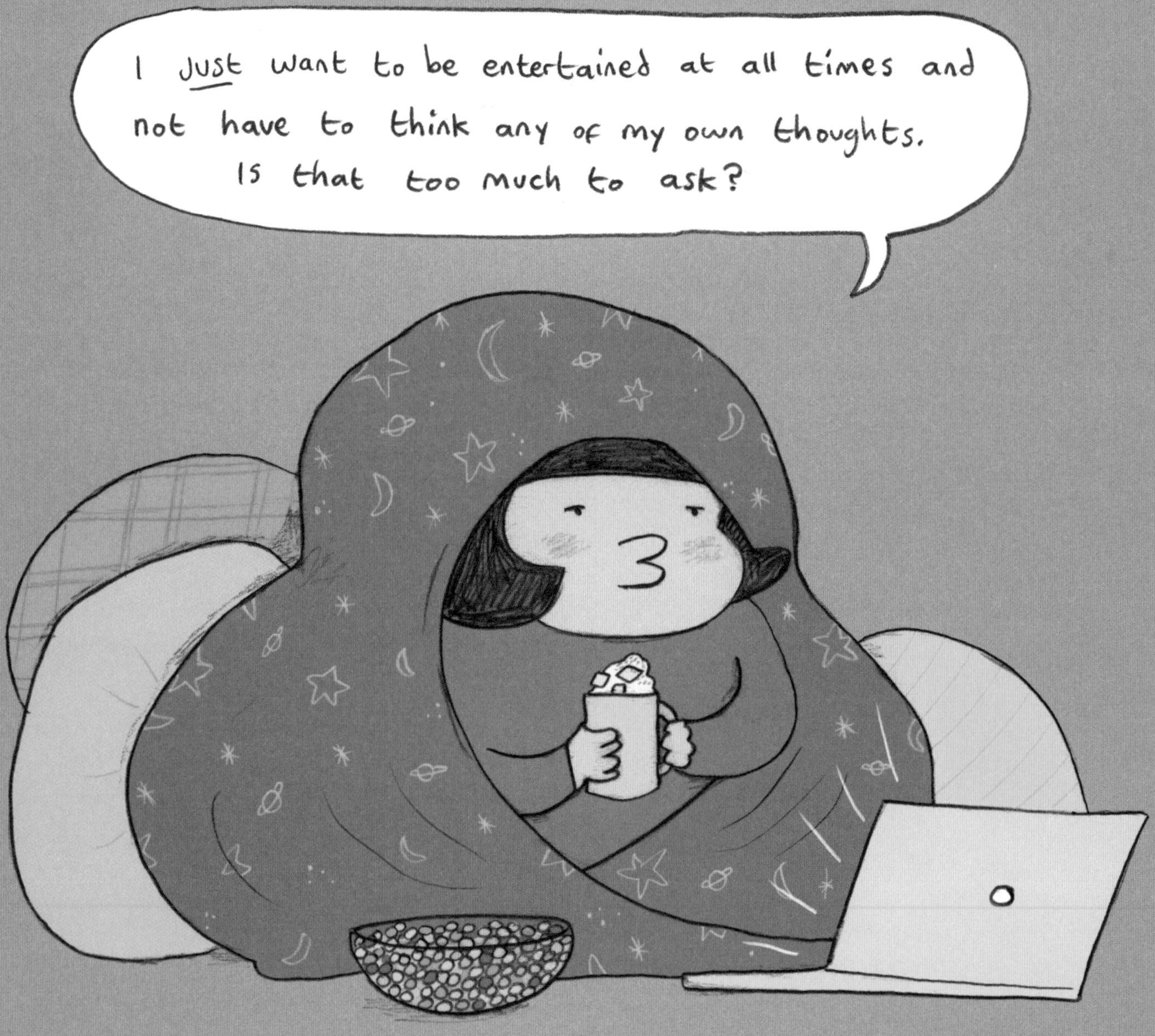
I JUST want to be entertained at all times and not have to think any of my own thoughts. Is that too much to ask?

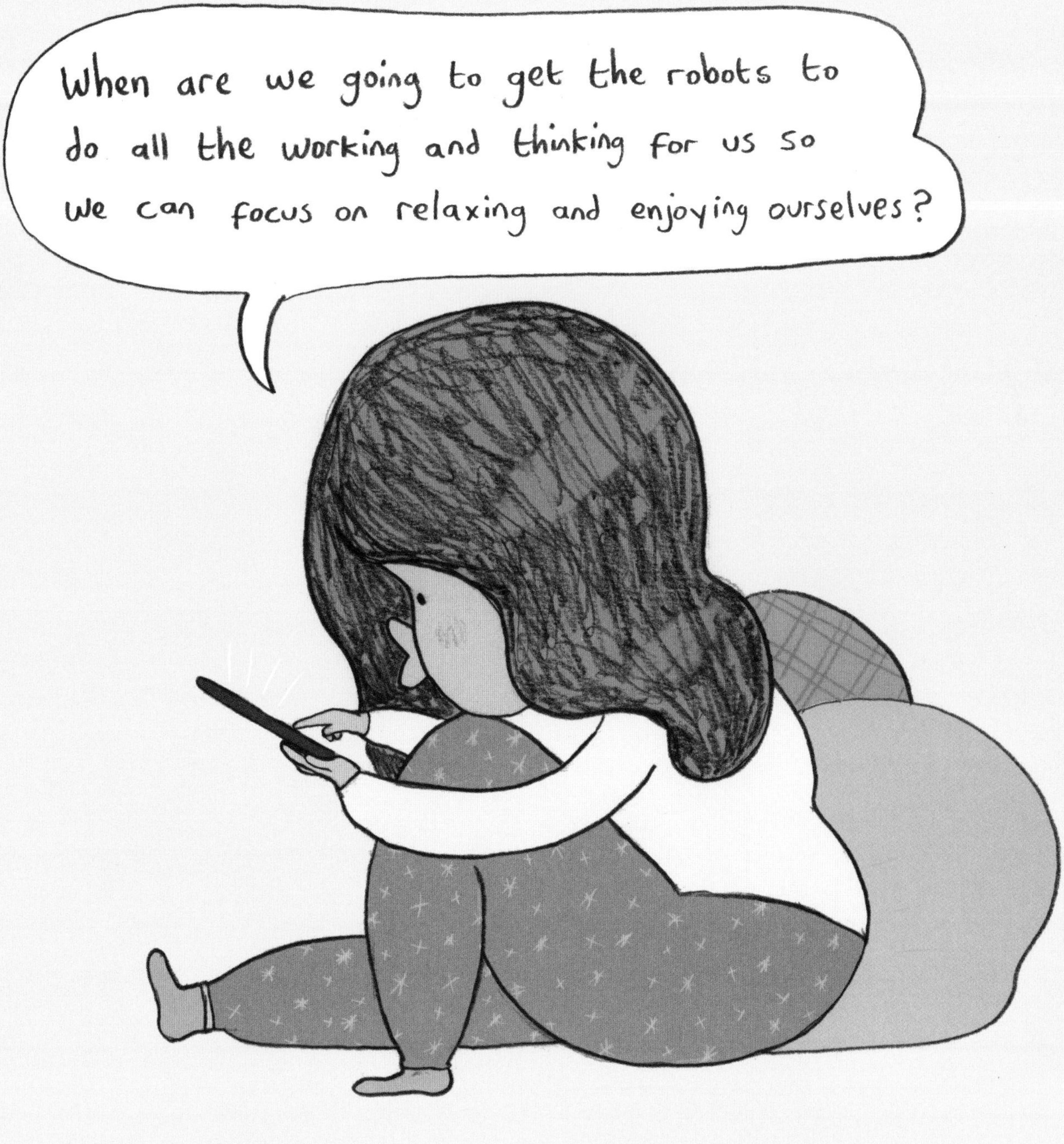
When are we going to get the robots to do all the working and thinking for us so we can focus on relaxing and enjoying ourselves?

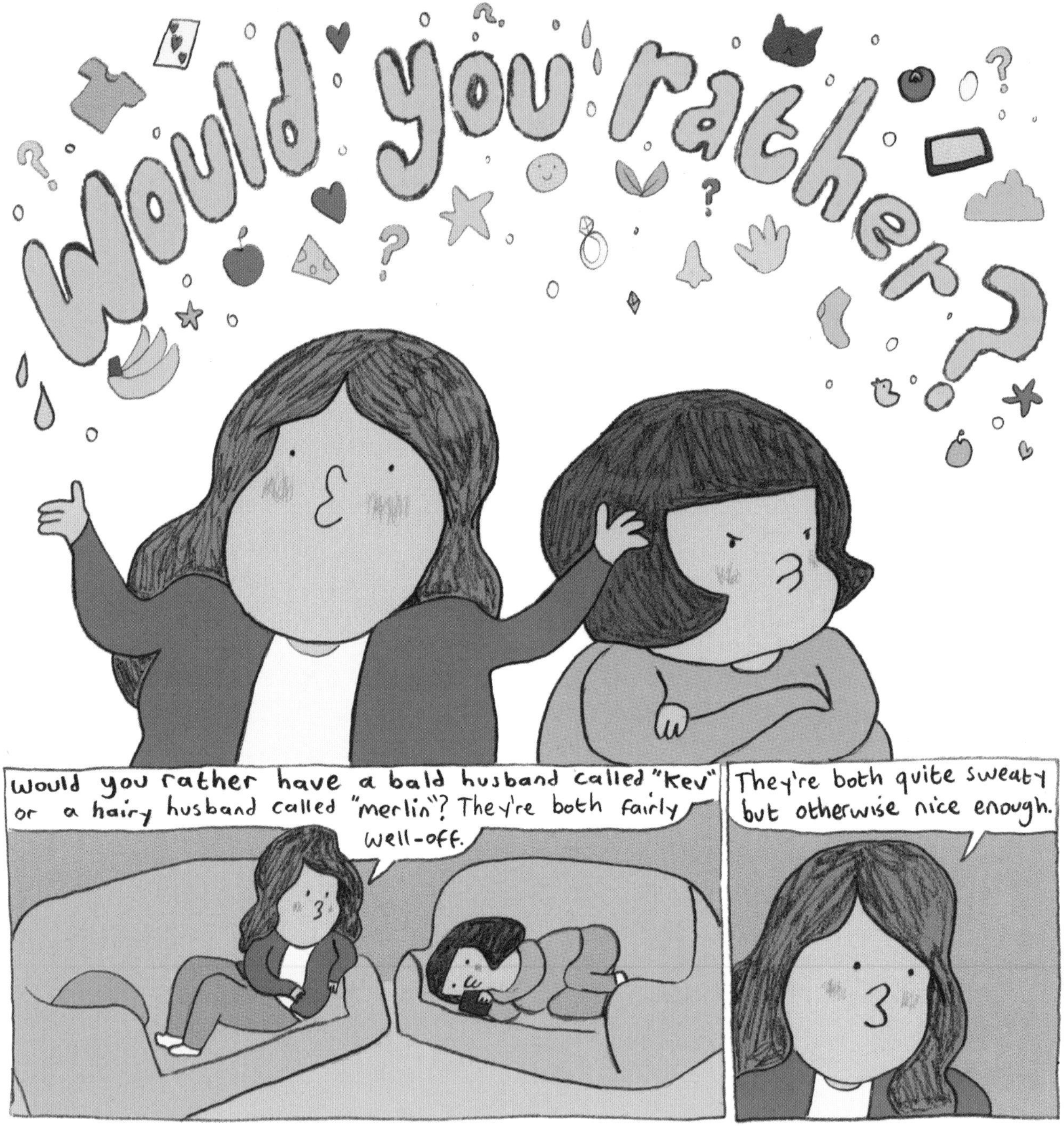

Would you rather?
Would you rather have a bald husband called "Kev" or a hairy husband called "Merlin"? They're both fairly well-off.
They're both quite sweaty but otherwise nice enough.

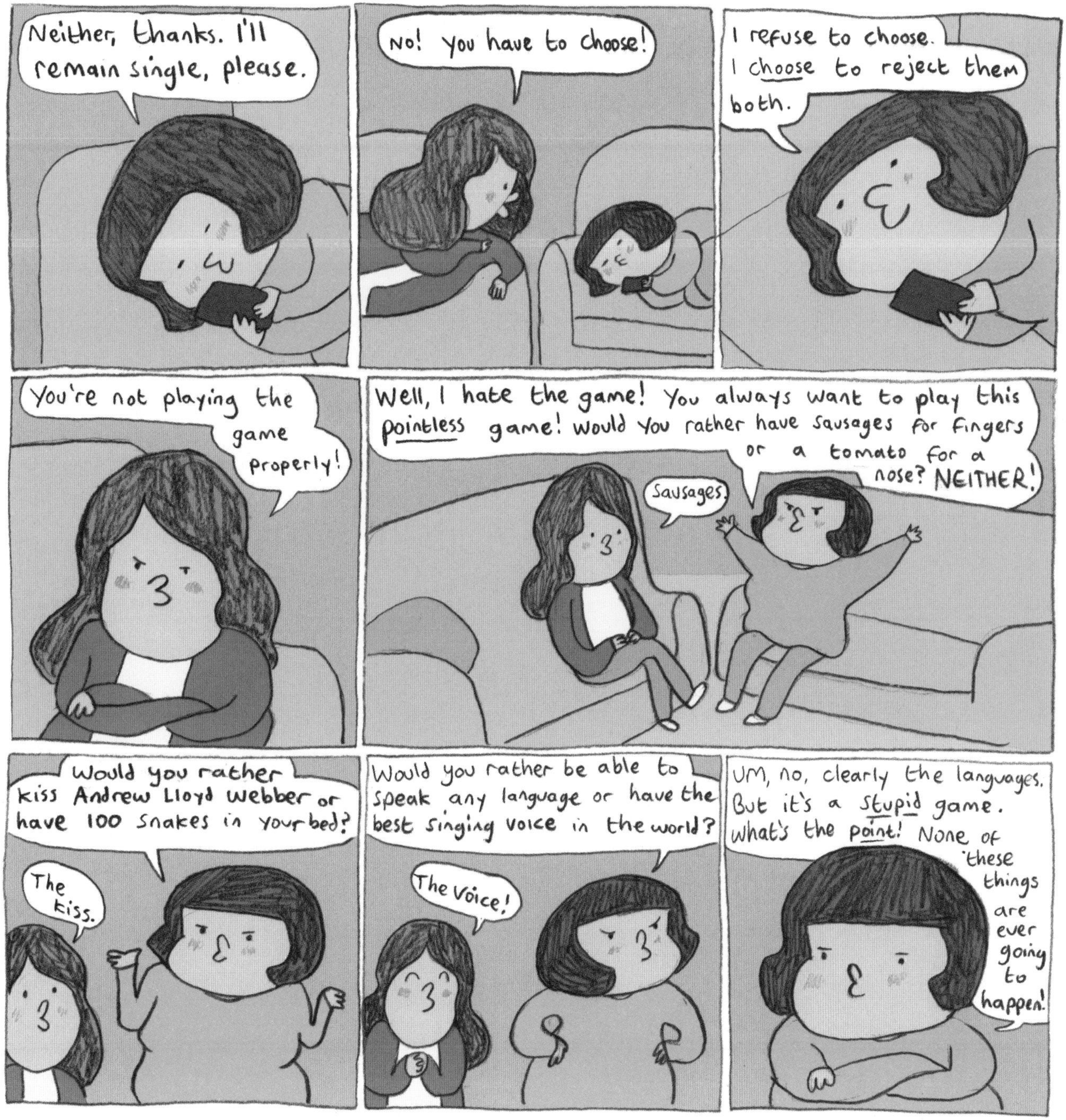
Neither, thanks. I'll remain single, please.
No! You have to choose!
I refuse to choose. I choose to reject them both.
You're not playing the game properly!
Well, I hate the game! You always want to play this pointless game! Would you rather have sausages for fingers or a tomato for a nose? NEITHER!
Sausages.
Would you rather kiss Andrew Lloyd Webber or have 100 snakes in your bed?
The kiss.
Would you rather be able to speak any language or have the best singing voice in the world?
The Voice!
Um, no, clearly the languages. But it's a stupid game. What's the point! None of these things are ever going to happen!

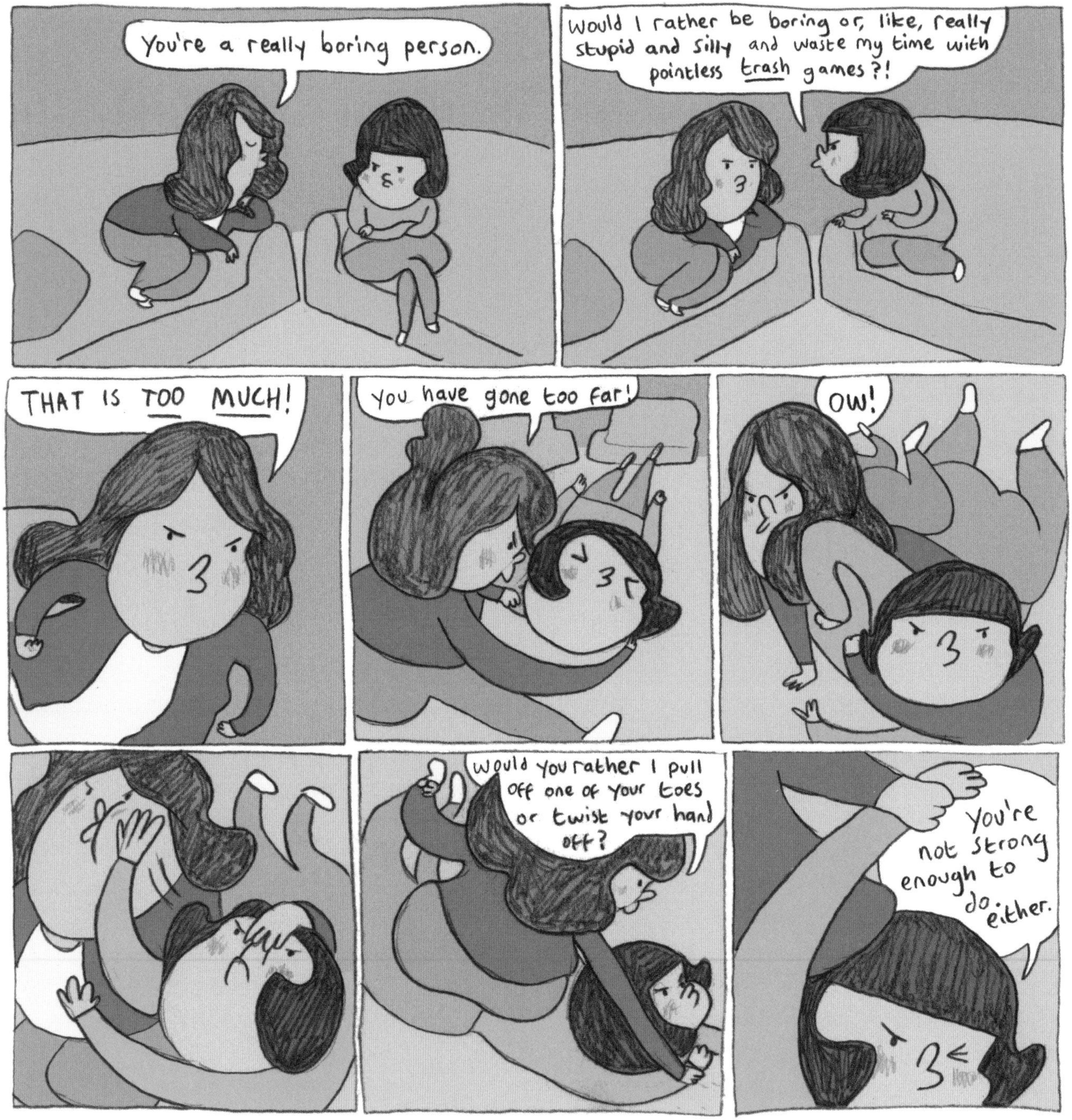
You're a really boring person.
Would I rather be boring or, like, really stupid and silly and waste my time with pointless trash games?!
THAT IS TOO MUCH!
You have gone too far!
OW!
Would you rather I pull off one of your toes or twist your hand off?
You're not strong enough to do either.

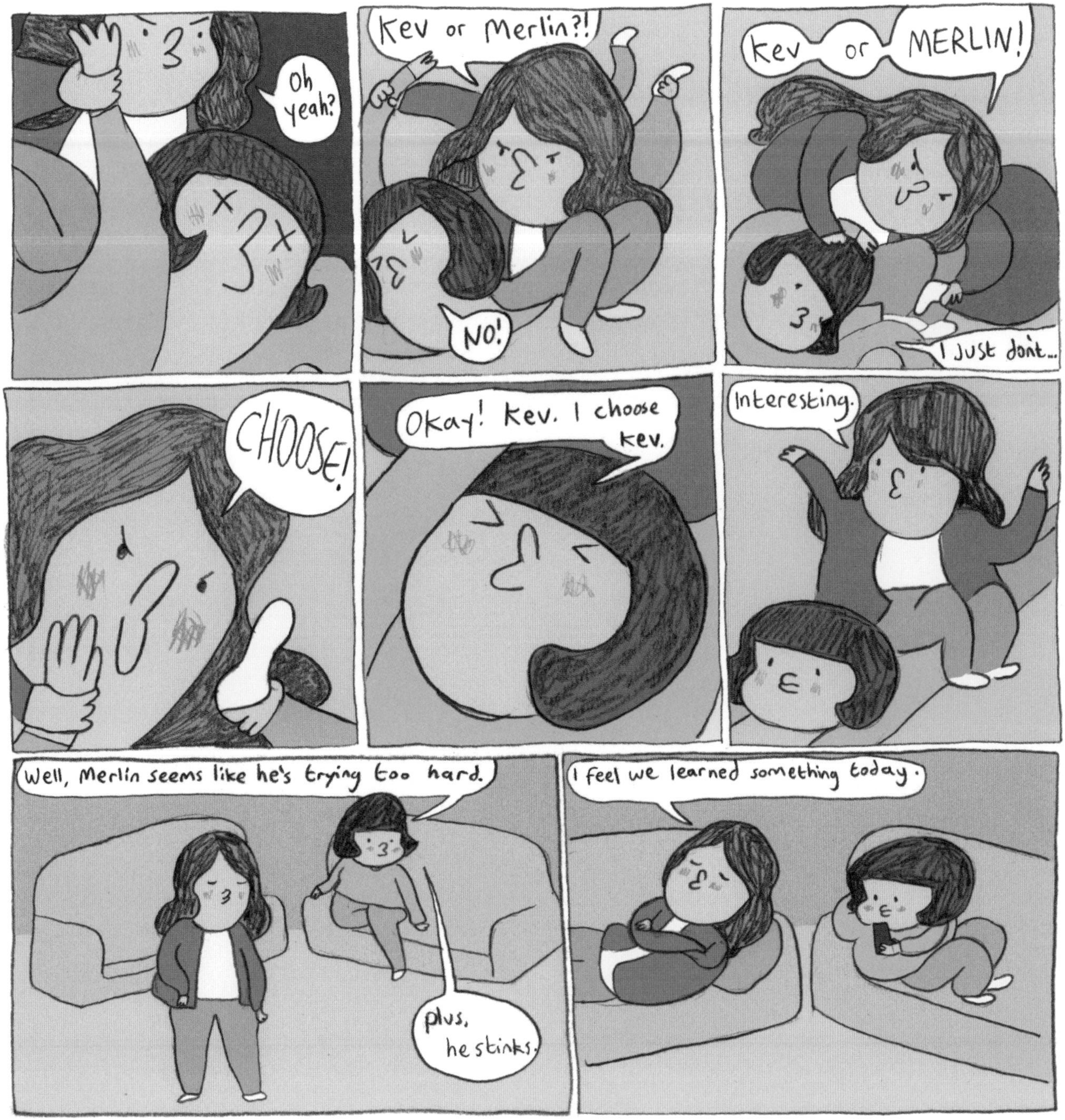
Oh yeah?
Kev or Merlin?!
NO!
Kev or MERLIN!
I just don't...
CHOOSE!
Okay! Kev. I choose Kev.
Interesting.
Well, Merlin seems like he's trying too hard.
plus, he stinks.
I feel we learned something today.

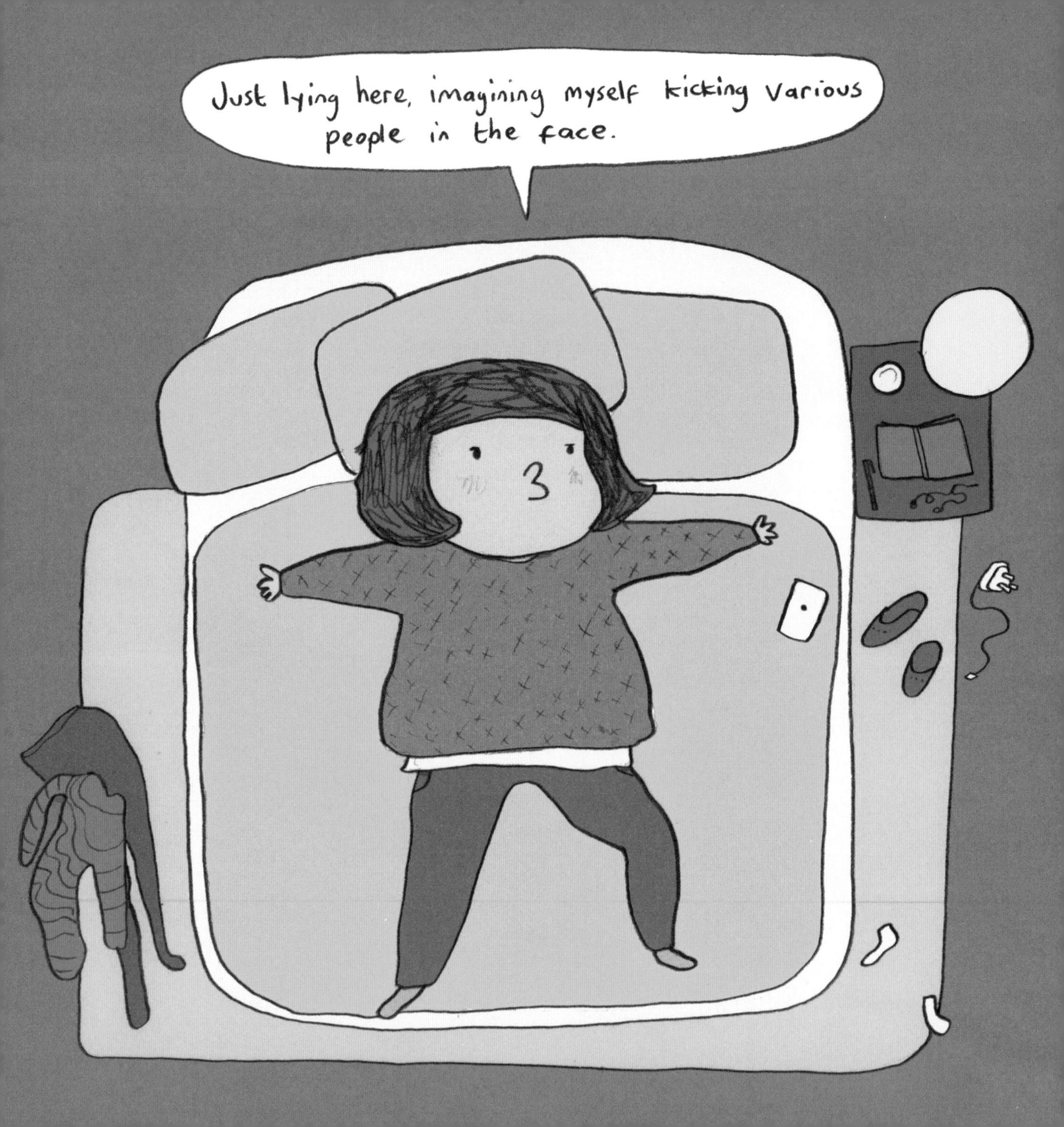
Just lying here, imagining myself kicking various people in the face.

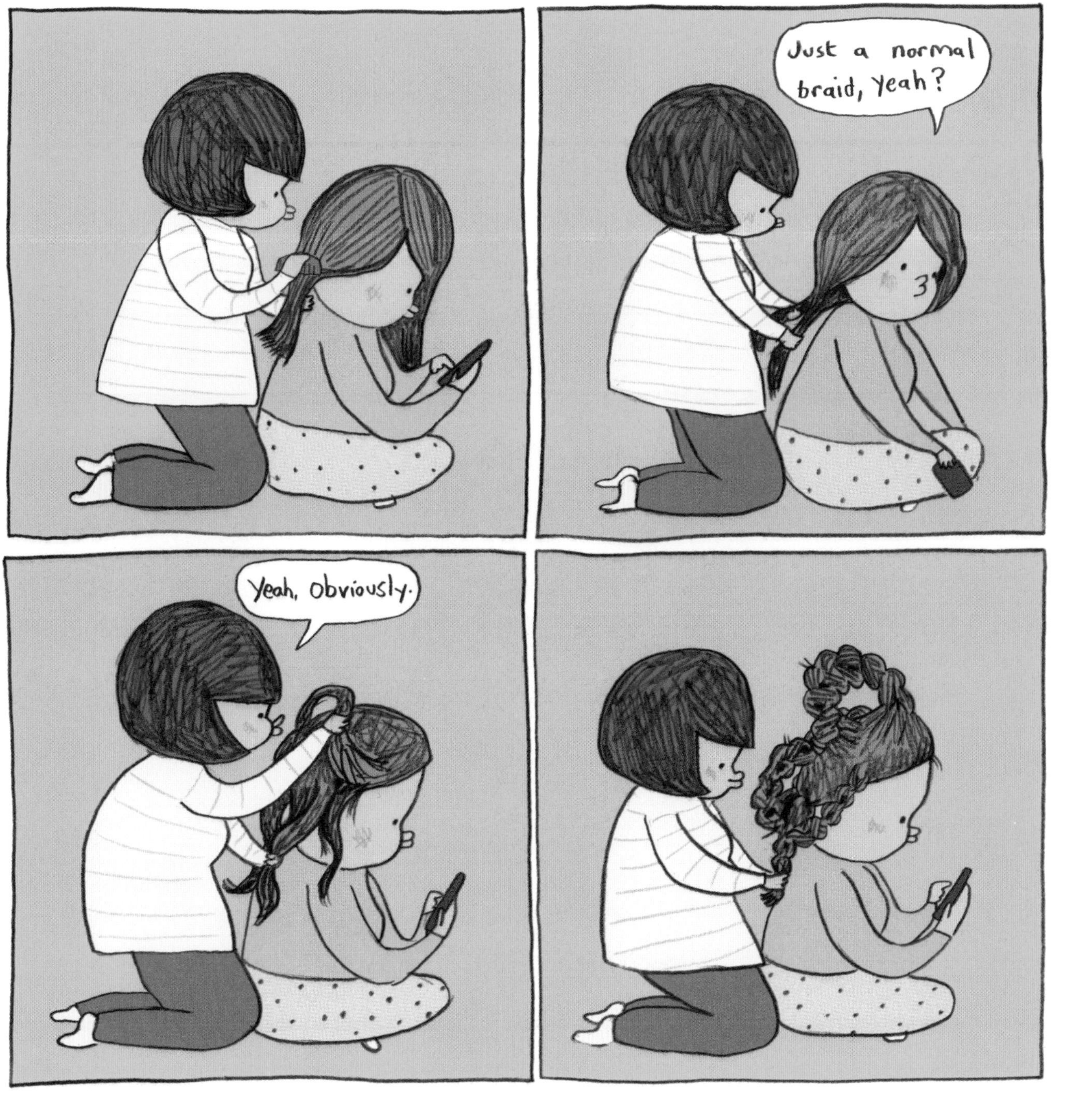
Just a normal braid, Yeah?
Yeah, obviously.

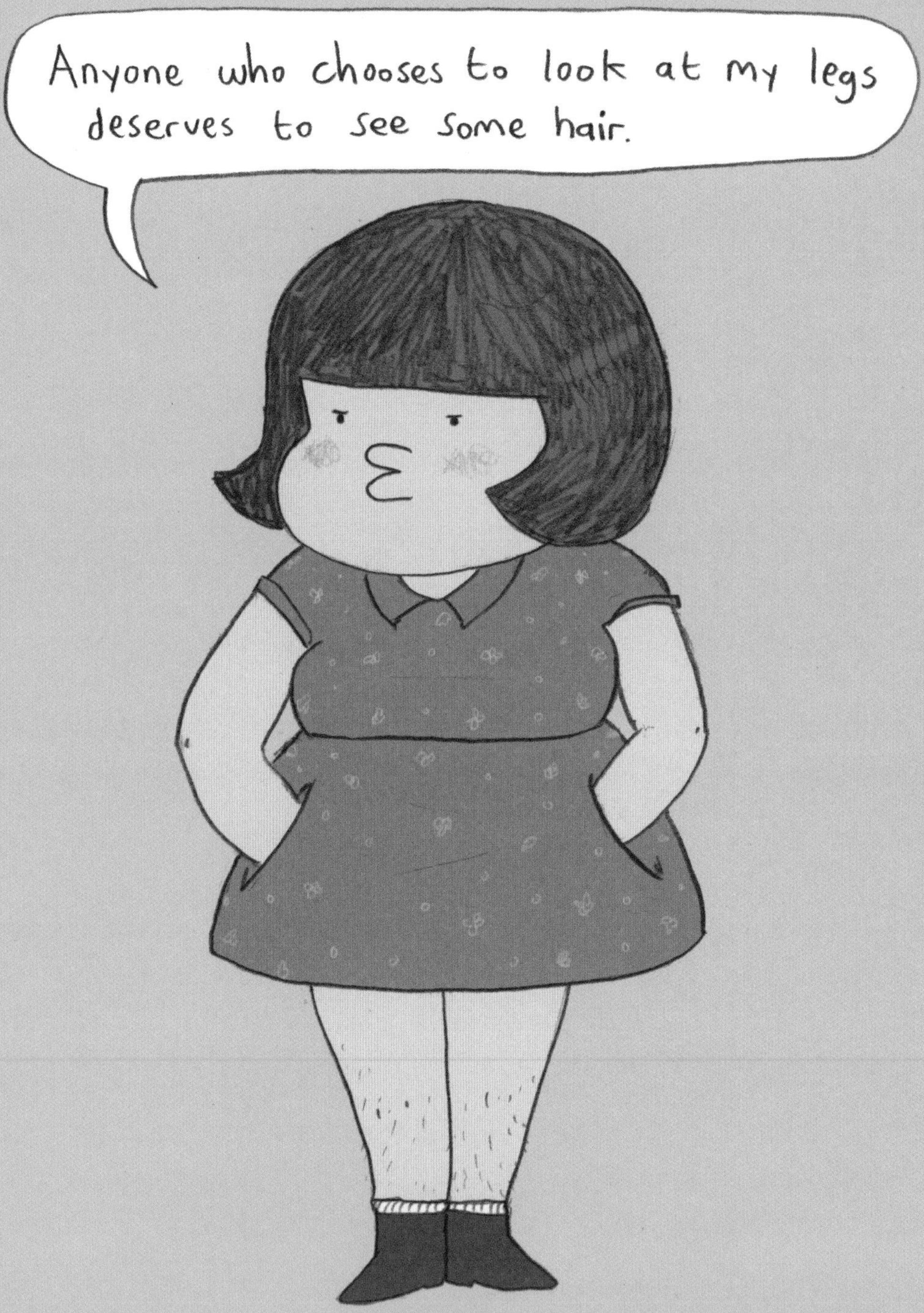
Anyone who chooses to look at my legs deserves to see some hair.

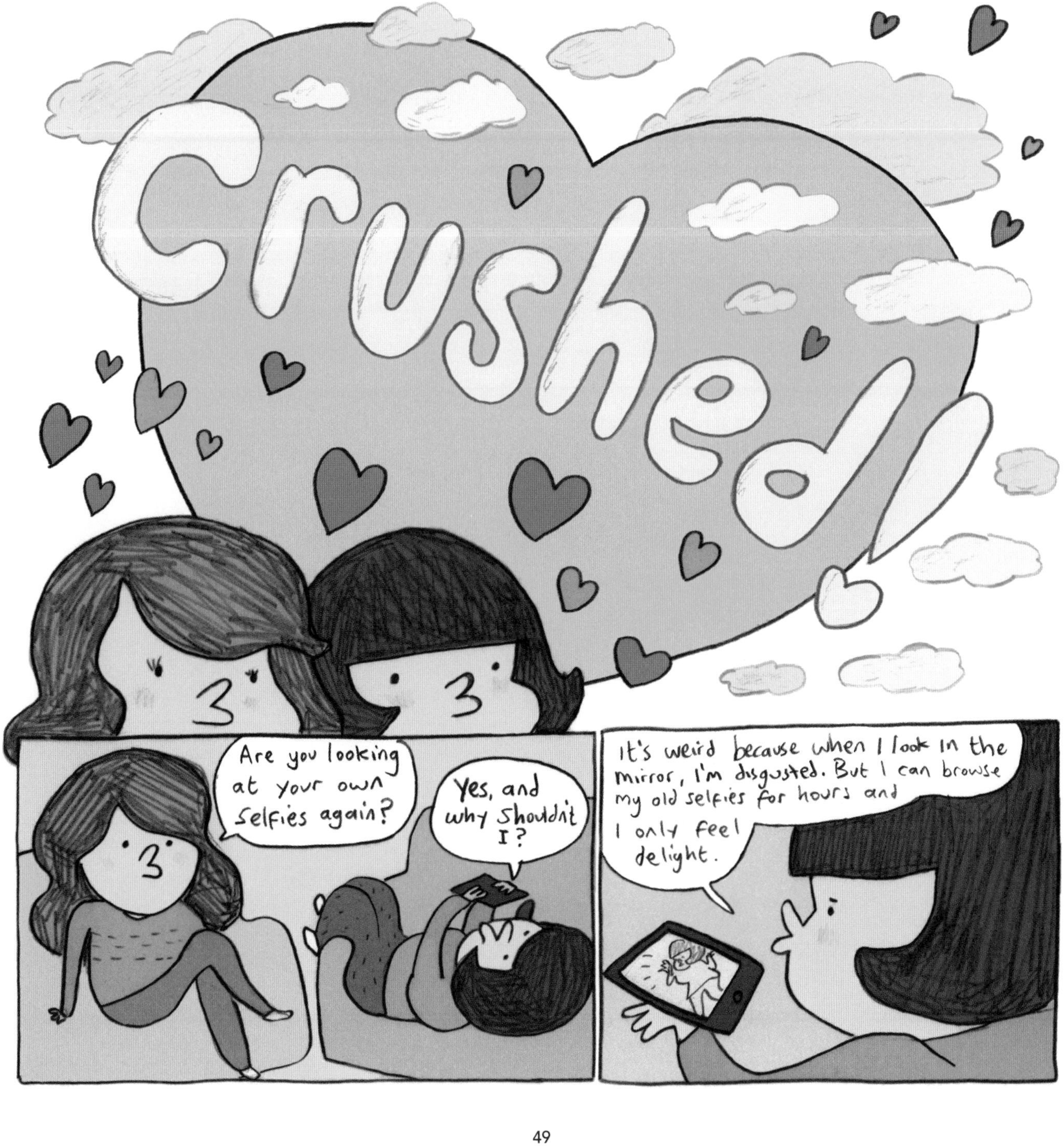
Crushed!
Are you looking at your own selfies again?
Yes, and why shouldn't I?
It's weird because when I look in the mirror, I'm disgusted. But I can browse my old selfies for hours and I only feel delight.

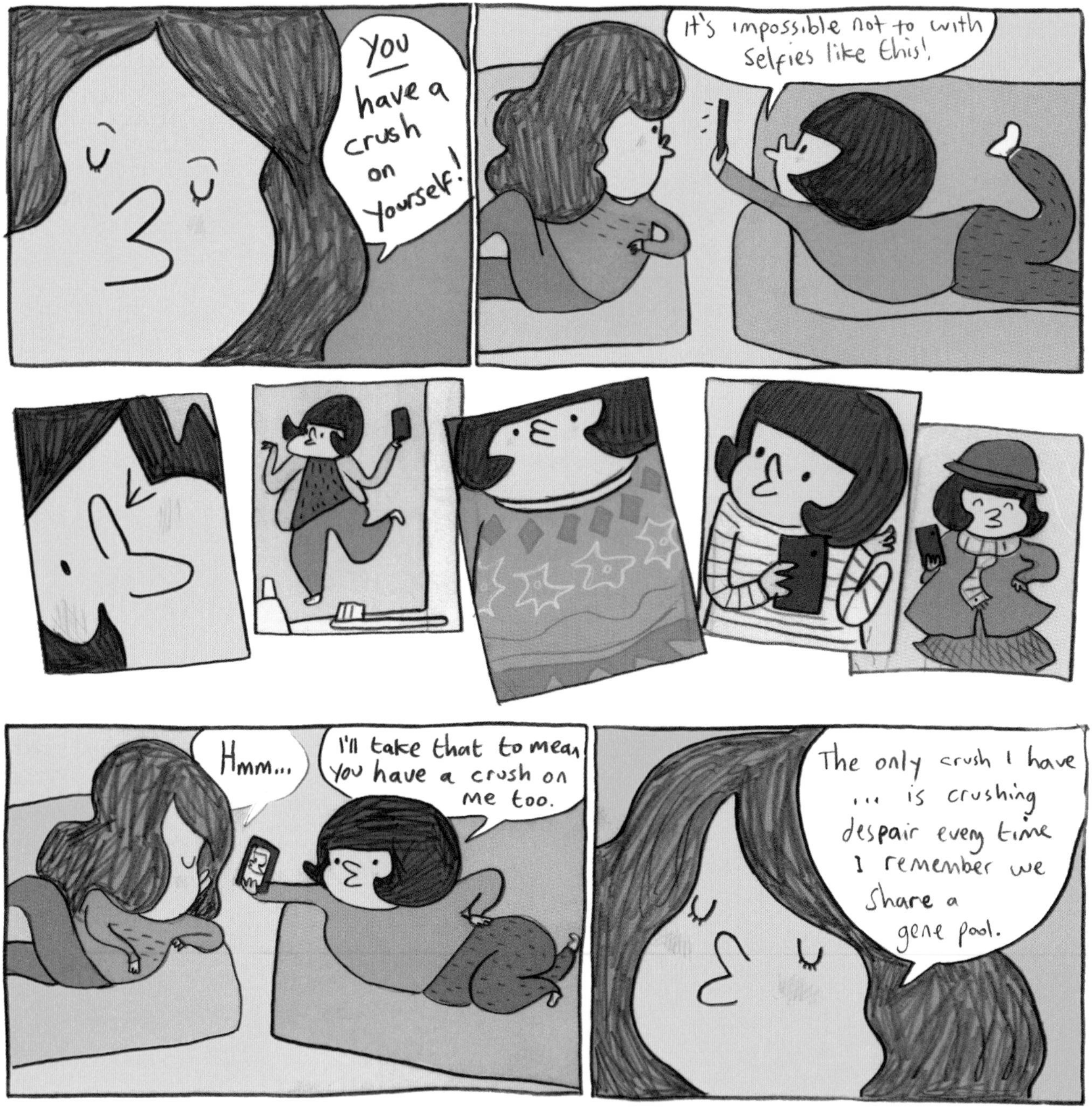
YOU have a crush on yourself!
It's impossible not to with selfies like this!
Hmm...
I'll take that to mean you have a crush on me too.
The only crush I have ... is crushing despair every time I remember we share a gene pool.

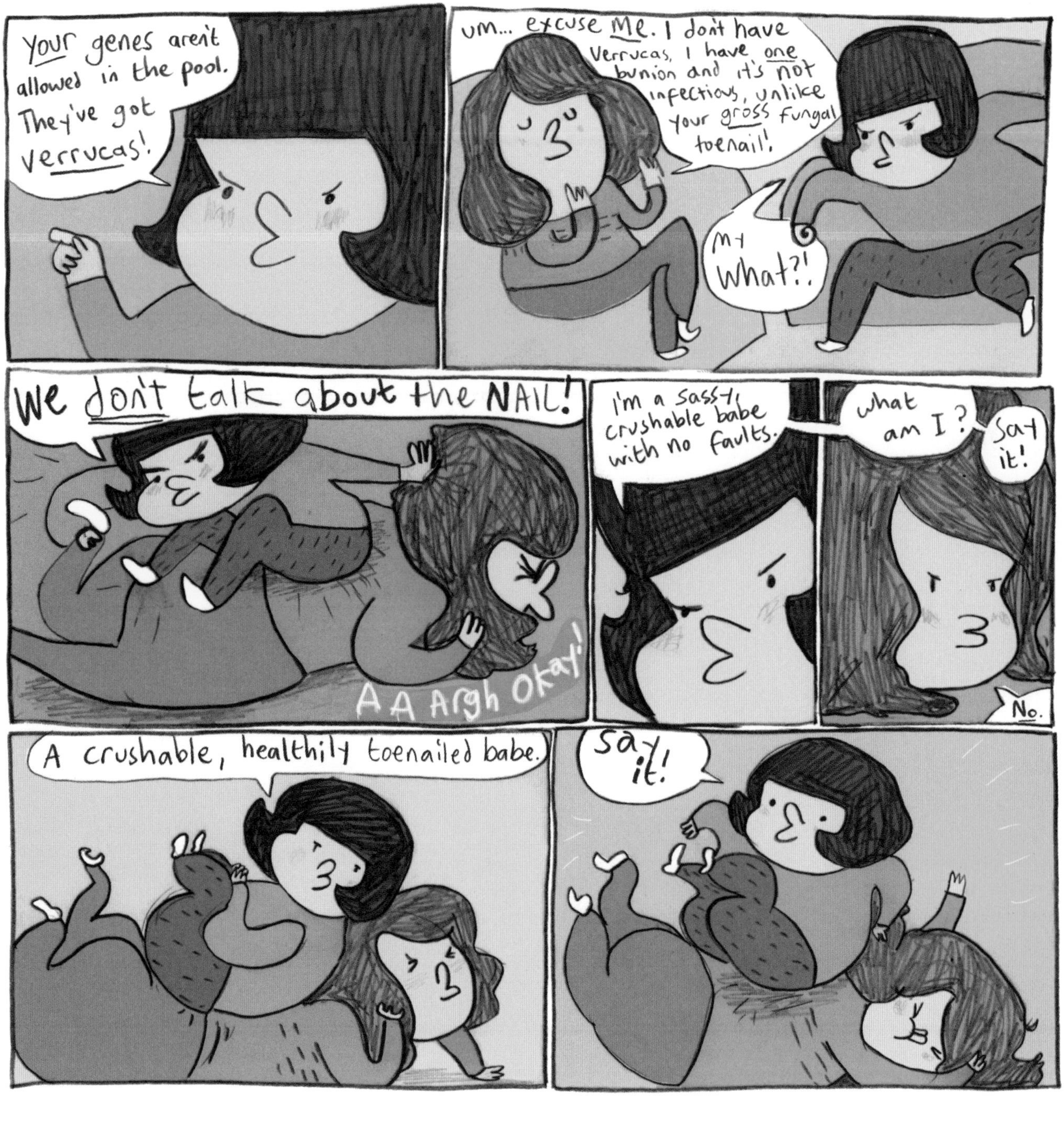
Your genes aren't allowed in the pool. They've got verrucas!
um... excuse Me. I don't have verrucas, I have one bunion and it's not infectious, unlike your gross fungal toenail!
My what?!
We don't talk about the NAIL!
A A Argh Okay!
I'm a sassy, crushable babe with no faults.
what am I?
Say it!
No.
A crushable, healthily toenailed babe.
Say it!

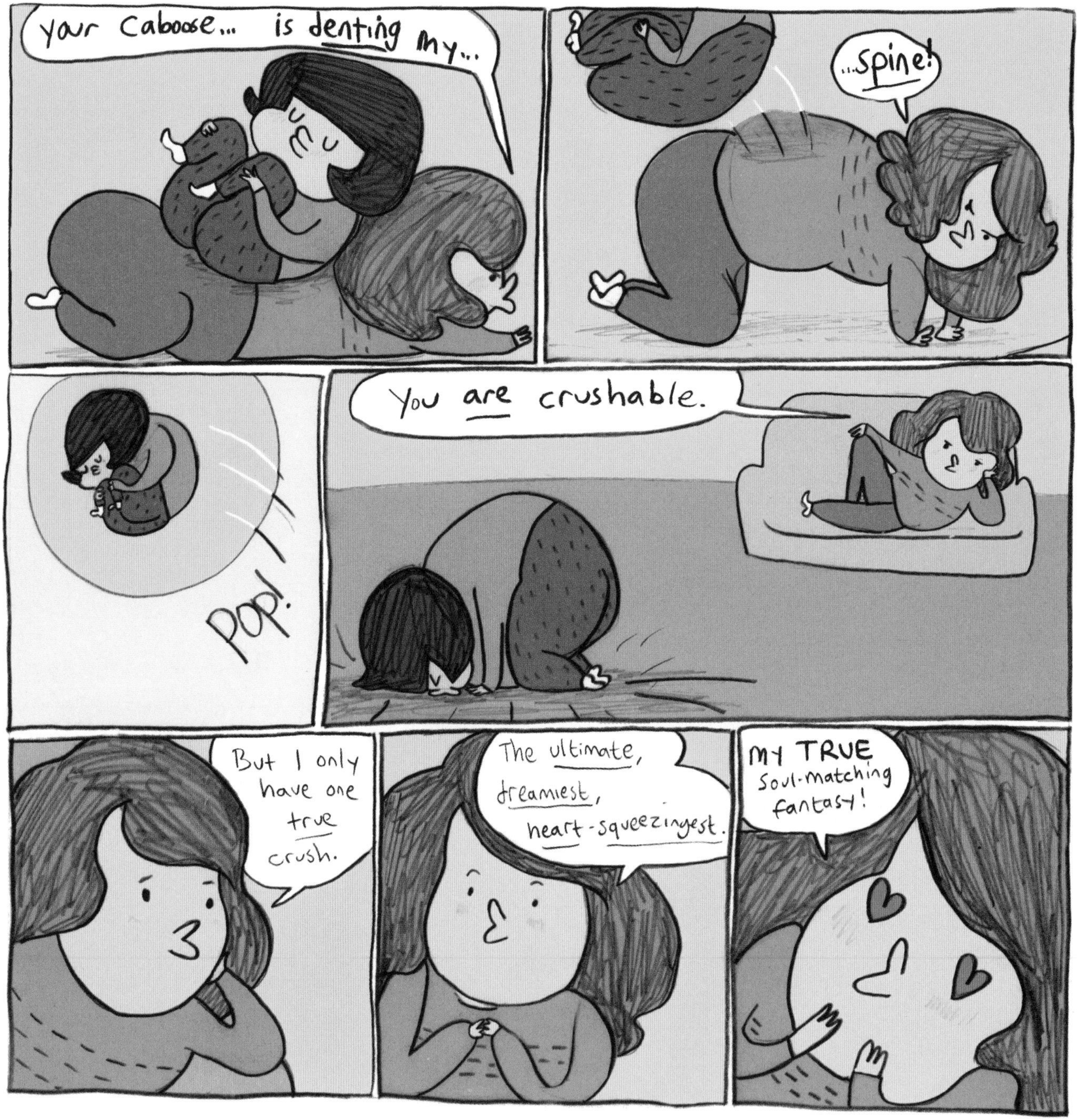
your Caboose... is denting my...
...spine!
POP!
You are crushable.
But I only have one true crush.
The ultimate, dreamiest, heart-squeezingest.
MY TRUE soul-matching fantasy!

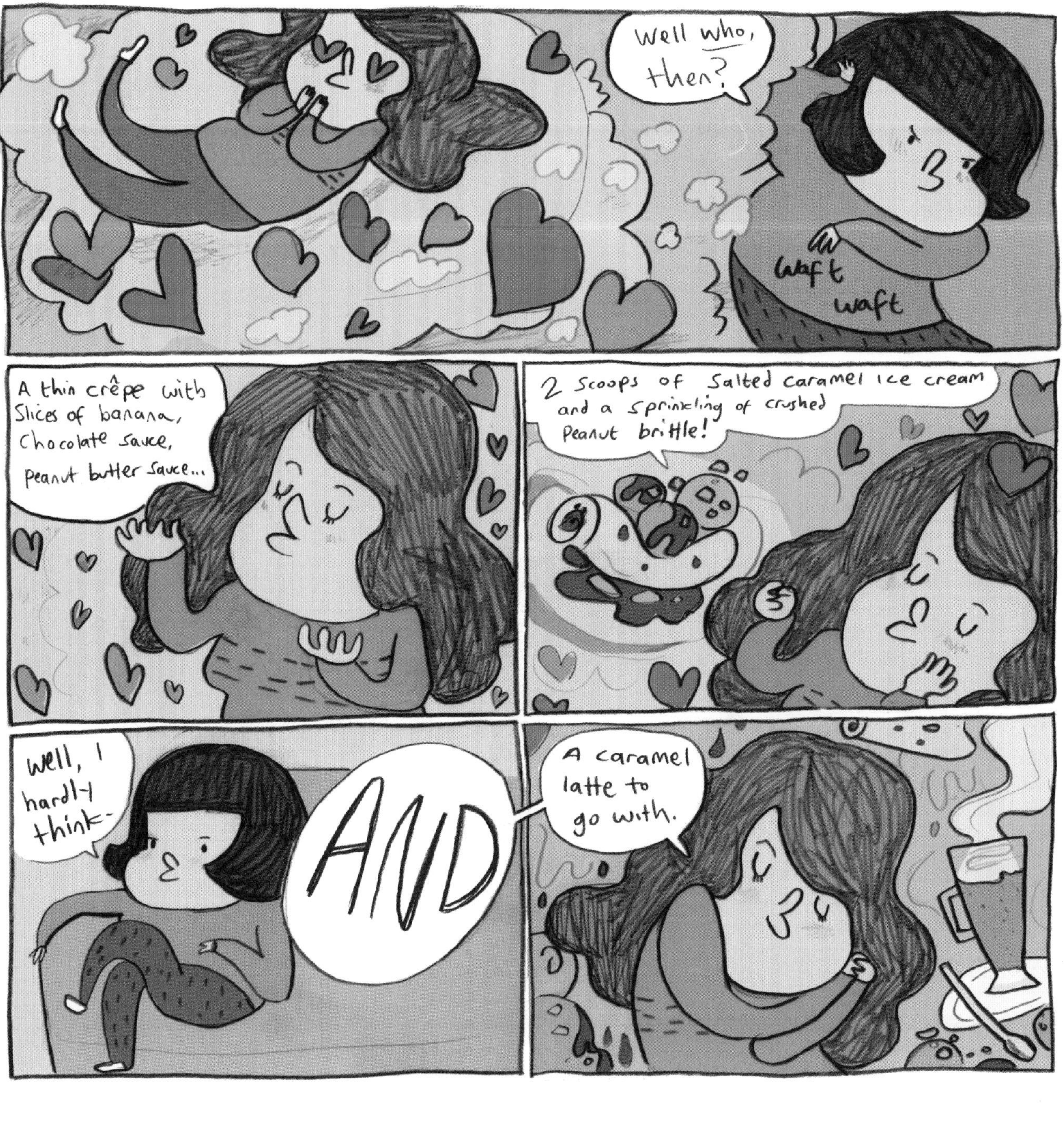

Well who, then?
waft
waft
A thin crêpe with Slices of banana, Chocolate sauce, peanut butter sauce...
2 Scoops of Salted caramel ice cream and a sprinkling of crushed Peanut brittle!
Well, I hardly think-
AND
A caramel latte to go with.

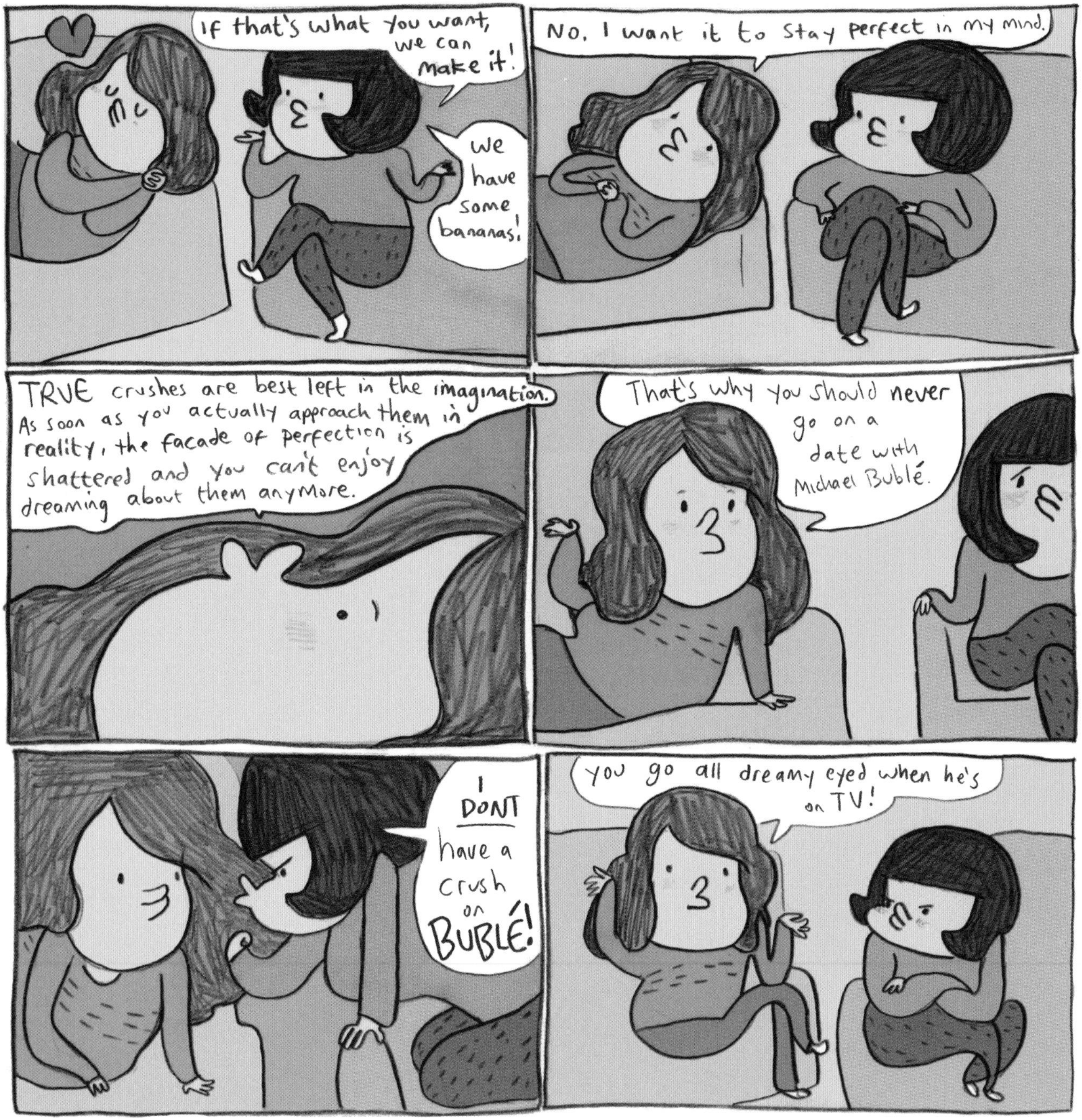
If that's what you want, we can make it!
We have some bananas!
No. I want it to stay perfect in my mind.
TRUE crushes are best left in the imagination. As soon as you actually approach them in reality, the facade of perfection is shattered and you can't enjoy dreaming about them anymore.
That's why you should never go on a date with Michael Bublé.
I DONT have a crush on BUBLÉ!
You go all dreamy eyed when he's on TV!

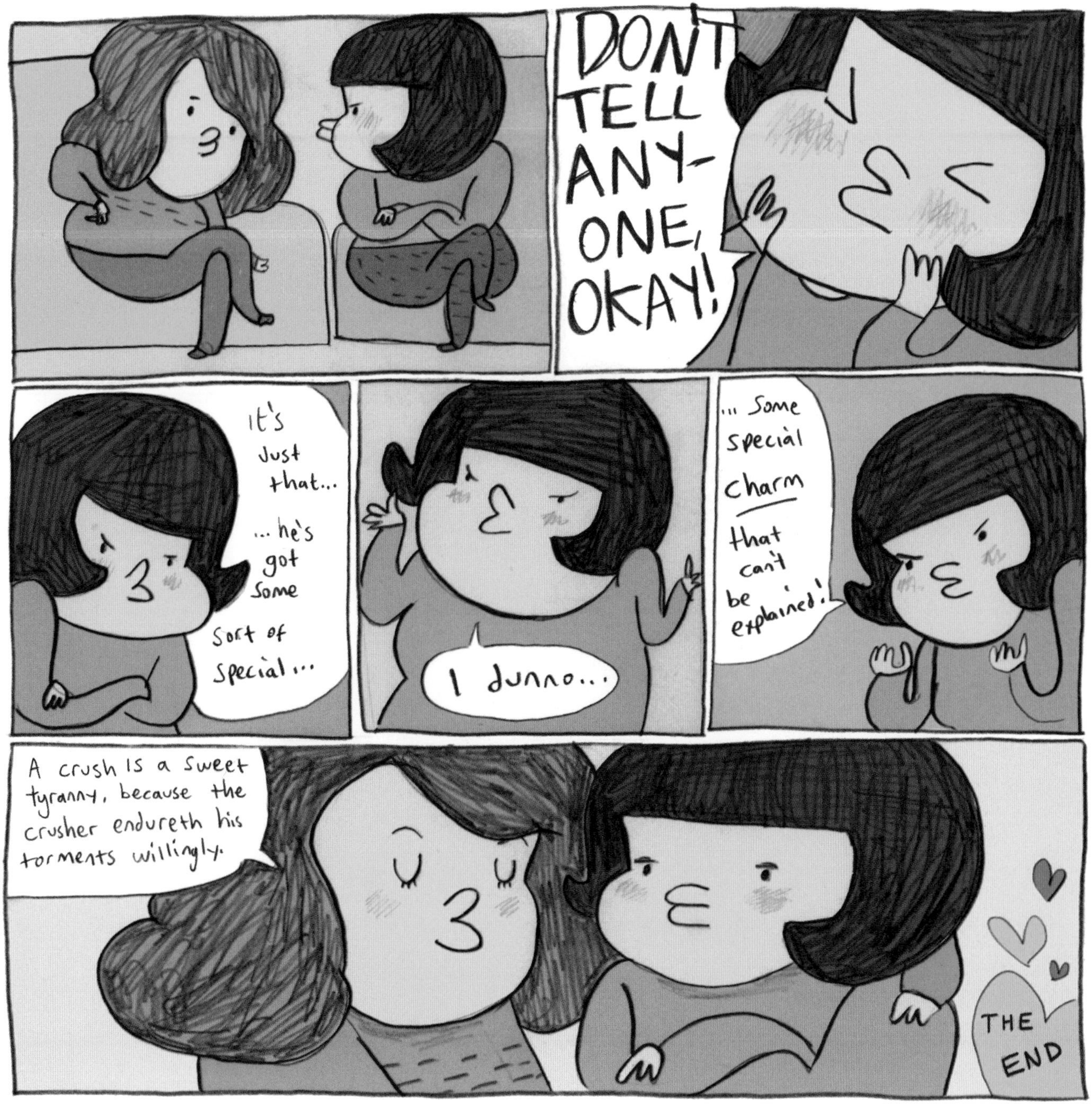

DON'T TELL ANY-ONE, OKAY!
It's just that...
...he's got some sort of special...
I dunno...
...some special charm that can't be explained!
A crush is a sweet tyranny, because the crusher endureth his torments willingly.
THE END

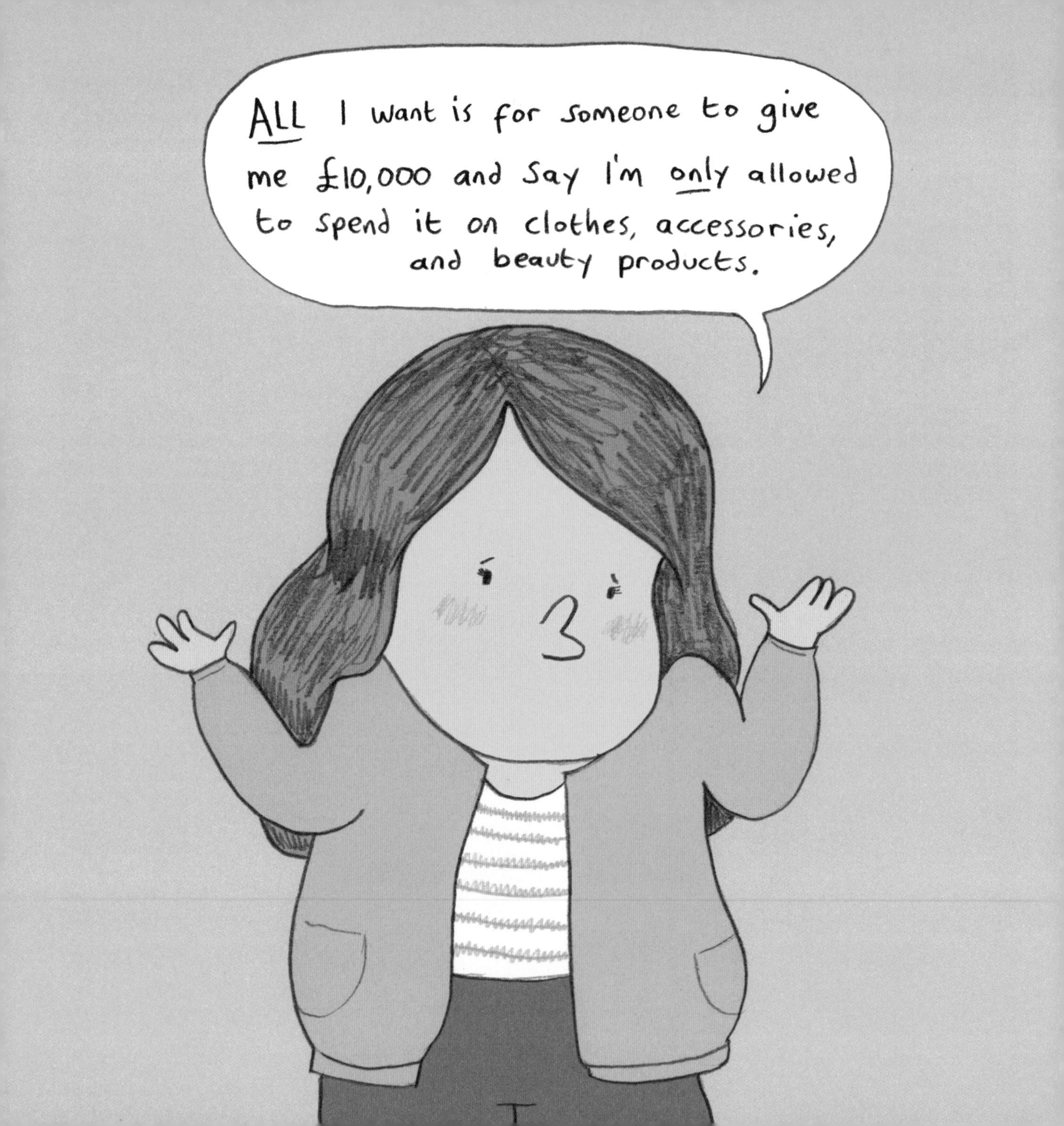
ALL I want is for someone to give me £10,000 and say I'm only allowed to spend it on clothes, accessories, and beauty products.

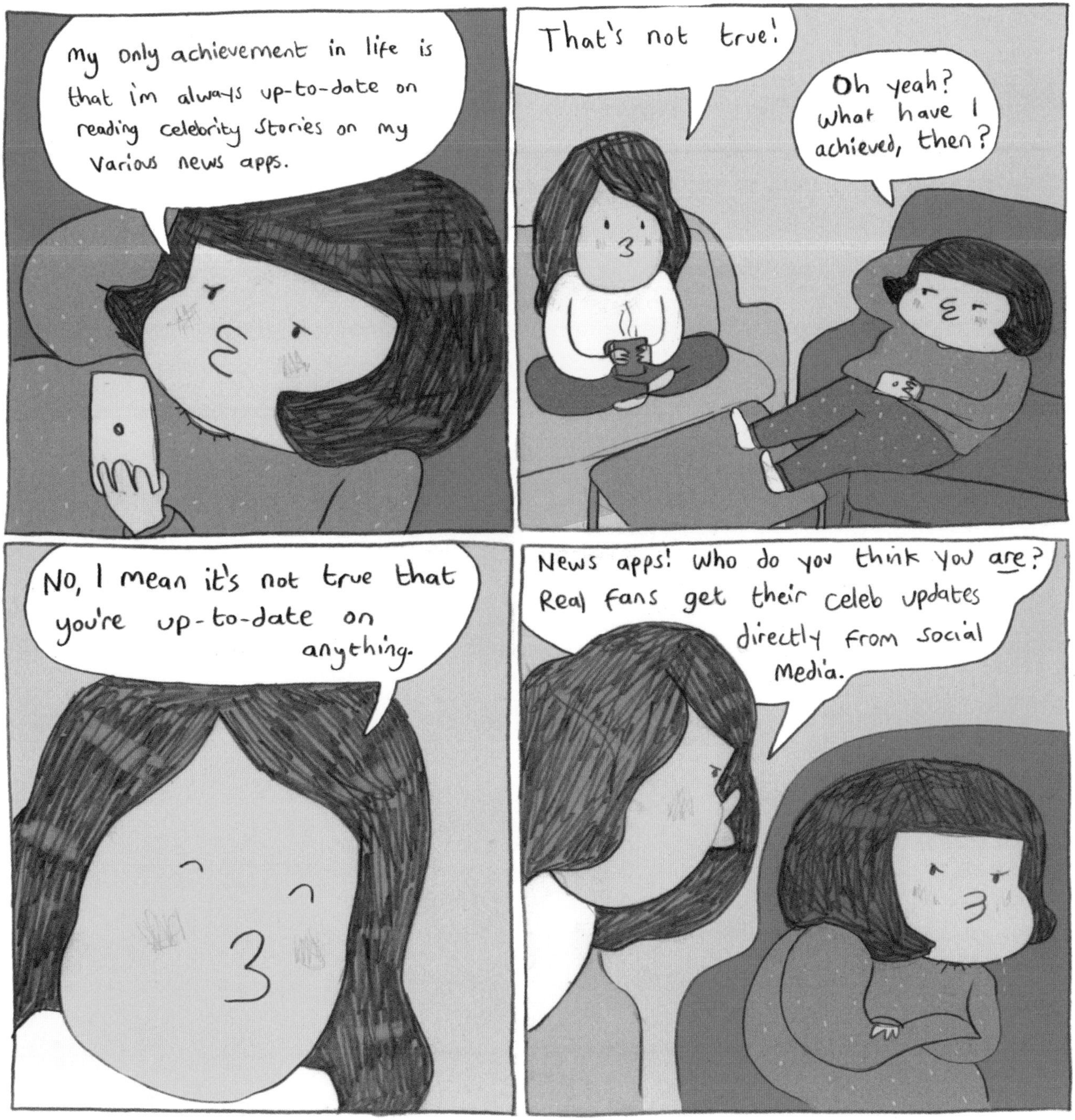
My only achievement in life is that i'm always up-to-date on reading celebrity stories on my various news apps.
That's not true!
Oh yeah? What have I achieved, then?
No, I mean it's not true that you're up-to-date on anything.
News apps! Who do you think you are? Real fans get their celeb updates directly from social media.

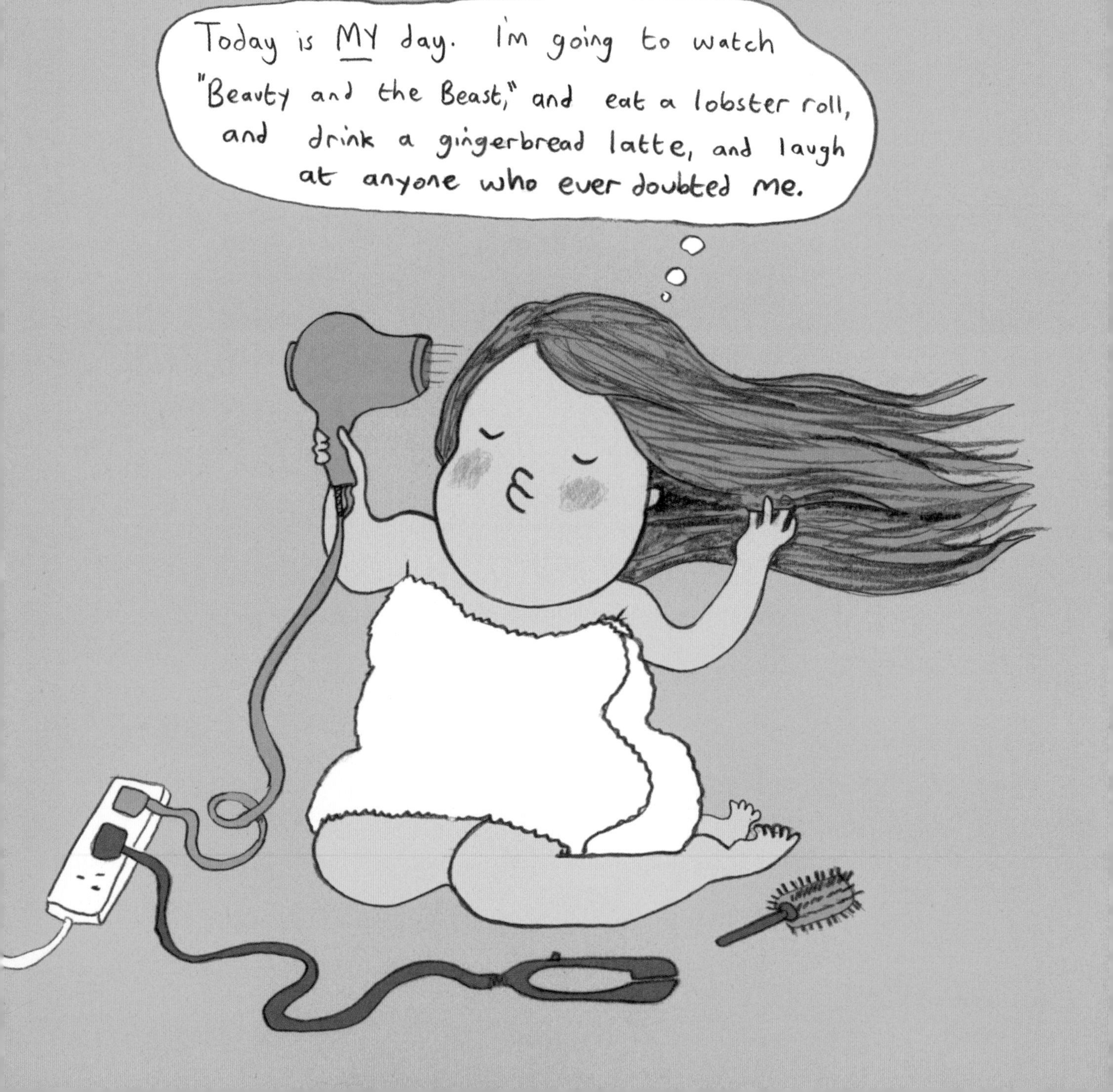
Today is MY day. I'm going to watch "Beauty and the Beast," and eat a lobster roll, and drink a gingerbread latte, and laugh at anyone who ever doubted me.

Clothes

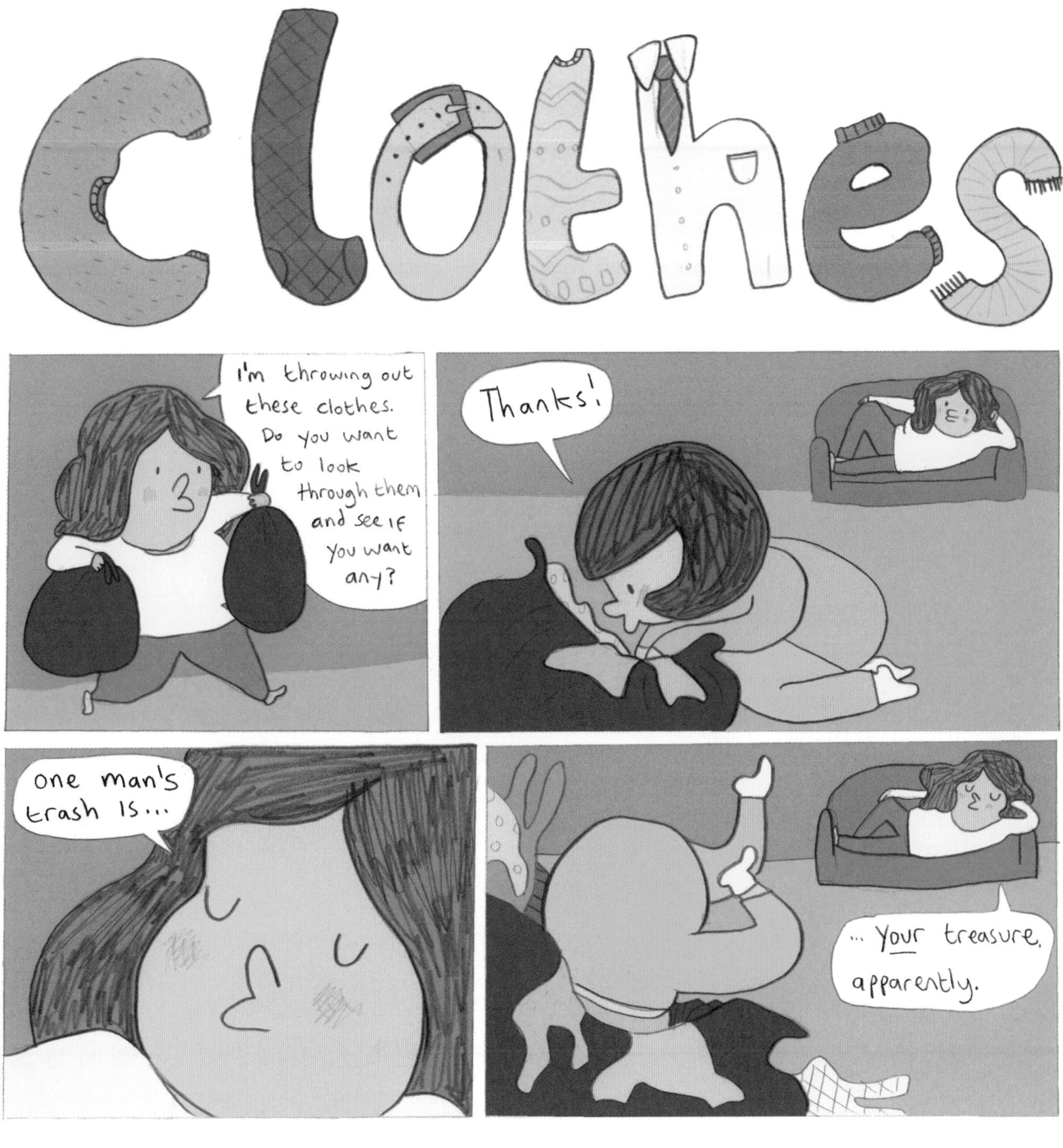

I'm throwing out these clothes. Do you want to look through them and see if you want any?
Thanks!
one man's trash is...
... your treasure, apparently.

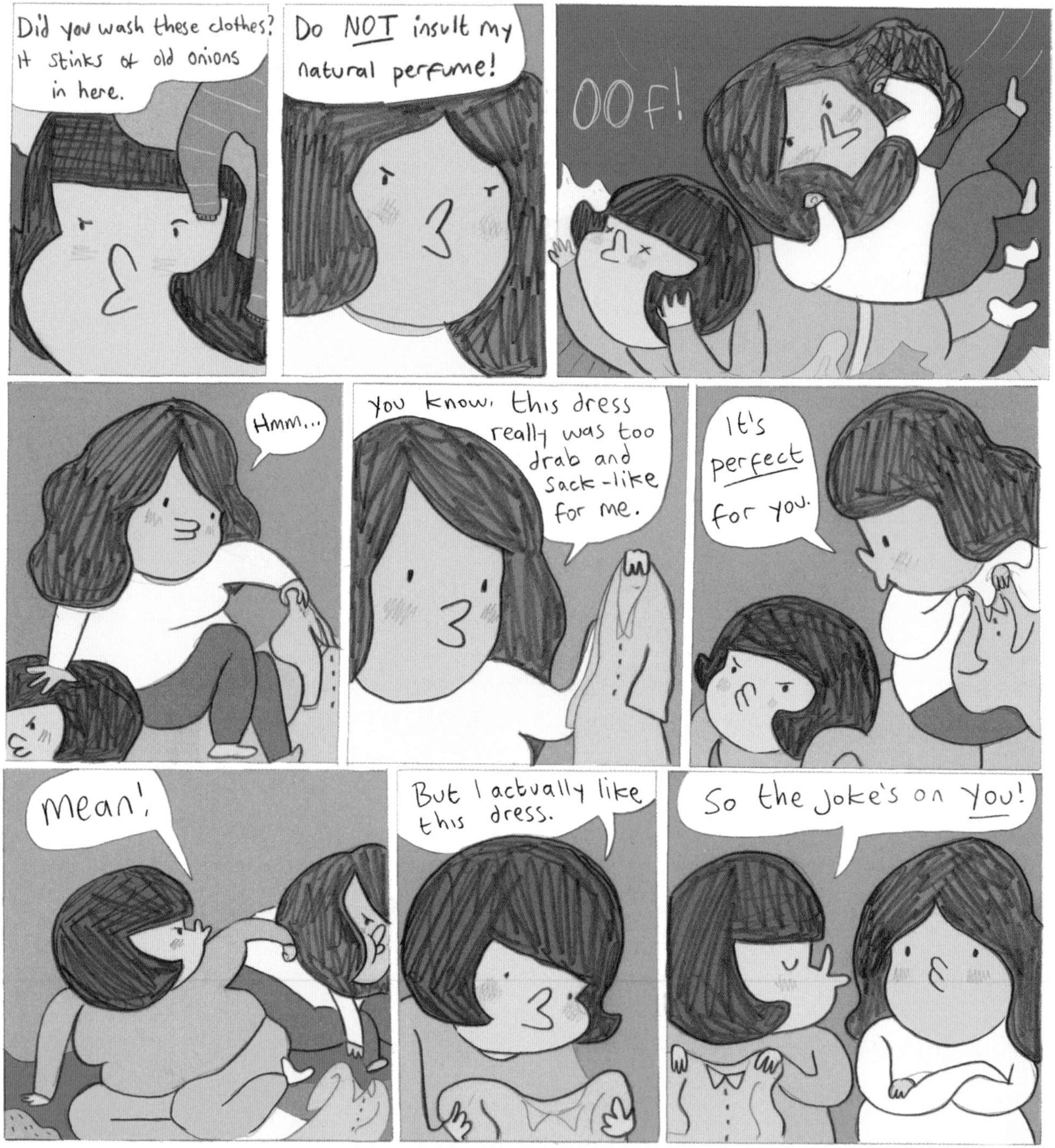
Did you wash these clothes? It stinks of old onions in here.
Do NOT insult my natural perfume!
OOF!
Hmm...
You know, this dress really was too drab and sack-like for me.
It's perfect for you.
Mean!
But I actually like this dress.
So the joke's on You!

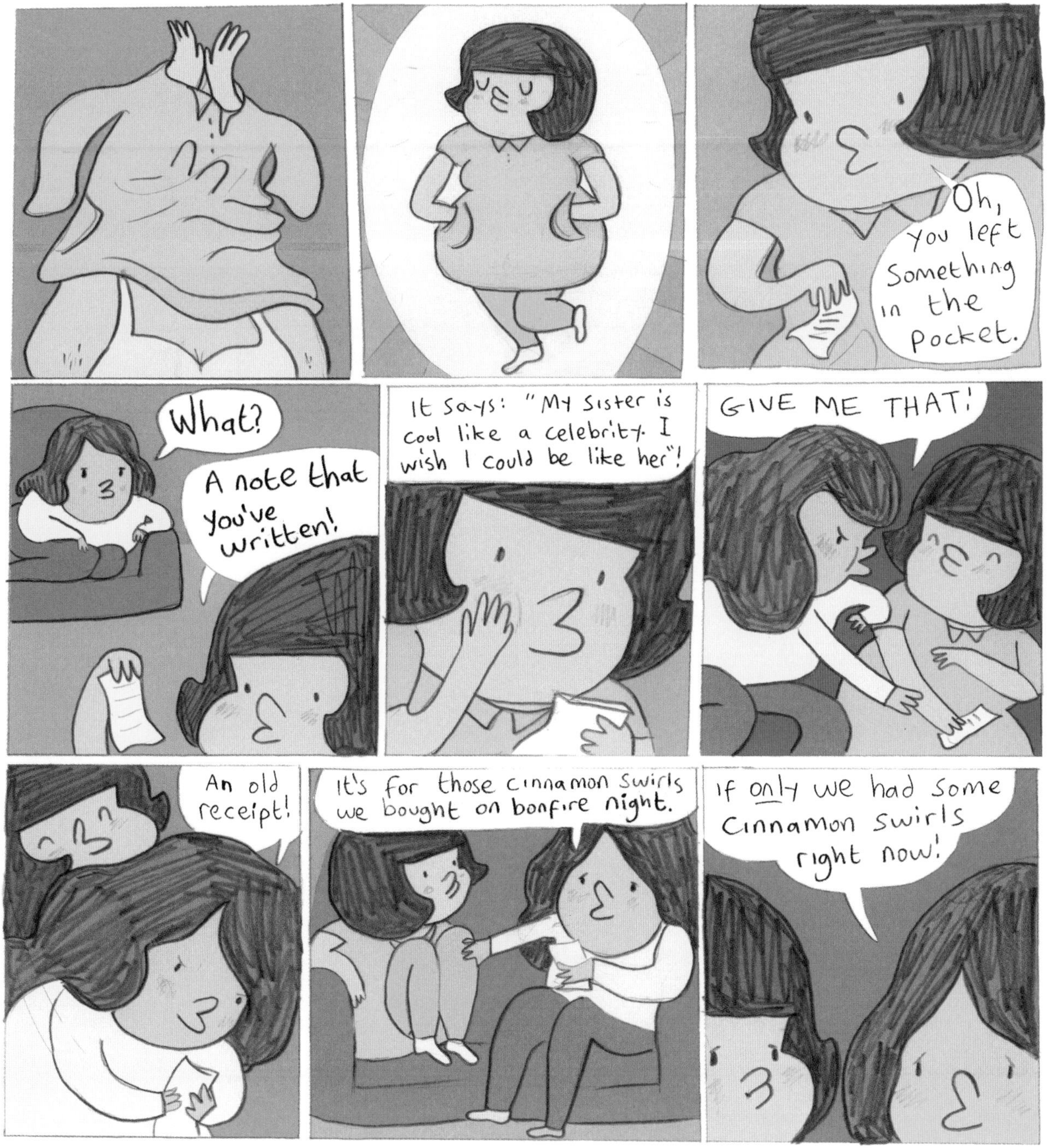

Oh, you left something in the pocket.
What?
A note that you've written!
It says: "My sister is cool like a celebrity. I wish I could be like her"!
GIVE ME THAT!
An old receipt!
It's for those cinnamon swirls we bought on bonfire night.
If only we had some cinnamon swirls right now!

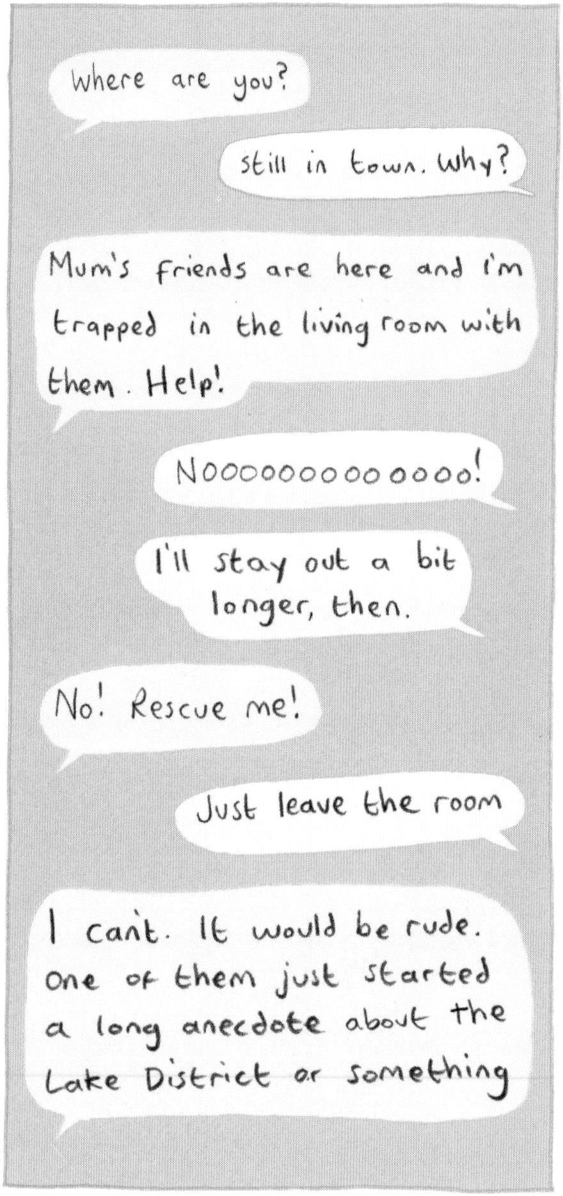
Where are you?
Still in town. Why?
Mum's friends are here and I'm trapped in the living room with them. Help!
Nooooooooooooo!
I'll stay out a bit longer, then.
No! Rescue me!
Just leave the room
I can't. It would be rude. One of them just started a long anecdote about the Lake District or something

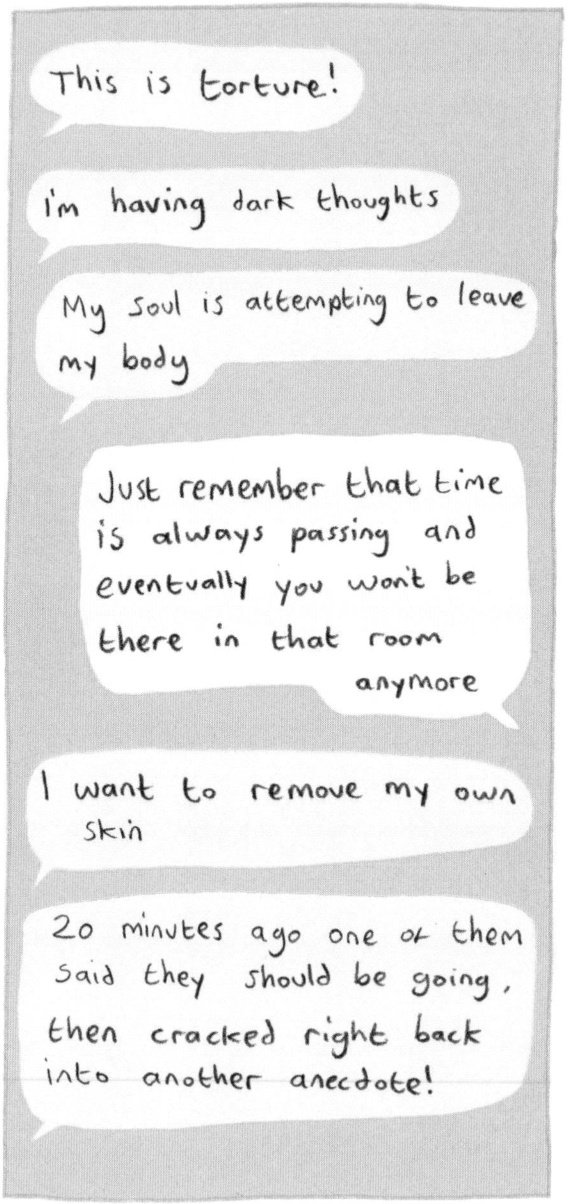
This is torture!
I'm having dark thoughts
My soul is attempting to leave my body
Just remember that time is always passing and eventually you won't be there in that room anymore
I want to remove my own skin
20 minutes ago one of them said they should be going, then cracked right back into another anecdote!

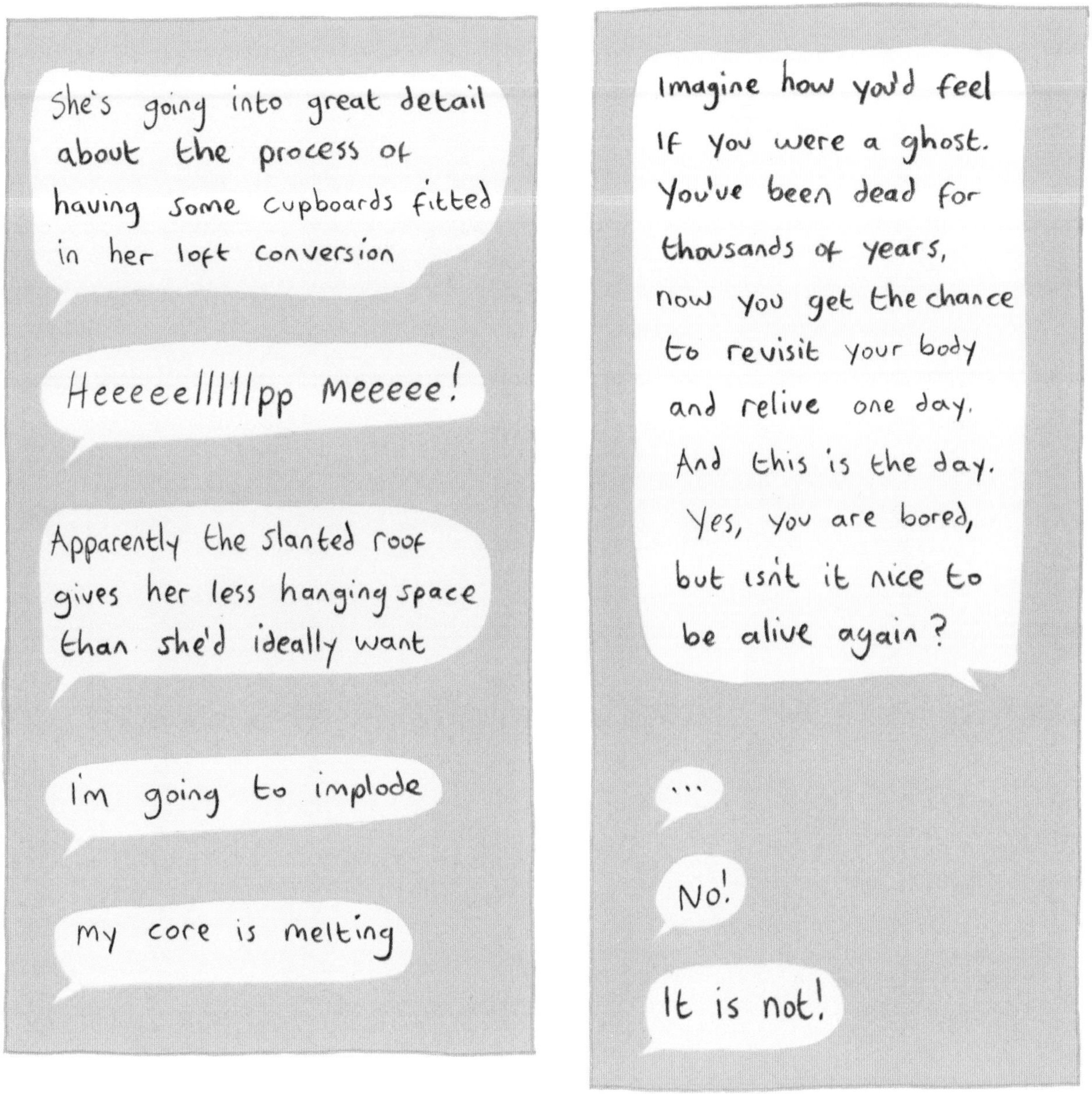
She's going into great detail about the process of having some cupboards fitted in her loft conversion
Heeeeellllllpp Meeeee!
Apparently the slanted roof gives her less hanging space than she'd ideally want
I'm going to implode
my core is melting
Imagine how you'd feel if you were a ghost. You've been dead for thousands of years, now you get the chance to revisit your body and relive one day. And this is the day. Yes, you are bored, but isn't it nice to be alive again?
...
No!
It is not!

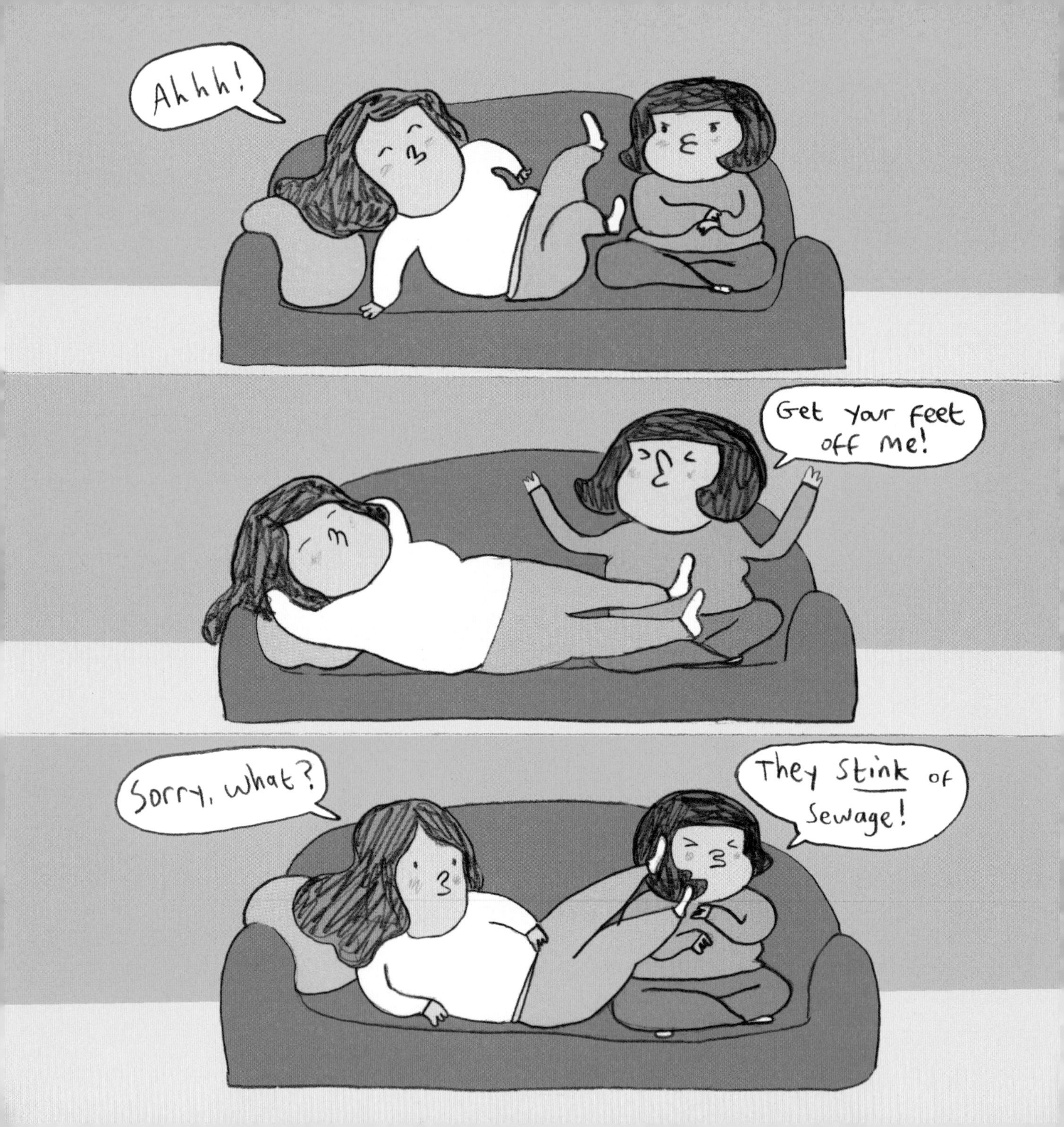
Ahhh!
Get your feet off me!
Sorry, what?
They stink of sewage!

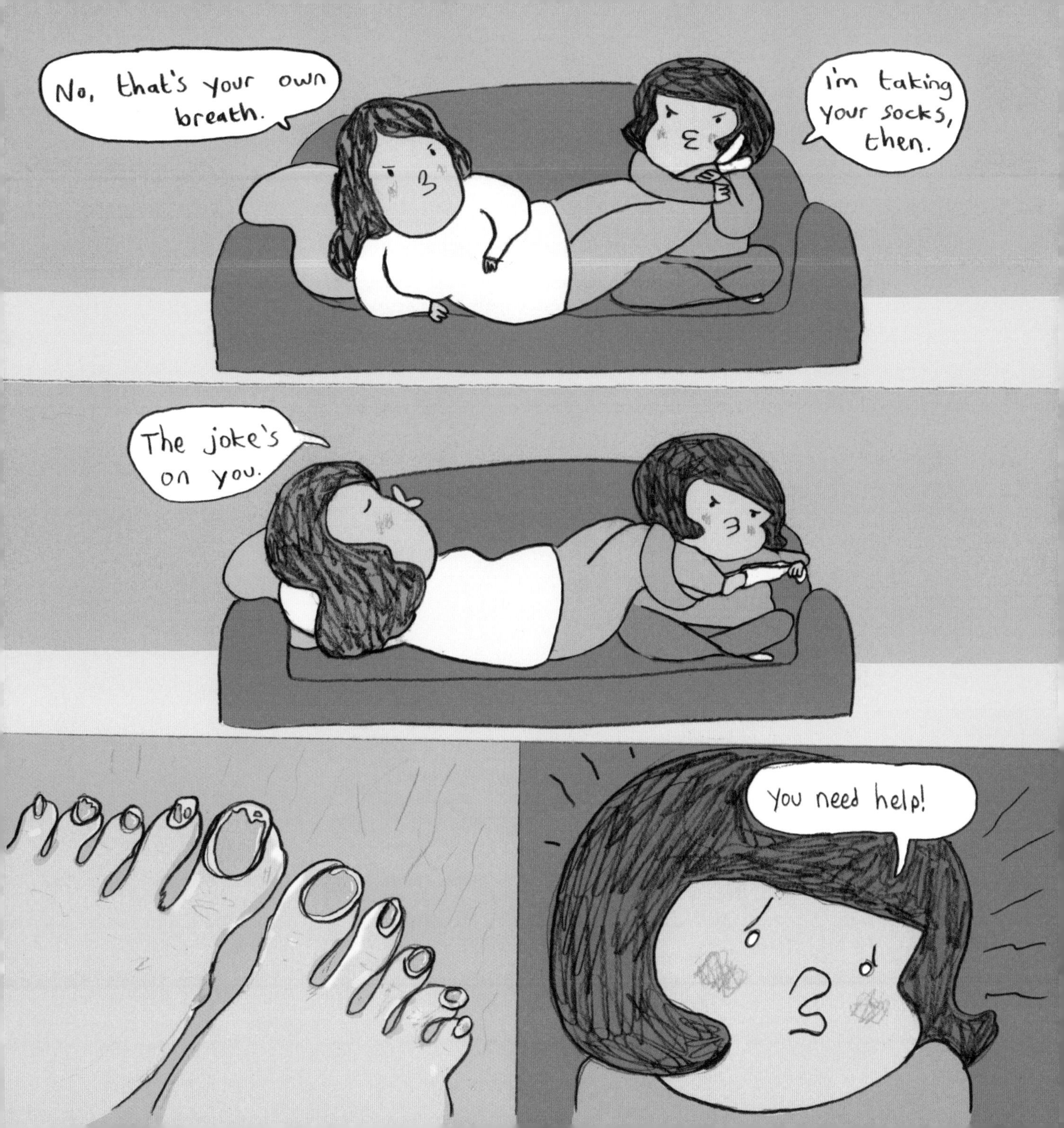
No, that's your own breath.
I'm taking your socks, then.
The joke's on you.
You need help!

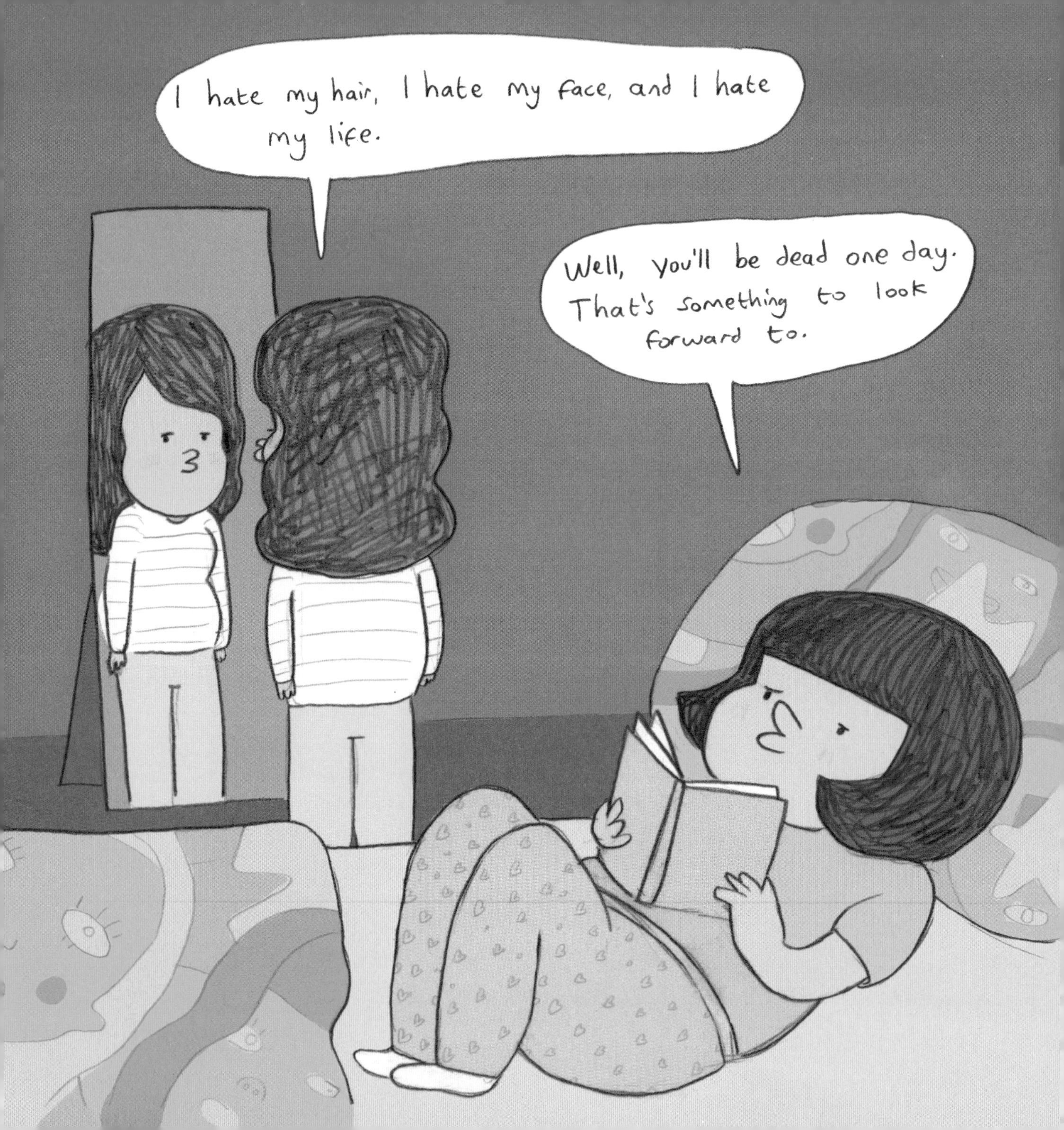
I hate my hair, I hate my face, and I hate my life.
Well, you'll be dead one day. That's something to look forward to.

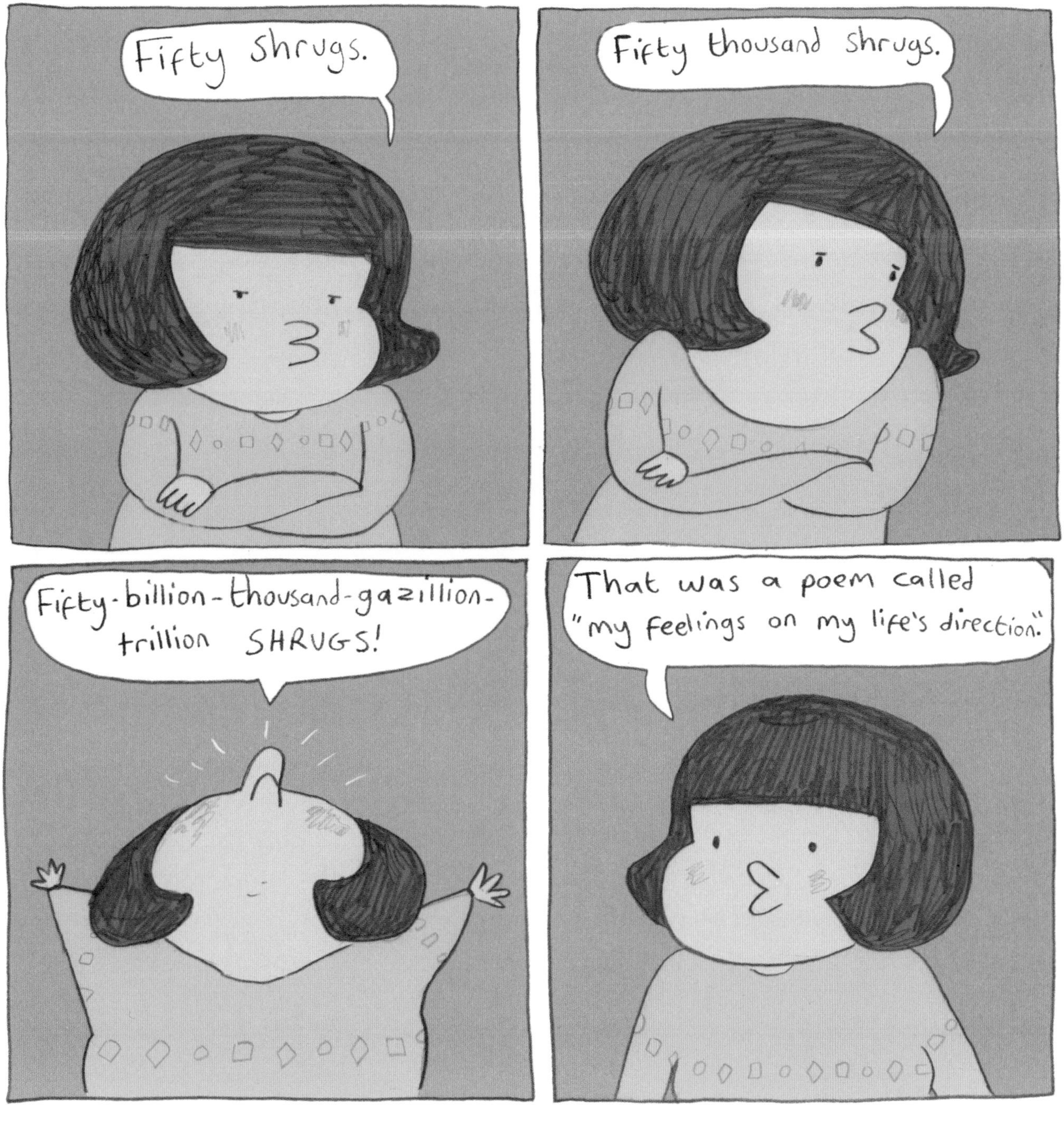
Fifty shrugs.
Fifty thousand shrugs.
Fifty-billion-thousand-gazillion-trillion SHRUGS!
That was a poem called "my feelings on my life's direction."

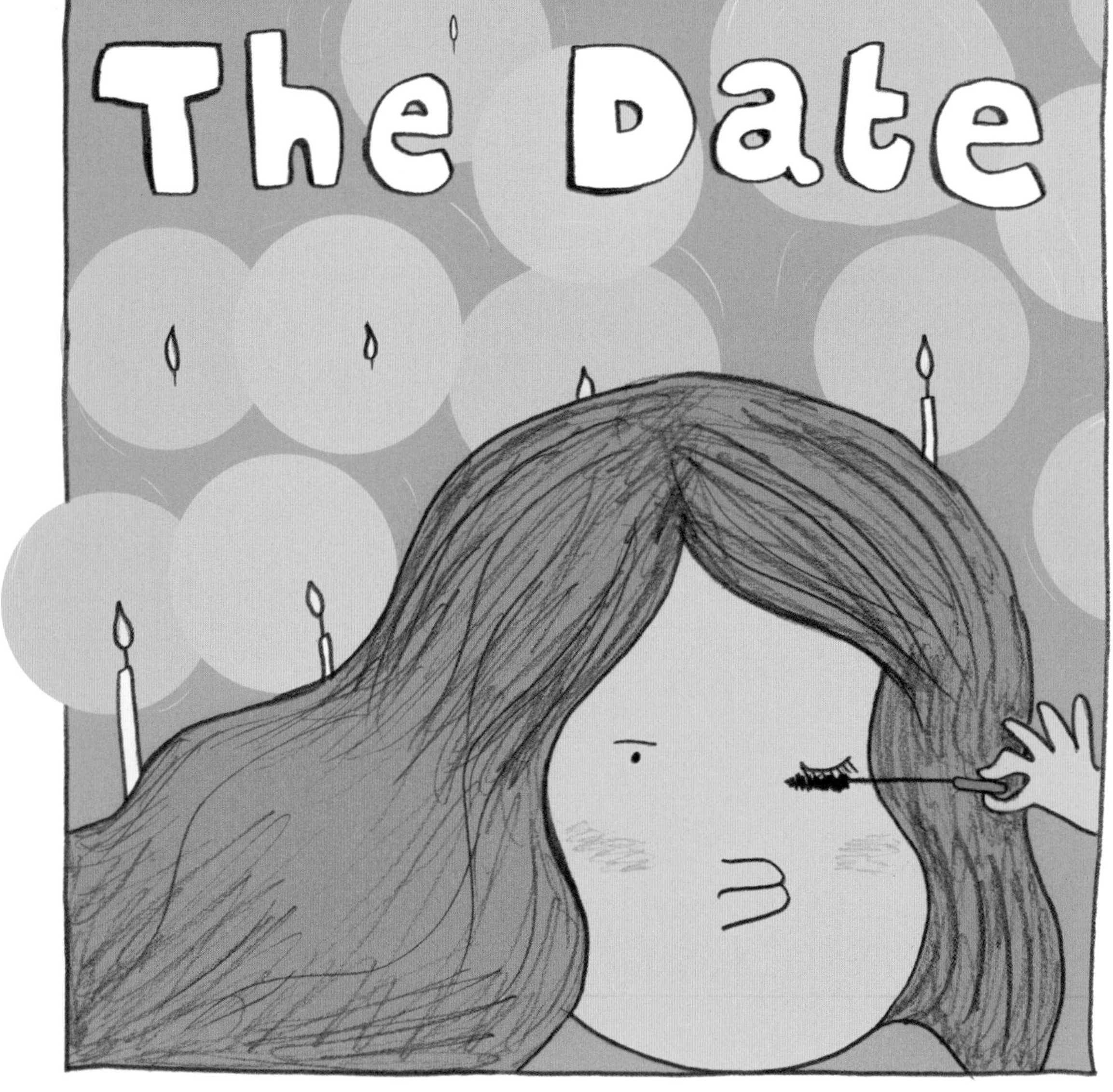
The Date

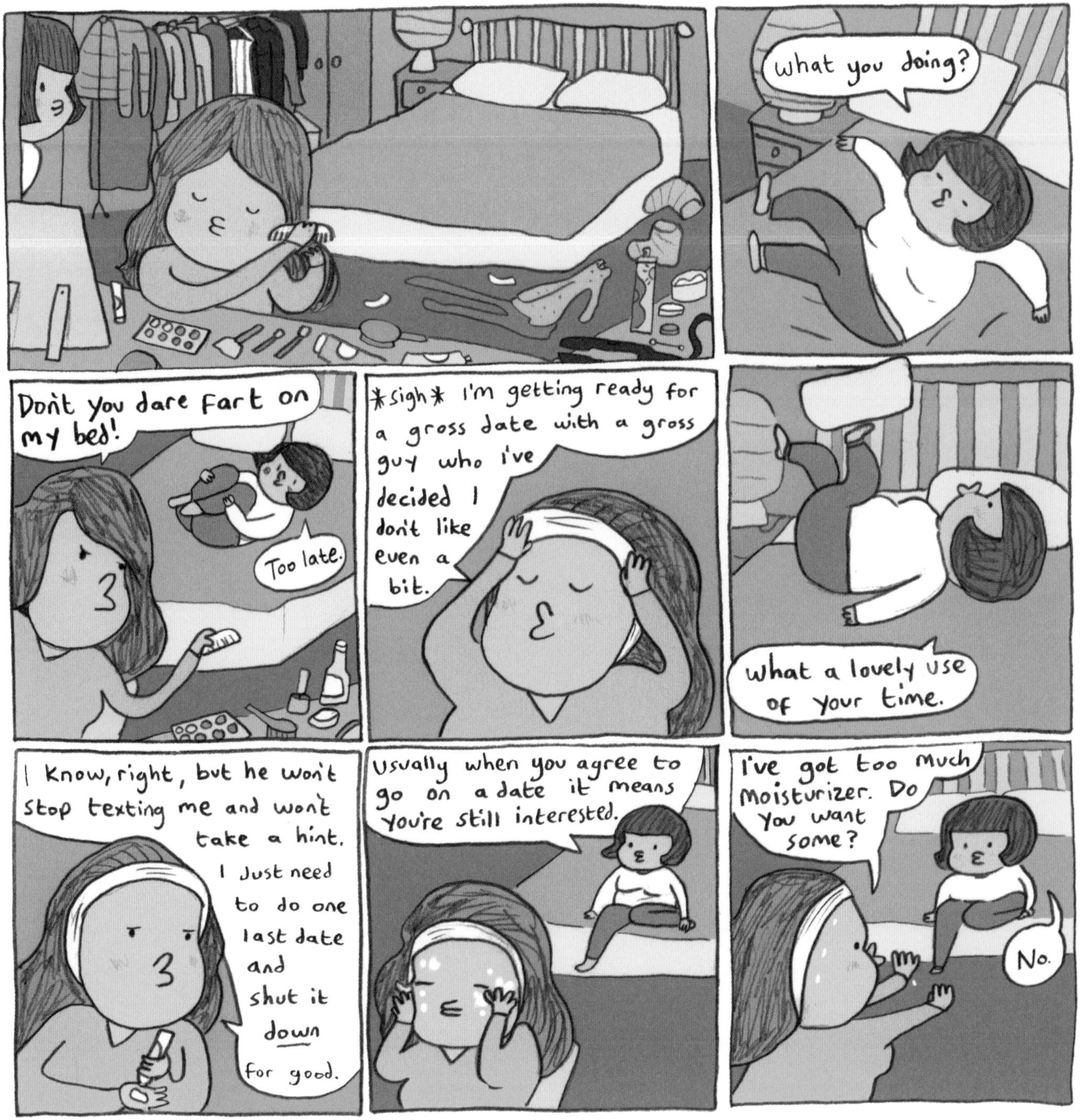
What you doing?
Don't you dare fart on my bed!
Too late.
sigh I'm getting ready for a gross date with a gross guy who I've decided I don't like even a bit.
What a lovely use of your time.
I know, right, but he won't stop texting me and won't take a hint.
I just need to do one last date and shut it down for good.
Usually when you agree to go on a date it means you're still interested.
I've got too much moisturizer. Do you want some?
No.

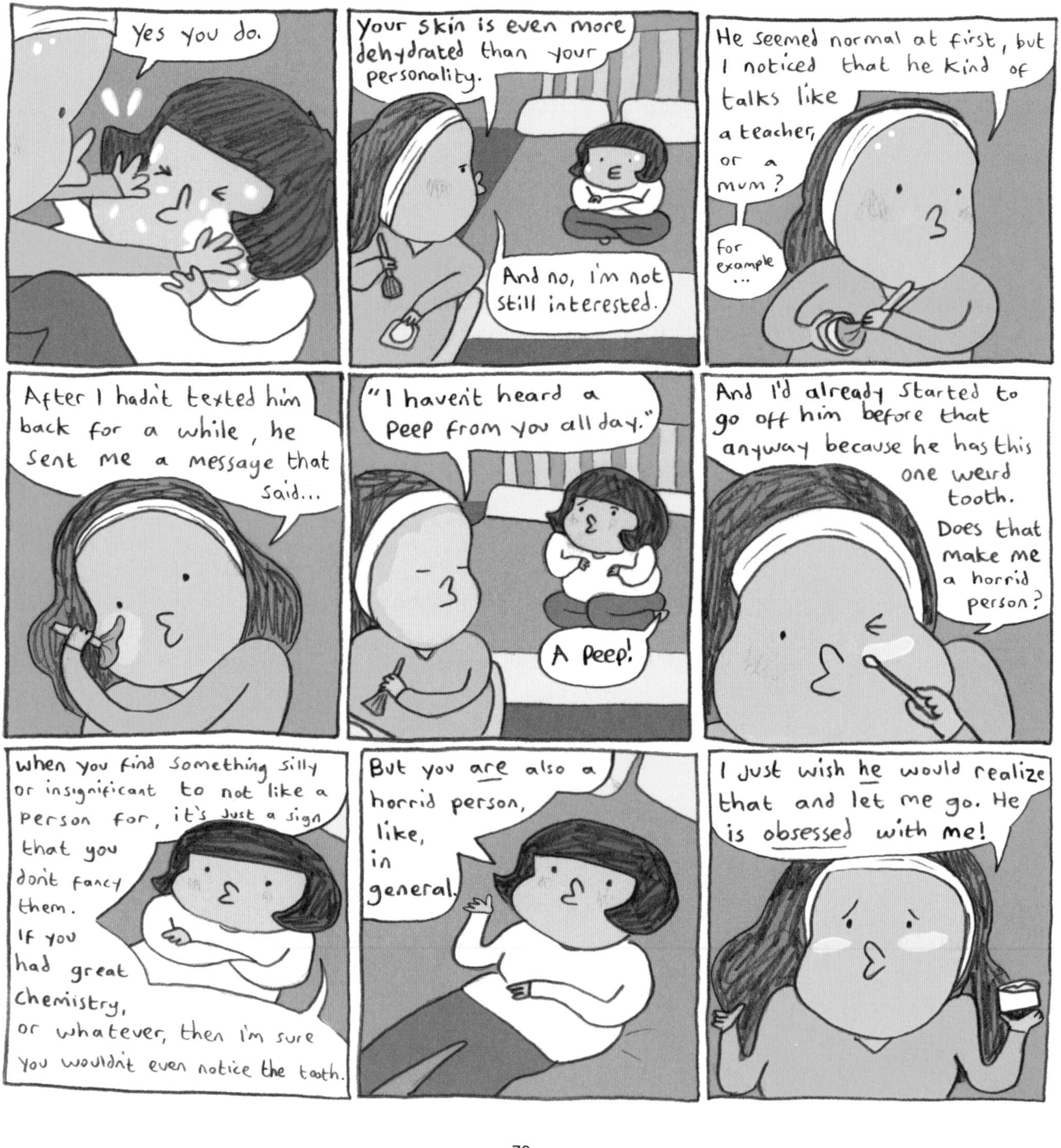
Yes you do.
Your skin is even more dehydrated than your personality.
And no, I'm not still interested.
He seemed normal at first, but I noticed that he kind of talks like
a teacher, or a mum?
For example...
After I hadn't texted him back for a while, he sent me a message that said...
"I haven't heard a peep from you all day."
A peep!
And I'd already started to go off him before that anyway because he has this one weird tooth.
Does that make me a horrid person?
When you find something silly or insignificant to not like a person for, it's just a sign that you don't fancy them.
If you had great chemistry, or whatever, then I'm sure you wouldn't even notice the tooth.
But you are also a horrid person, like, in general.
I just wish he would realize that and let me go. He is obsessed with me!

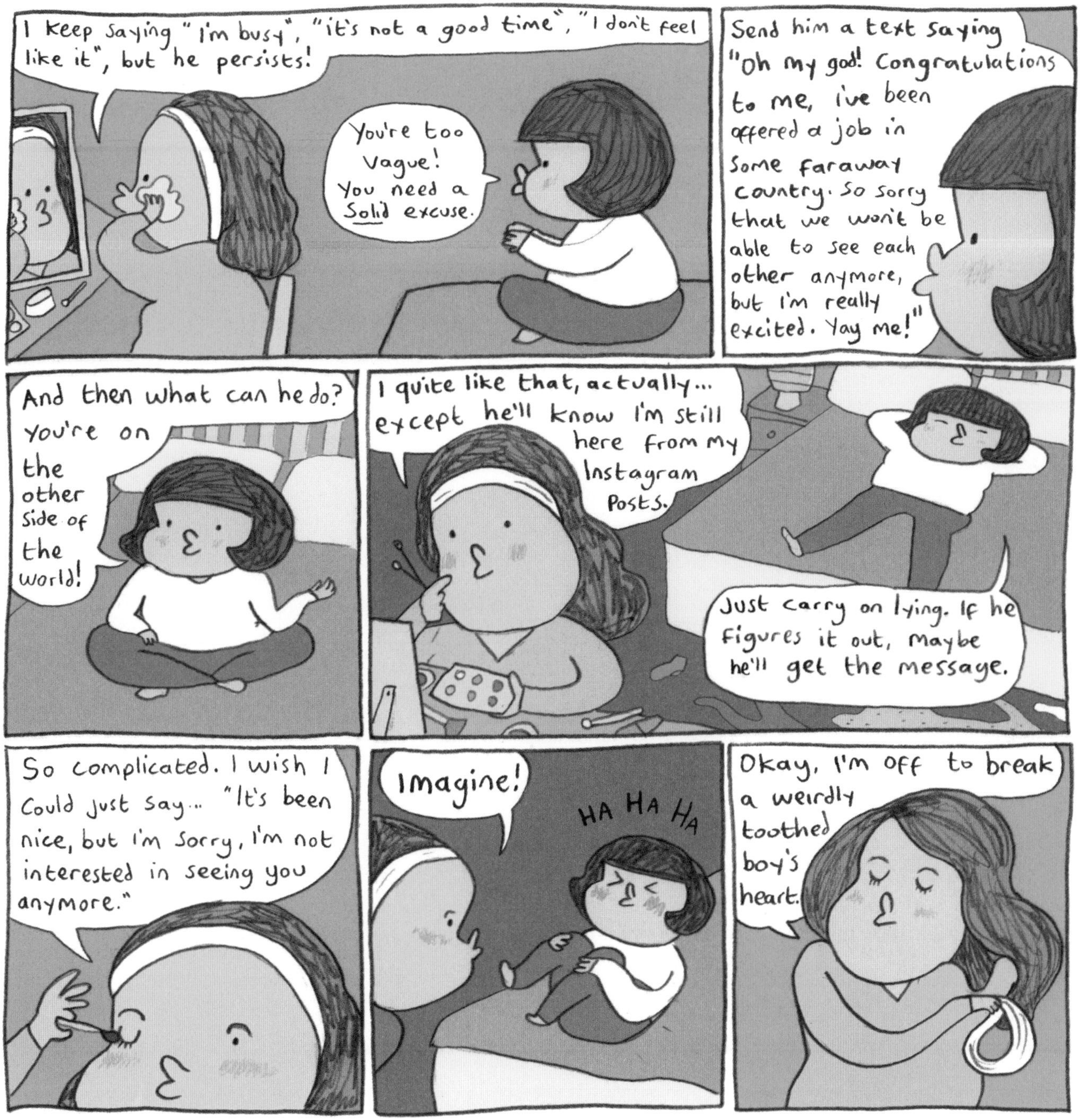
I keep saying "I'm busy", "it's not a good time", "I don't feel like it", but he persists!
You're too vague! You need a solid excuse.
Send him a text saying "Oh my god! Congratulations to me, I've been offered a job in some faraway country. So sorry that we won't be able to see each other anymore, but I'm really excited. Yay me!"
And then what can he do? You're on the other side of the world!
I quite like that, actually... except he'll know I'm still here from my Instagram posts.
Just carry on lying. If he figures it out, maybe he'll get the message.
So complicated. I wish I could just say... "It's been nice, but I'm sorry, I'm not interested in seeing you anymore."
Imagine!
HA HA HA
Okay, I'm off to break a weirdly toothed boy's heart.

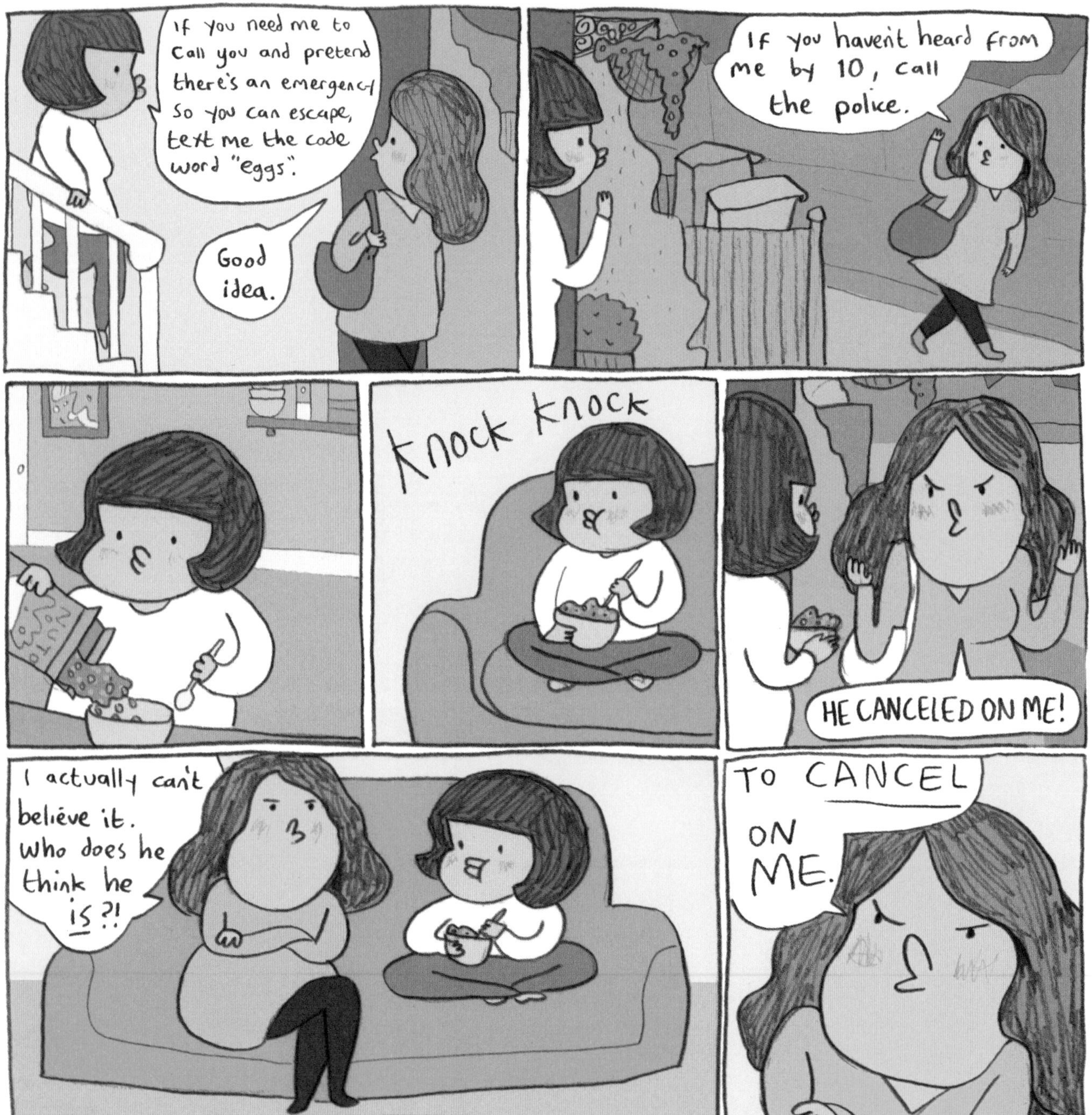
If you need me to call you and pretend there's an emergency so you can escape, text me the code word "eggs".
Good idea.
If you haven't heard from me by 10, call the police.
Knock Knock
HE CANCELED ON ME!
I actually can't believe it. Who does he think he is?!
TO CANCEL ON ME.

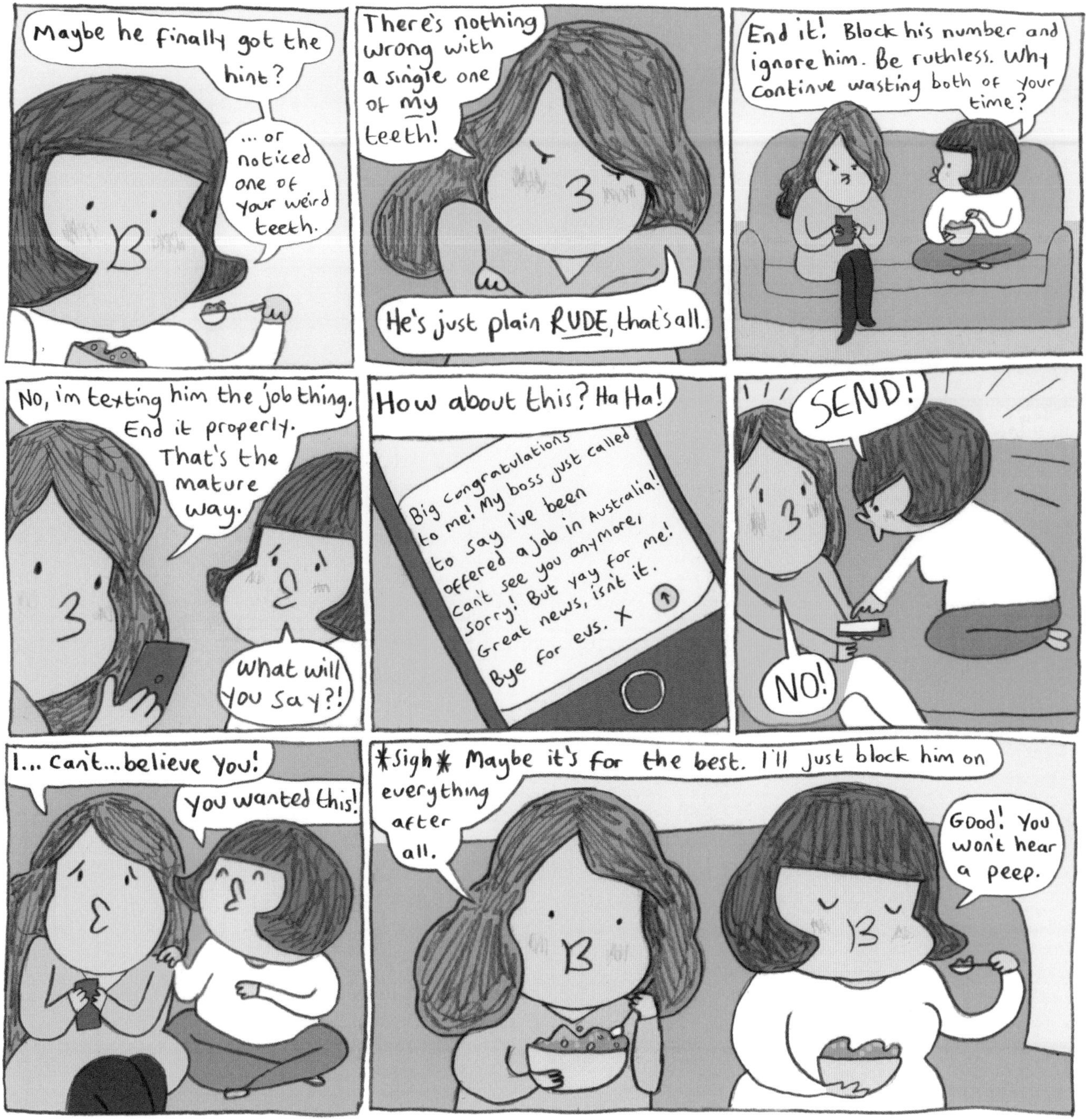

Maybe he finally got the hint?
... or noticed one of your weird teeth.
There's nothing wrong with a single one of my teeth!
He's just plain RUDE, that's all.
End it! Block his number and ignore him. Be ruthless. Why continue wasting both of your time?
No, im texting him the job thing. End it properly. That's the mature way.
What will you say?!
How about this? Ha Ha!
Big congratulations to me! My boss just called to say I've been offered a job in Australia! can't see you anymore, sorry! But yay for me! Great news, isn't it. Bye for evs. X
SEND!
NO!
I... can't... believe you!
You wanted this!
Sigh Maybe it's for the best. I'll just block him on everything after all.
Good! You won't hear a peep.

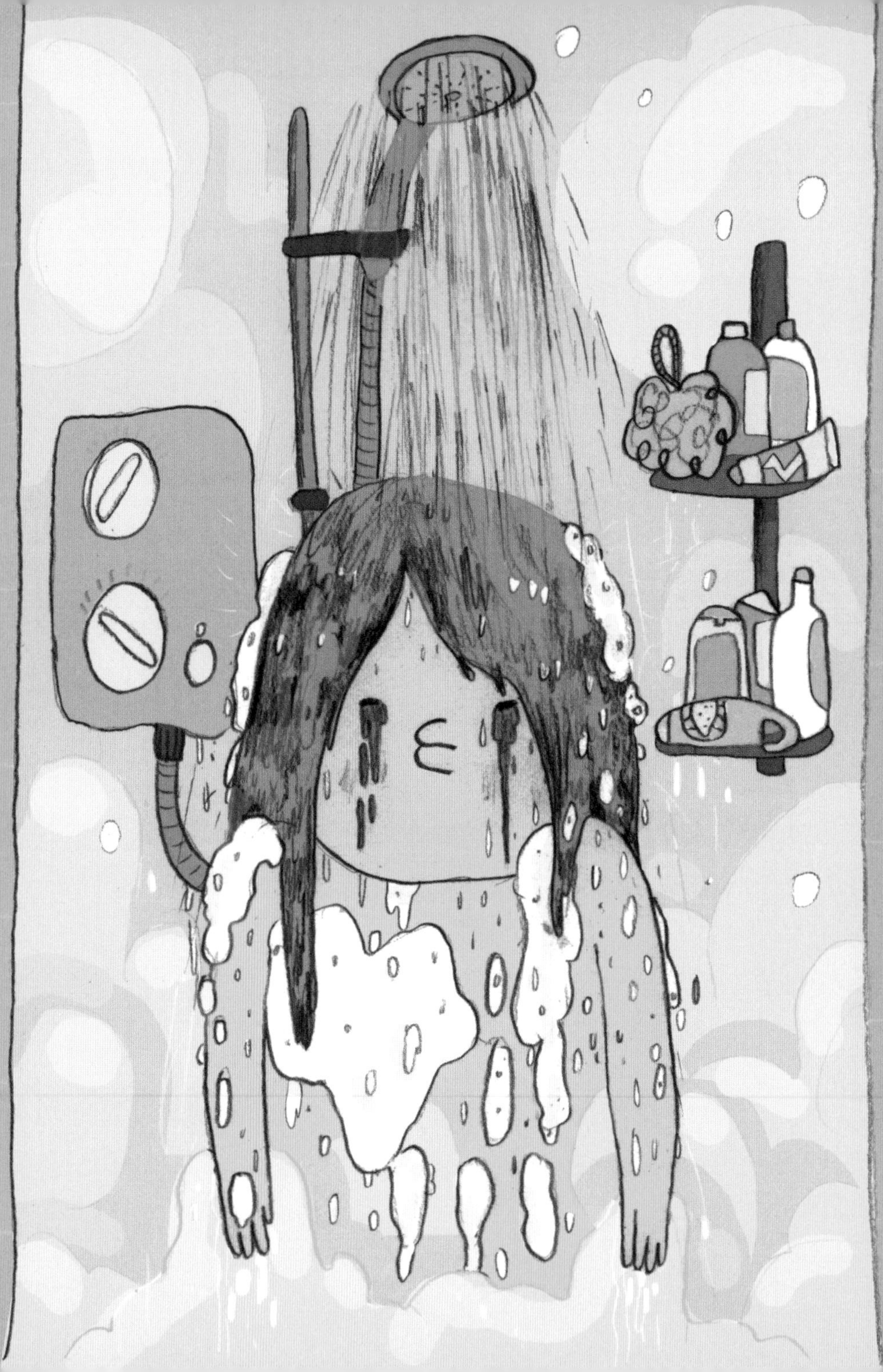

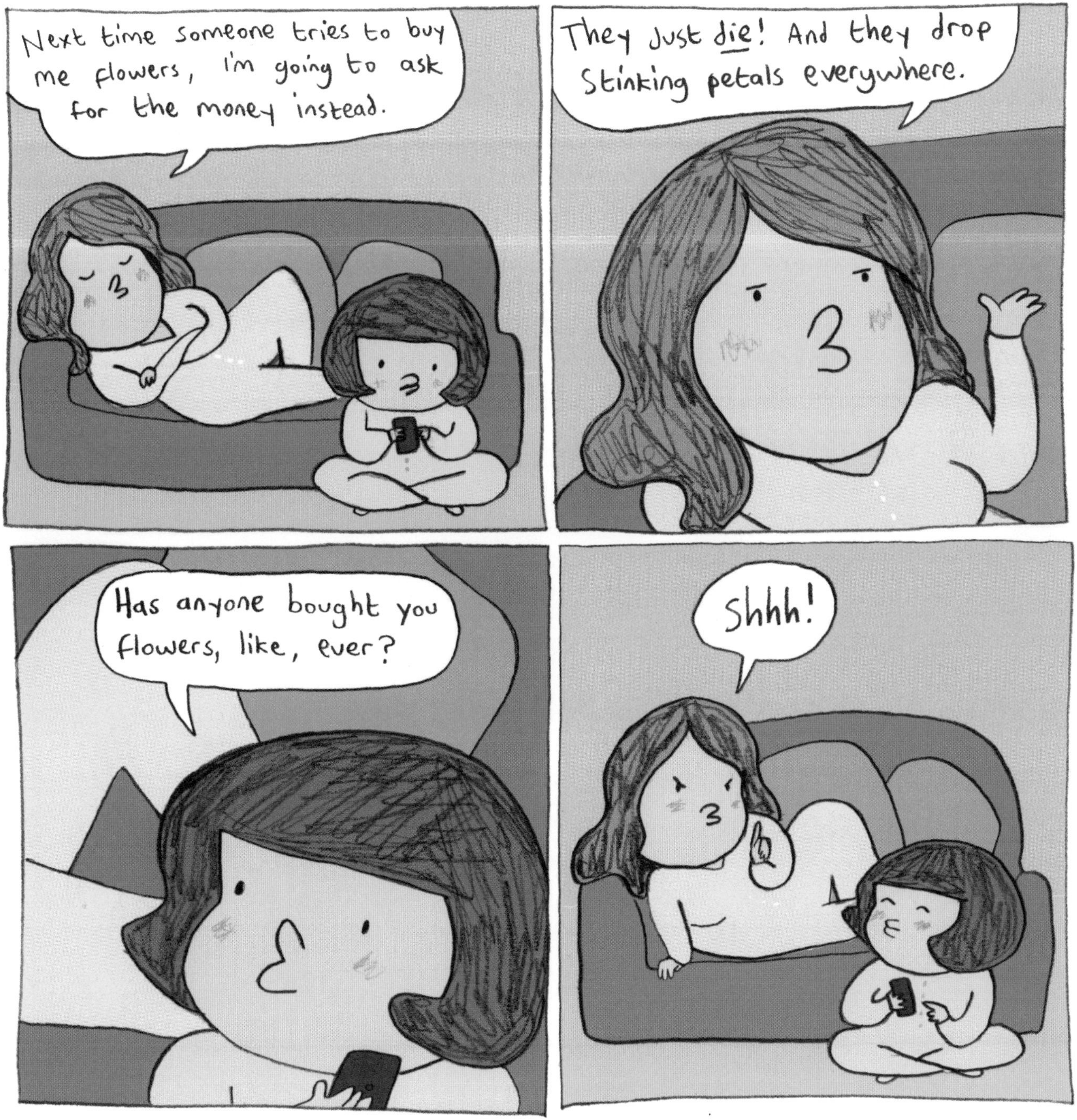
Next time someone tries to buy me flowers, I'm going to ask for the money instead.
They just die! And they drop stinking petals everywhere.
Has anyone bought you flowers, like, ever?
Shhh!

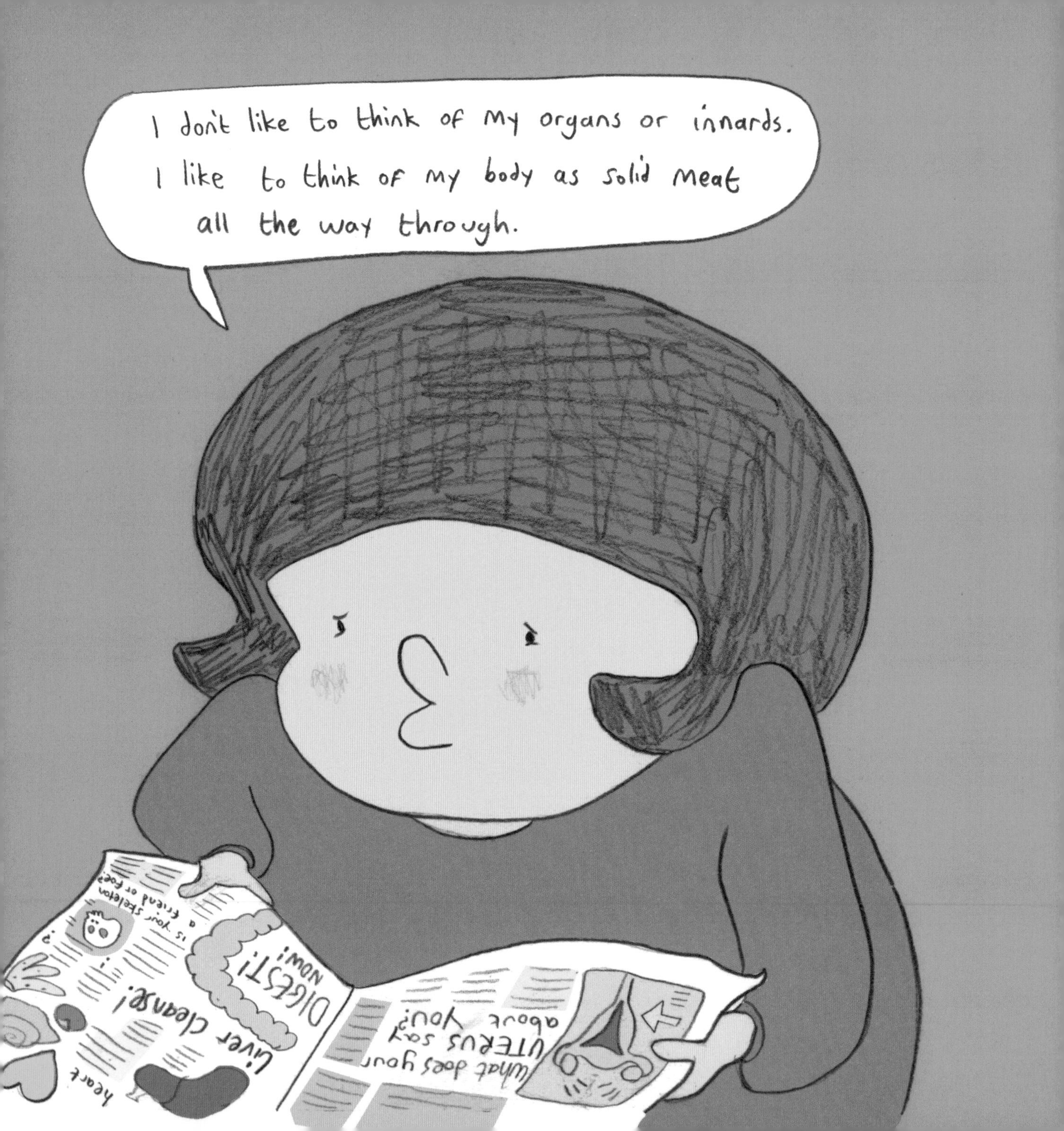
I don't like to think of my organs or innards. I like to think of my body as solid meat all the way through.
is your skeleton a friend or foe?
DIGEST!! NOW!
liver cleanse!
heart
what does your UTERUS say about you?

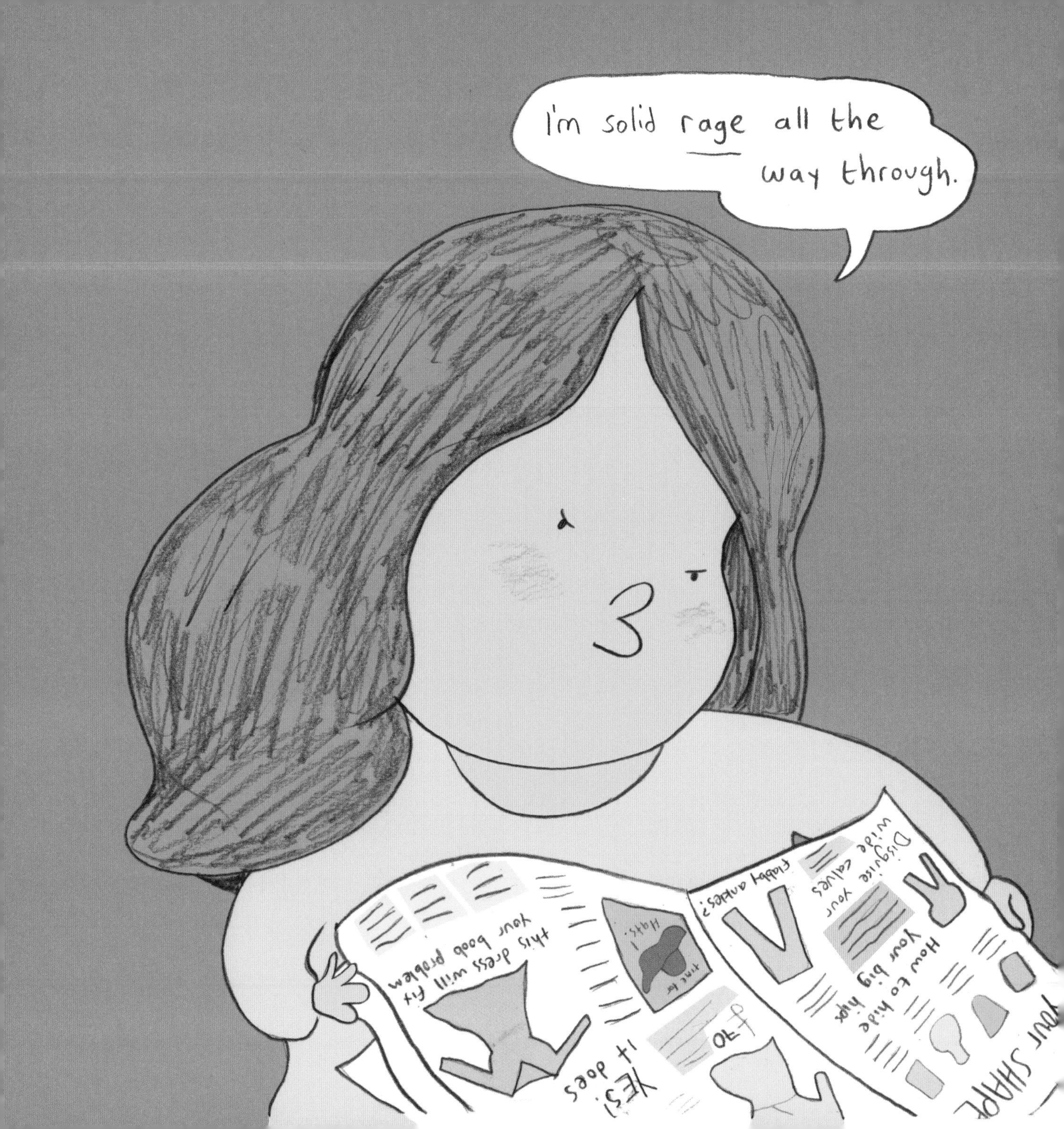
I'm solid rage all the way through.
this dress will fit your boob problem
YES! it does
Flabby ankles?
Disguise your wide calves
How to hide your big hips

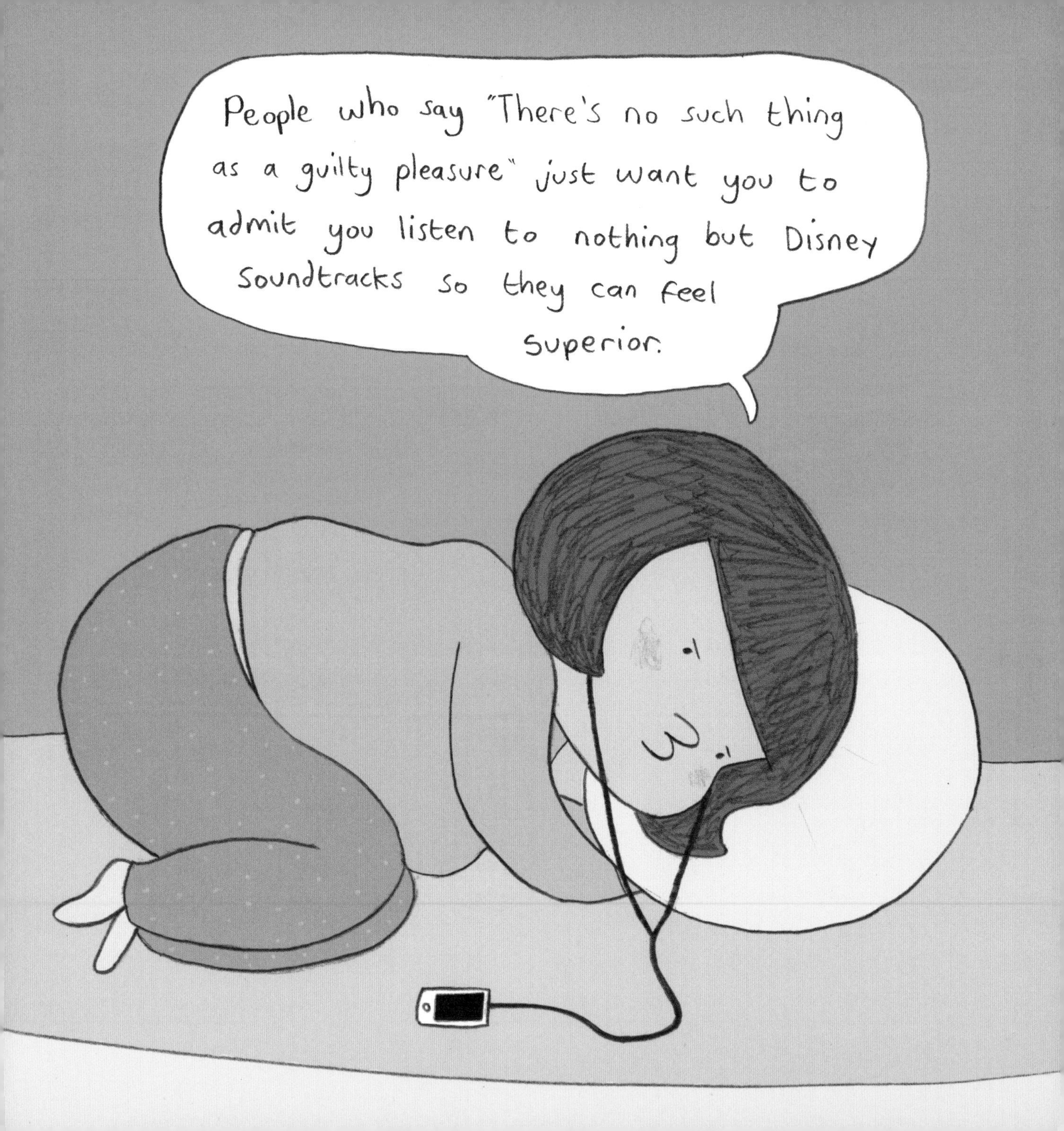
People who say "There's no such thing as a guilty pleasure" just want you to admit you listen to nothing but Disney soundtracks so they can feel superior.

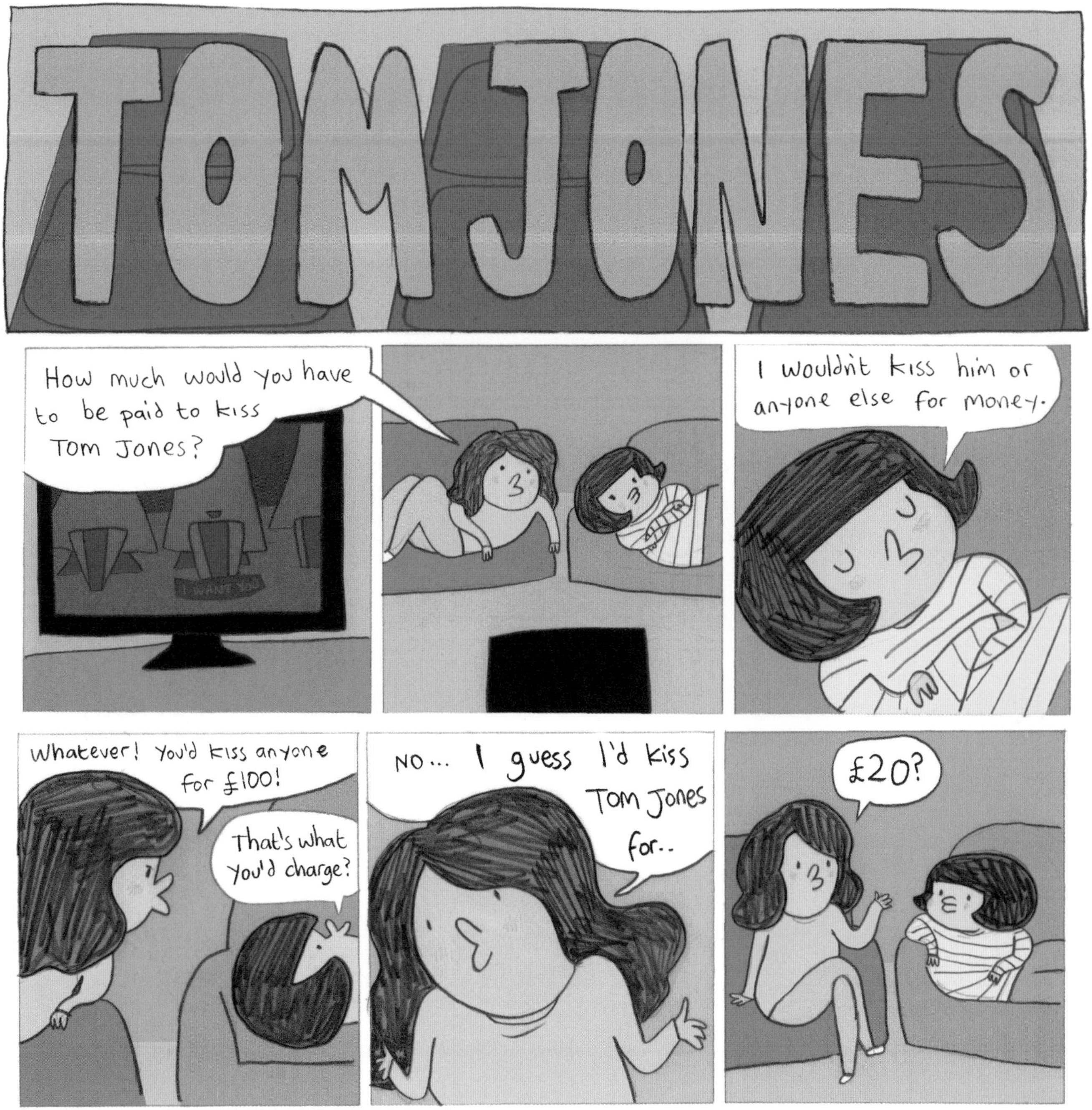
TOM JONES
How much would you have to be paid to kiss Tom Jones?
I wouldn't kiss him or anyone else for money.
Whatever! You'd kiss anyone for £100!
That's what you'd charge?
No... I guess I'd kiss Tom Jones for..
£20?

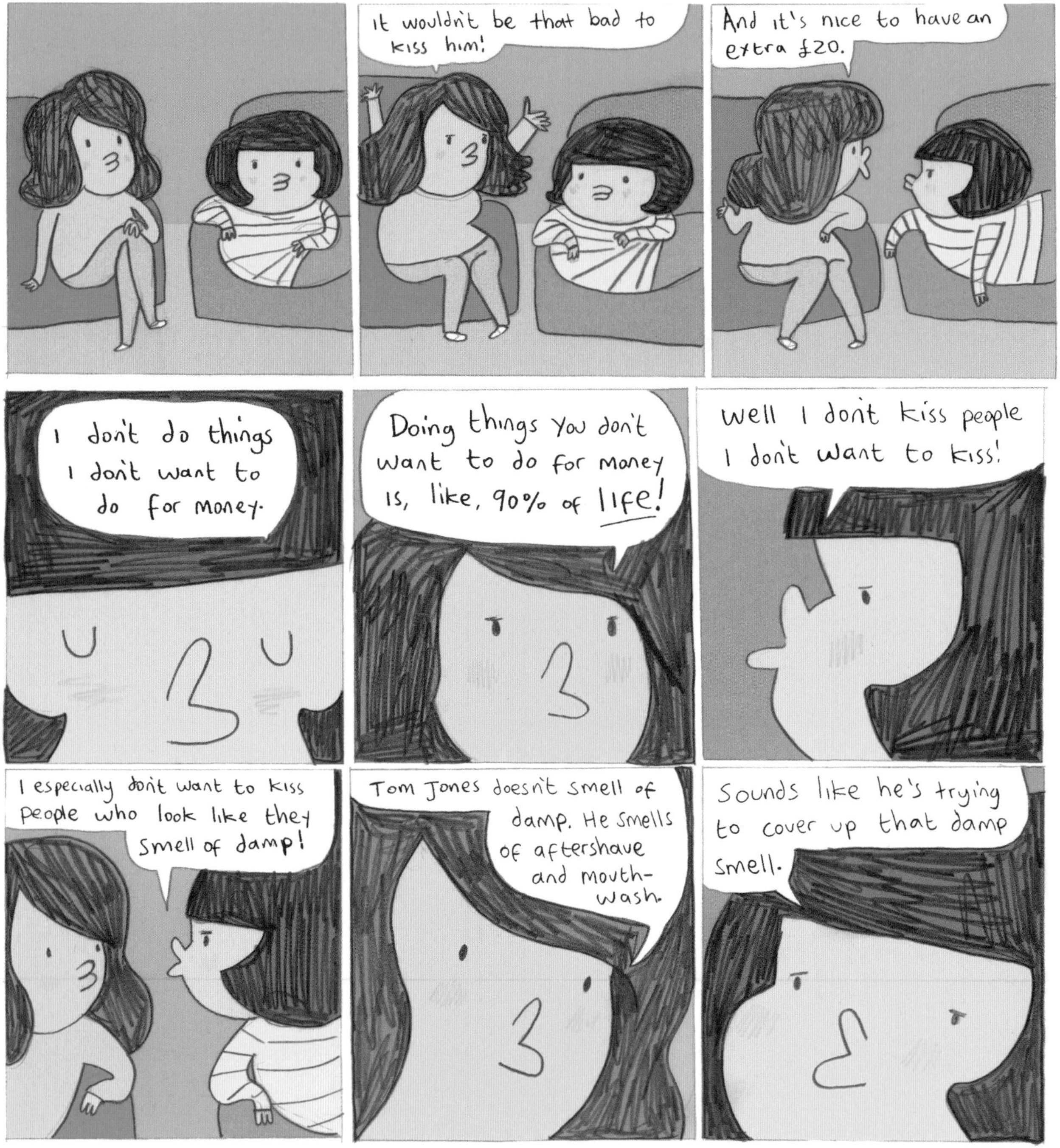
It wouldn't be that bad to kiss him!
And it's nice to have an extra £20.
I don't do things I don't want to do for money.
Doing things you don't want to do for money is, like, 90% of LIFE!
Well I don't kiss people I don't want to kiss!
I especially don't want to kiss people who look like they smell of damp!
Tom Jones doesn't smell of damp. He smells of aftershave and mouth-wash.
Sounds like he's trying to cover up that damp smell.

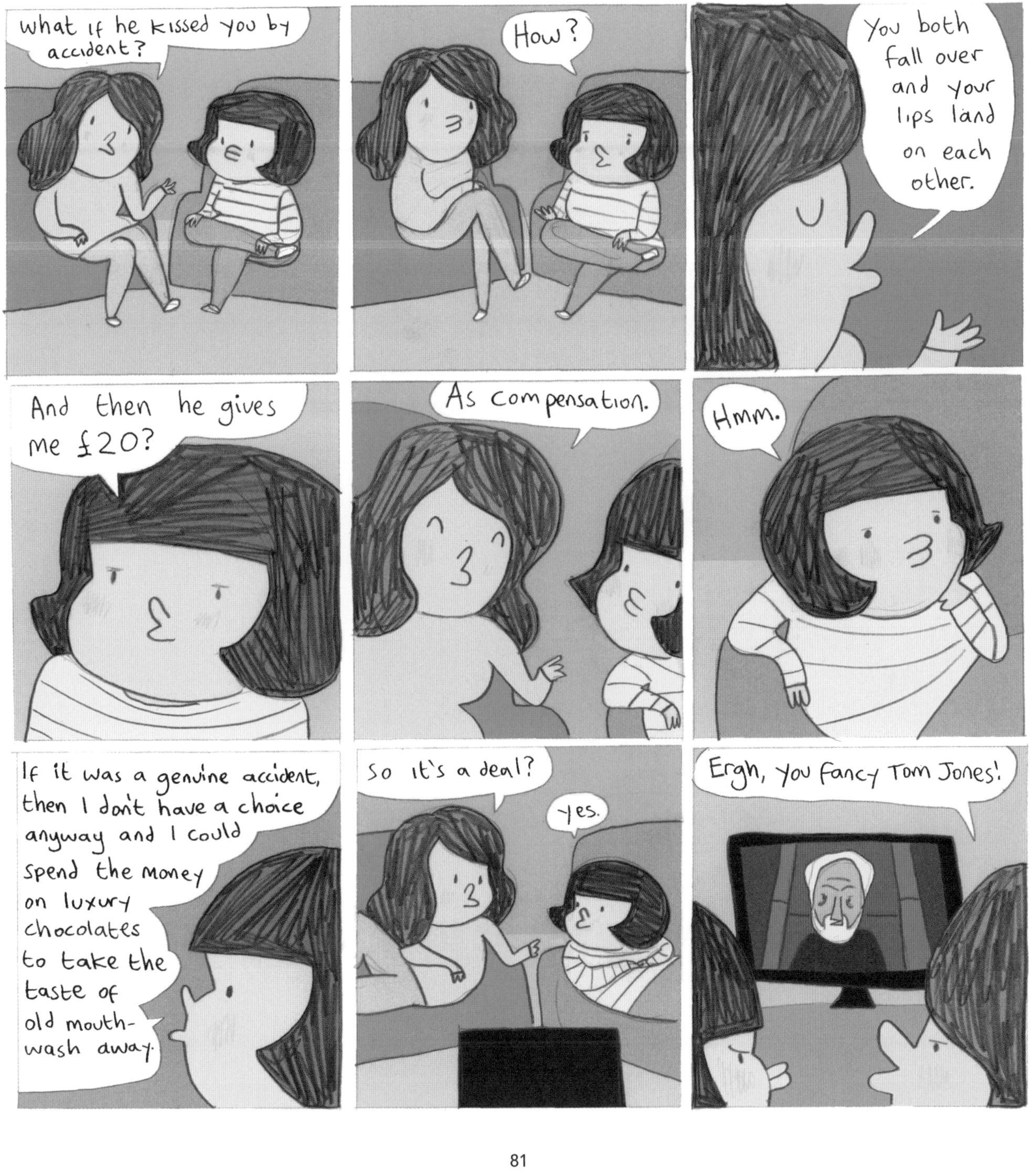
what if he kissed you by accident?
How?
You both fall over and your lips land on each other.
And then he gives me £20?
As compensation.
Hmm.
If it was a genuine accident, then I don't have a choice anyway and I could spend the money on luxury chocolates to take the taste of old mouth-wash away.
So it's a deal?
Yes.
Ergh, you fancy Tom Jones!

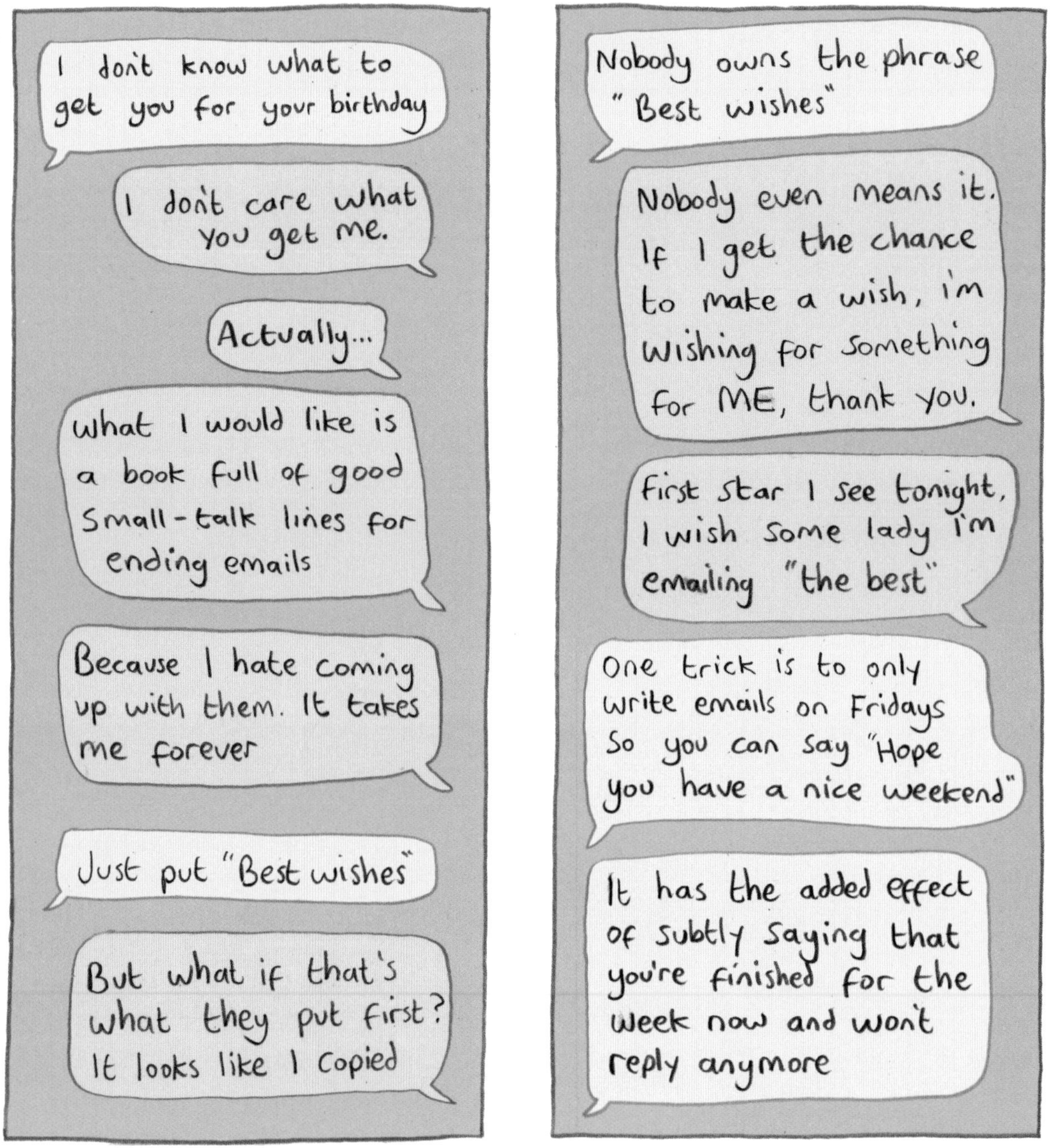
I don't know what to get you for your birthday
I don't care what you get me.
Actually...
What I would like is a book full of good small-talk lines for ending emails
Because I hate coming up with them. It takes me forever
Just put "Best wishes"
But what if that's what they put first? It looks like I copied
Nobody owns the phrase "Best wishes"
Nobody even means it. If I get the chance to make a wish, I'm wishing for something for ME, thank you.
First star I see tonight, I wish some lady I'm emailing "the best"
One trick is to only write emails on Fridays so you can say "Hope you have a nice weekend"
It has the added effect of subtly saying that you're finished for the week now and won't reply anymore

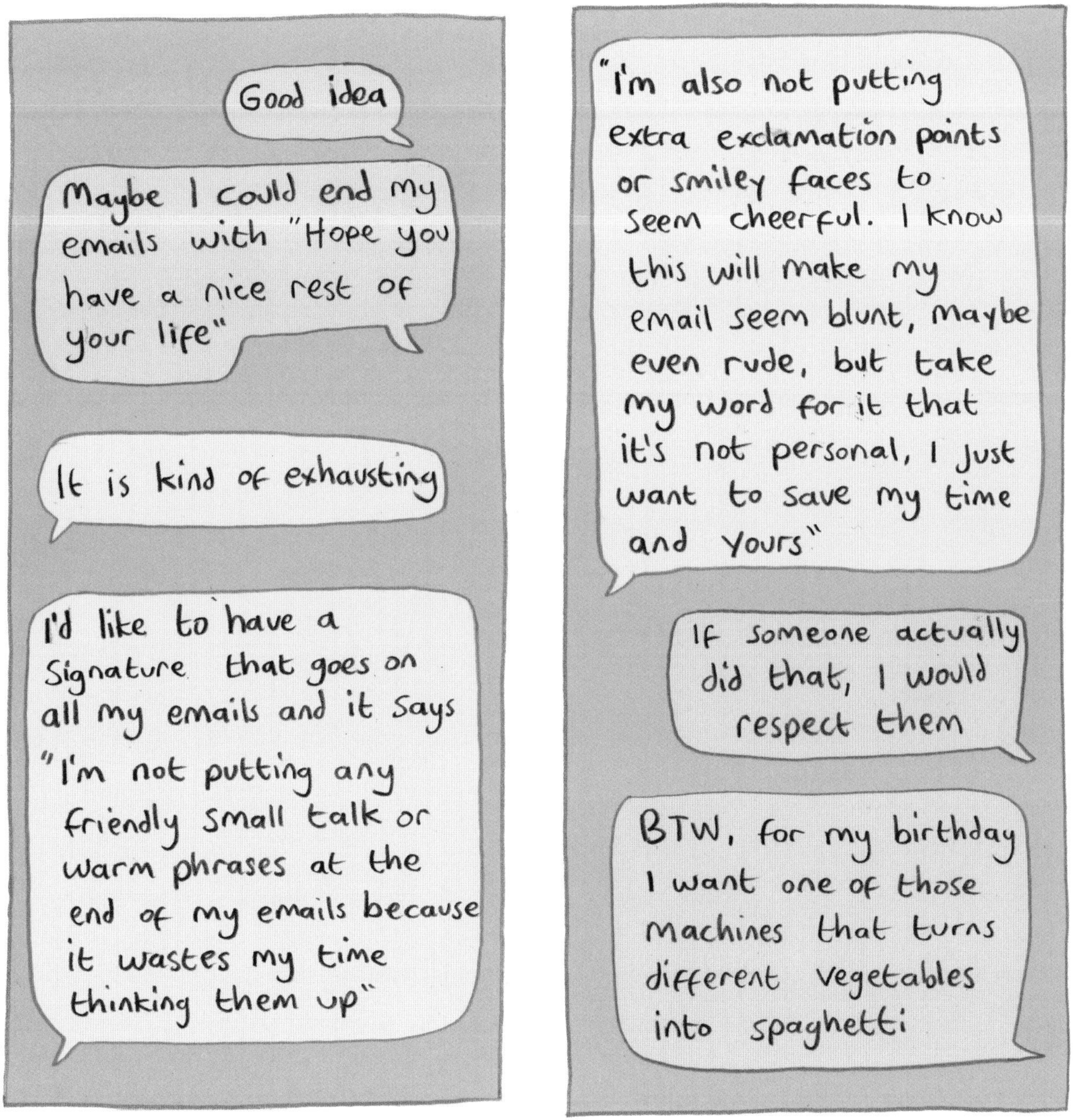
Good idea
Maybe I could end my emails with "Hope you have a nice rest of your life"
It is kind of exhausting
I'd like to have a signature that goes on all my emails and it says "I'm not putting any friendly small talk or warm phrases at the end of my emails because it wastes my time thinking them up"
"I'm also not putting extra exclamation points or smiley faces to seem cheerful. I know this will make my email seem blunt, maybe even rude, but take my word for it that it's not personal, I just want to save my time and yours"
If someone actually did that, I would respect them
BTW, for my birthday I want one of those machines that turns different vegetables into spaghetti

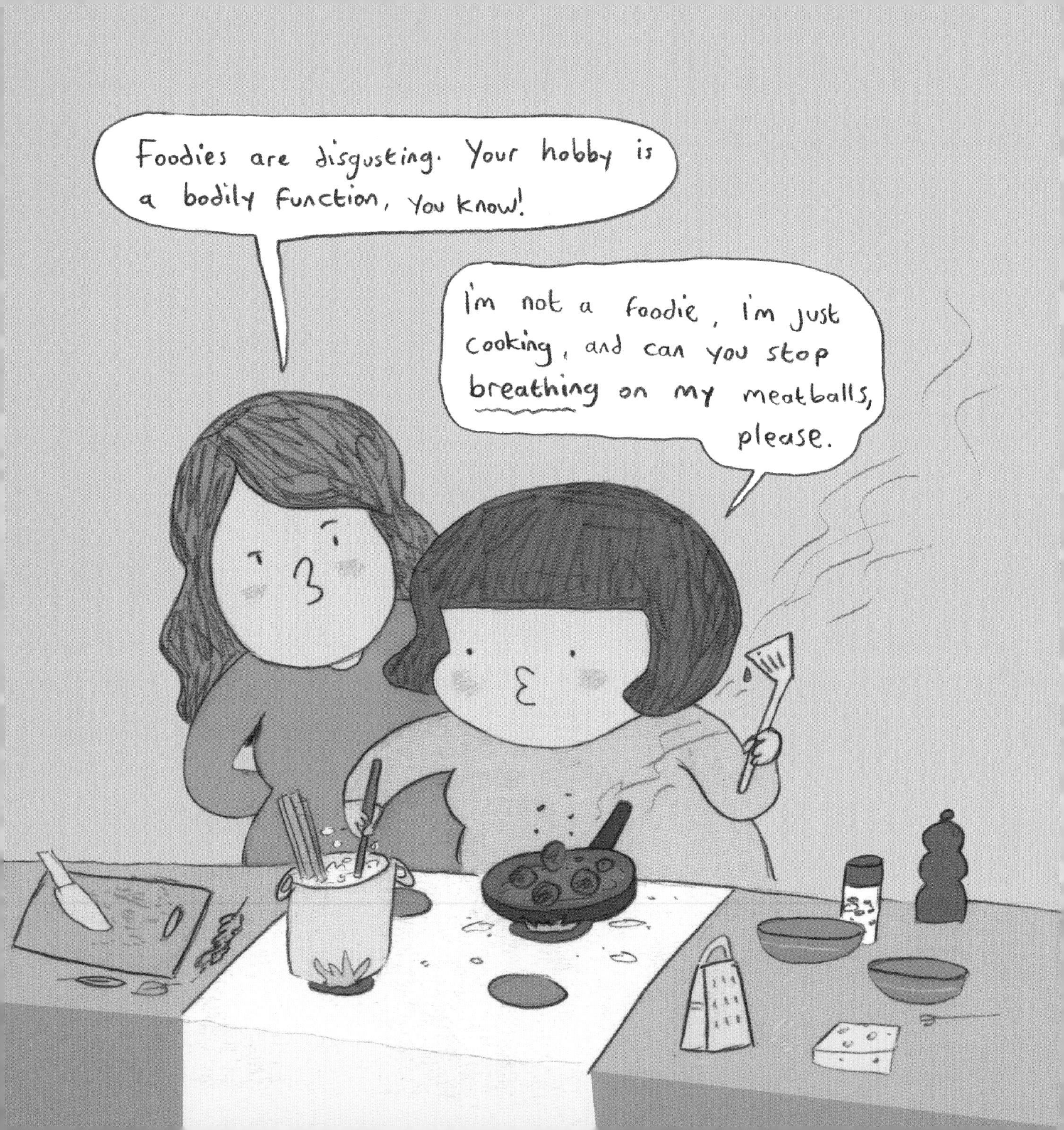
Foodies are disgusting. Your hobby is a bodily function, you know!
I'm not a foodie, I'm just cooking, and can you stop breathing on my meatballs, please.

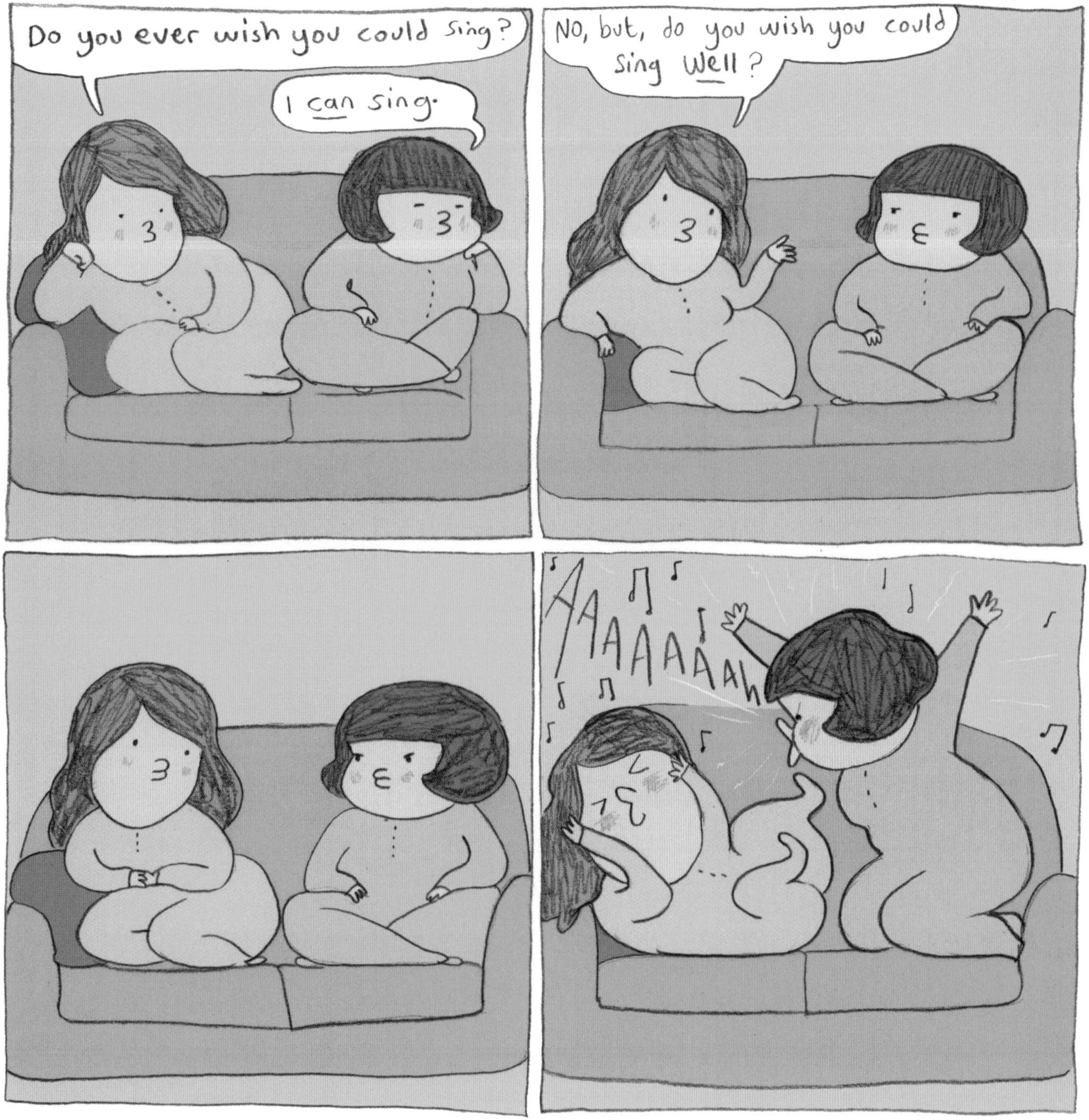
Do you ever wish you could sing?
I can sing.
No, but, do you wish you could sing well?
AAAAAAAAAh

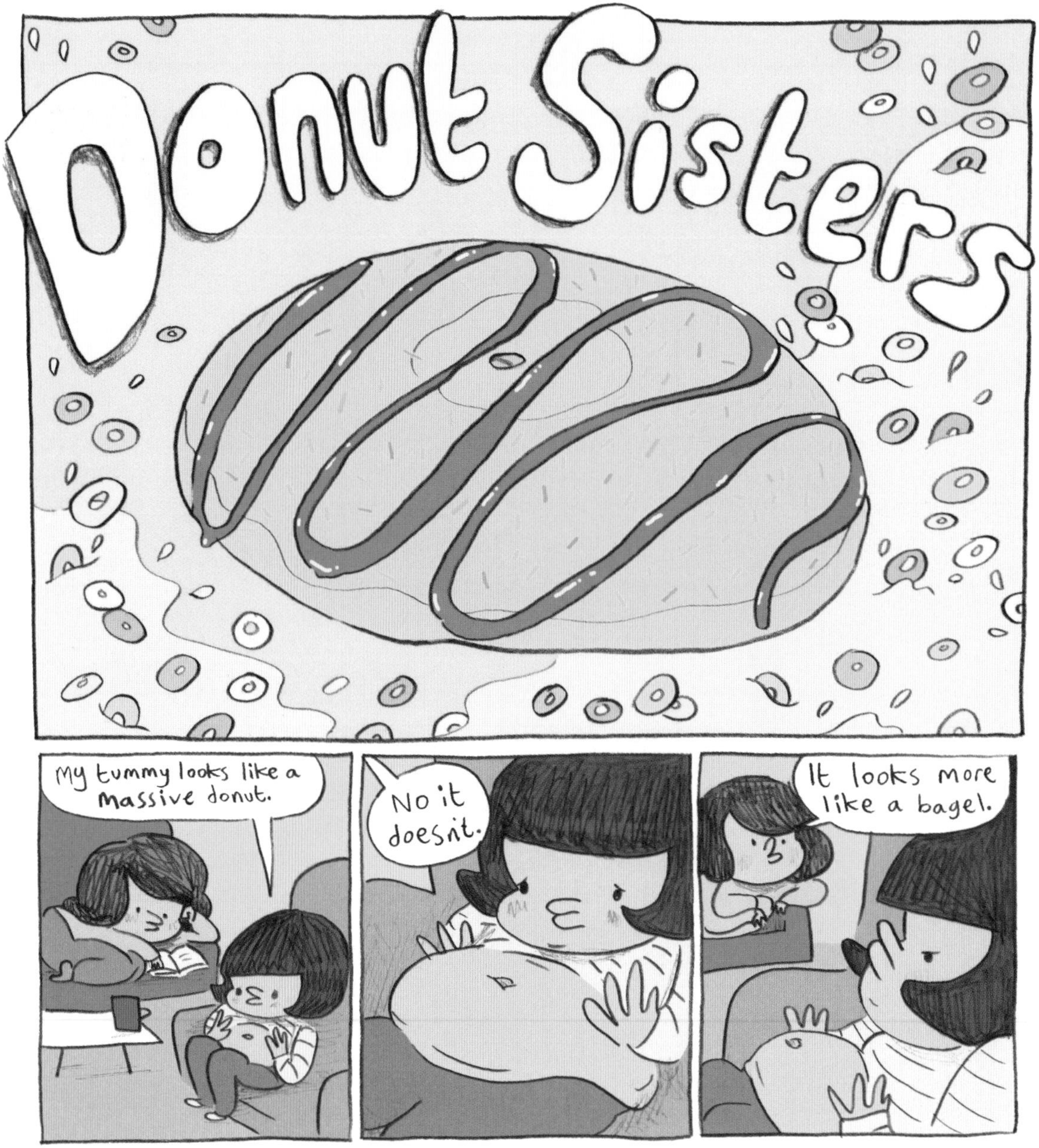
Donut Sisters
My tummy looks like a massive donut.
No it doesn't.
It looks more like a bagel.

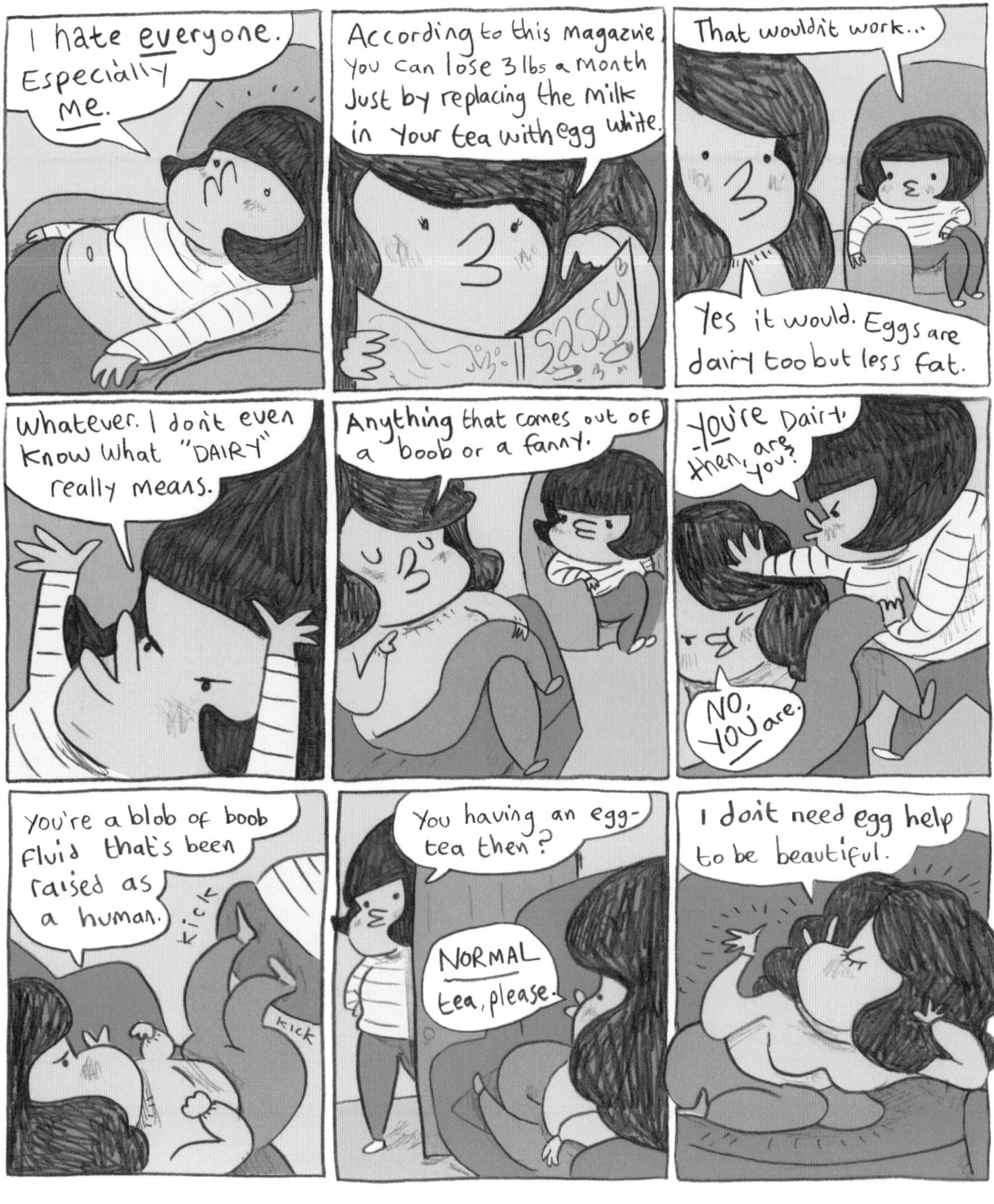

I hate everyone. Especially me.
According to this magazine you can lose 3lbs a month just by replacing the milk in your tea with egg white.
SASSY
That wouldn't work...
Yes it would. Eggs are dairy too but less fat.
Whatever. I don't even know what "DAIRY" really means.
Anything that comes out of a boob or a fanny.
You're dairy then, are you?
NO, YOU are.
You're a blob of boob fluid that's been raised as a human.
KICK
KICK
You having an egg-tea then?
NORMAL tea, please.
I don't need egg help to be beautiful.

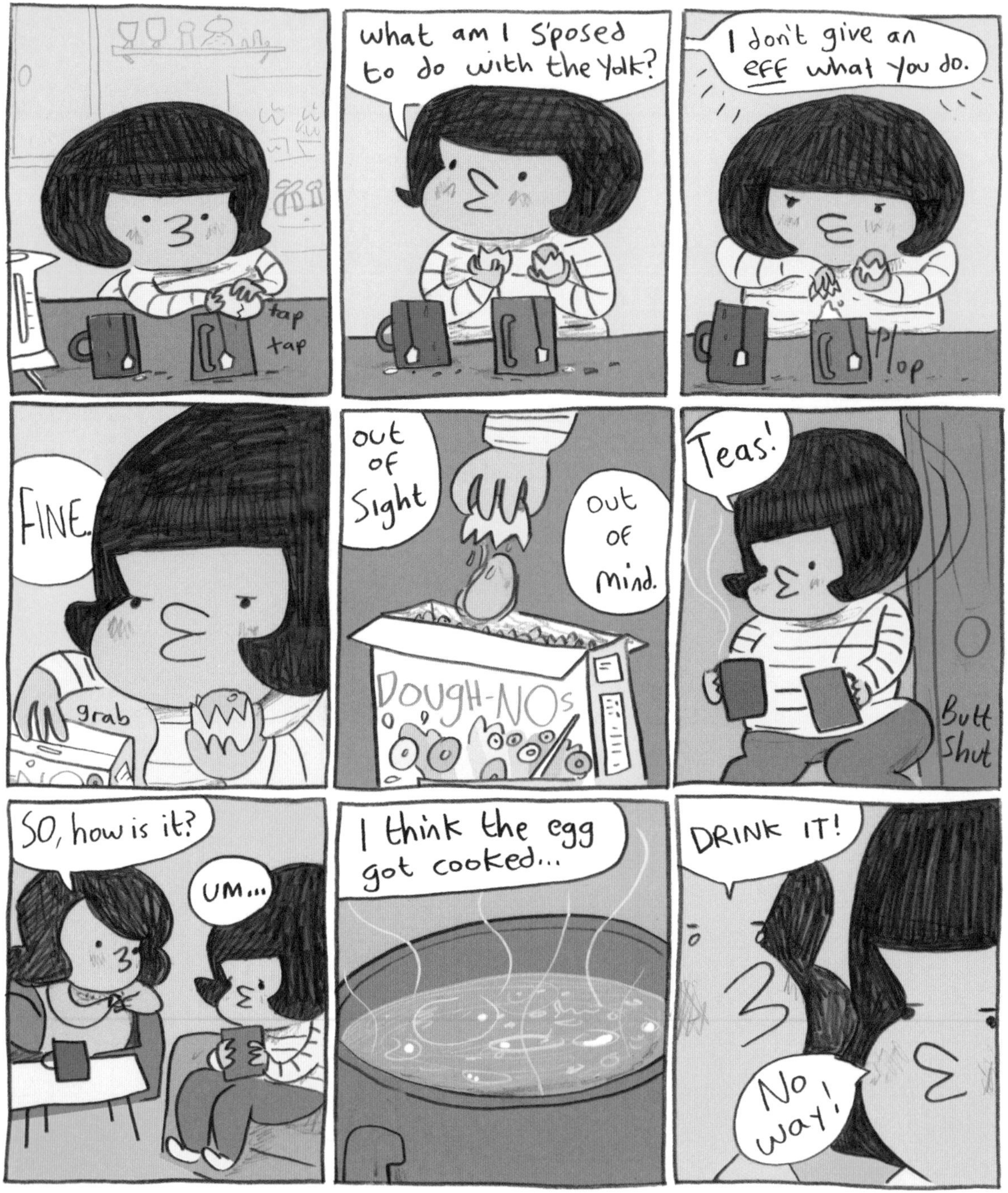
tap
tap
what am I s'posed to do with the yolk?
I don't give an EFF what you do.
Plop
FINE.
grab
out of sight
Out of mind.
DOUGH-NOs
Teas!
Butt Shut
SO, how is it?
UM...
I think the egg got cooked...
DRINK IT!
No way!

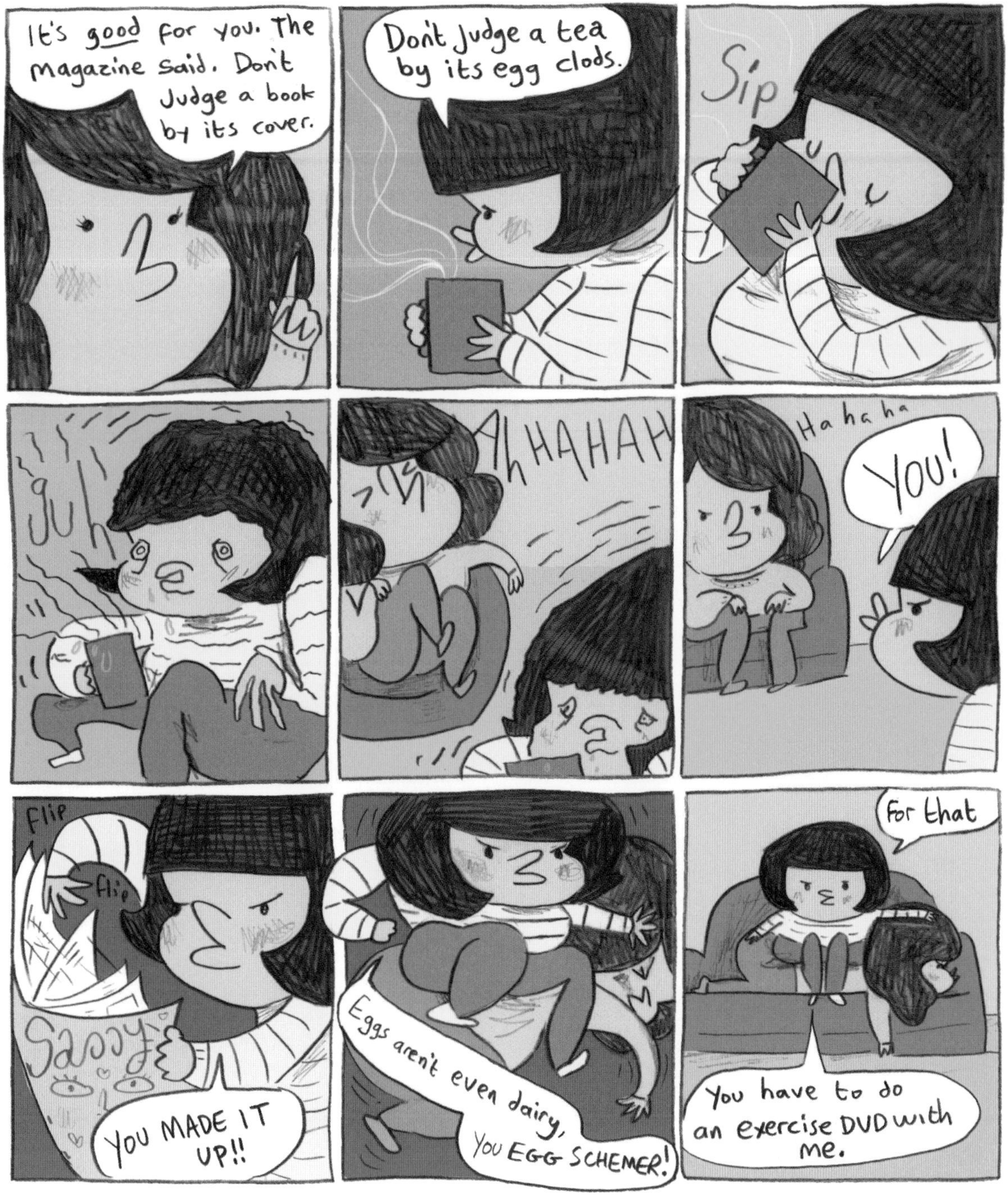
It's good for you. The magazine said. Don't judge a book by its cover.
Don't judge a tea by its egg clods.
Sip
guh
AhHAHAH
Ha ha ha
YOU!
Flip
flip
Sassy
YOU MADE IT UP!!
Eggs aren't even dairy, YOU EGG SCHEMER!
For that
You have to do an exercise DVD with me.

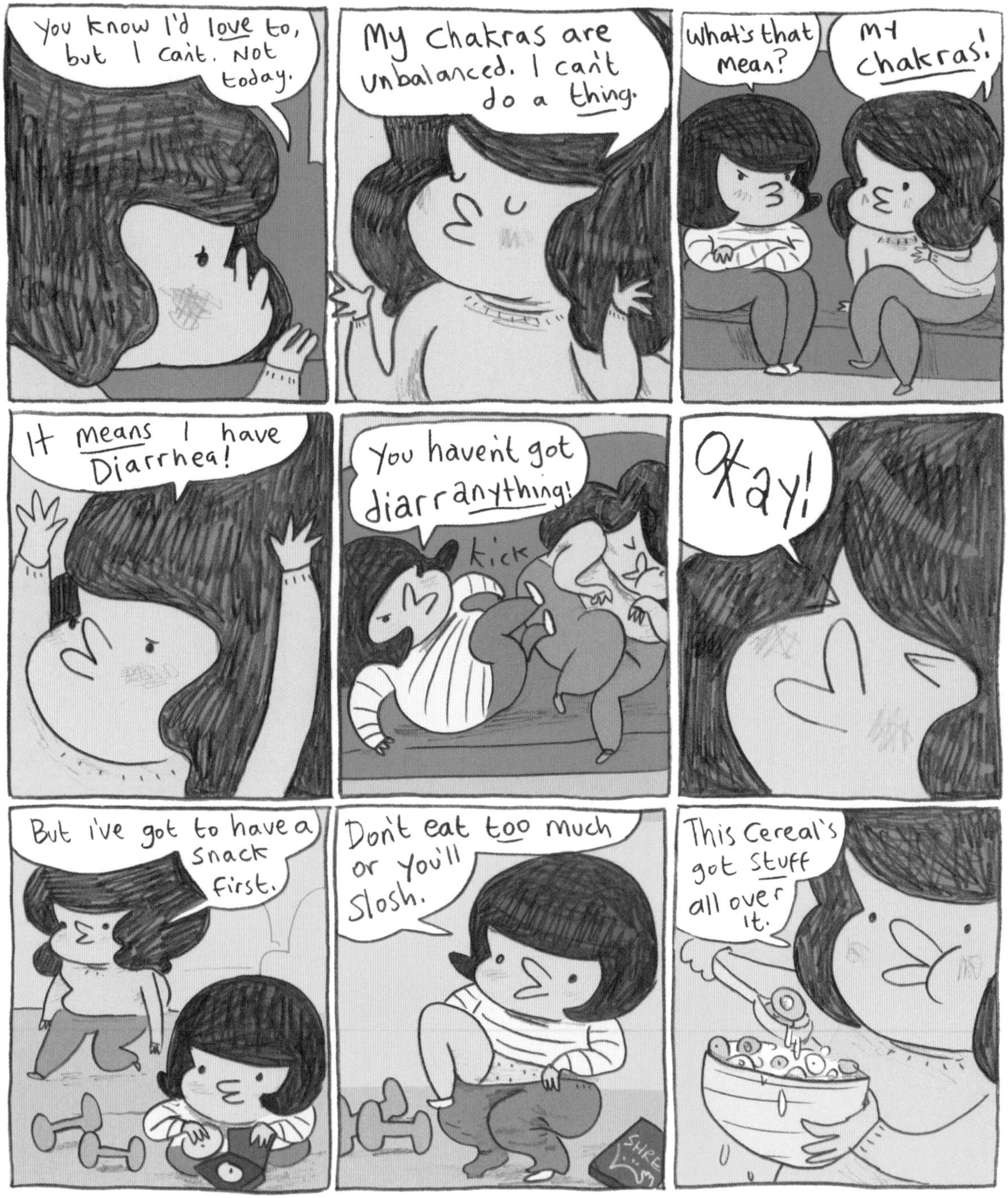
You know I'd love to, but I can't. Not today.
My chakras are unbalanced. I can't do a thing.
What's that mean?
My chakras!
It means I have diarrhea!
You haven't got diarranything!
kick
Okay!
But I've got to have a snack first.
Don't eat too much or you'll slosh.
This cereal's got stuff all over it.

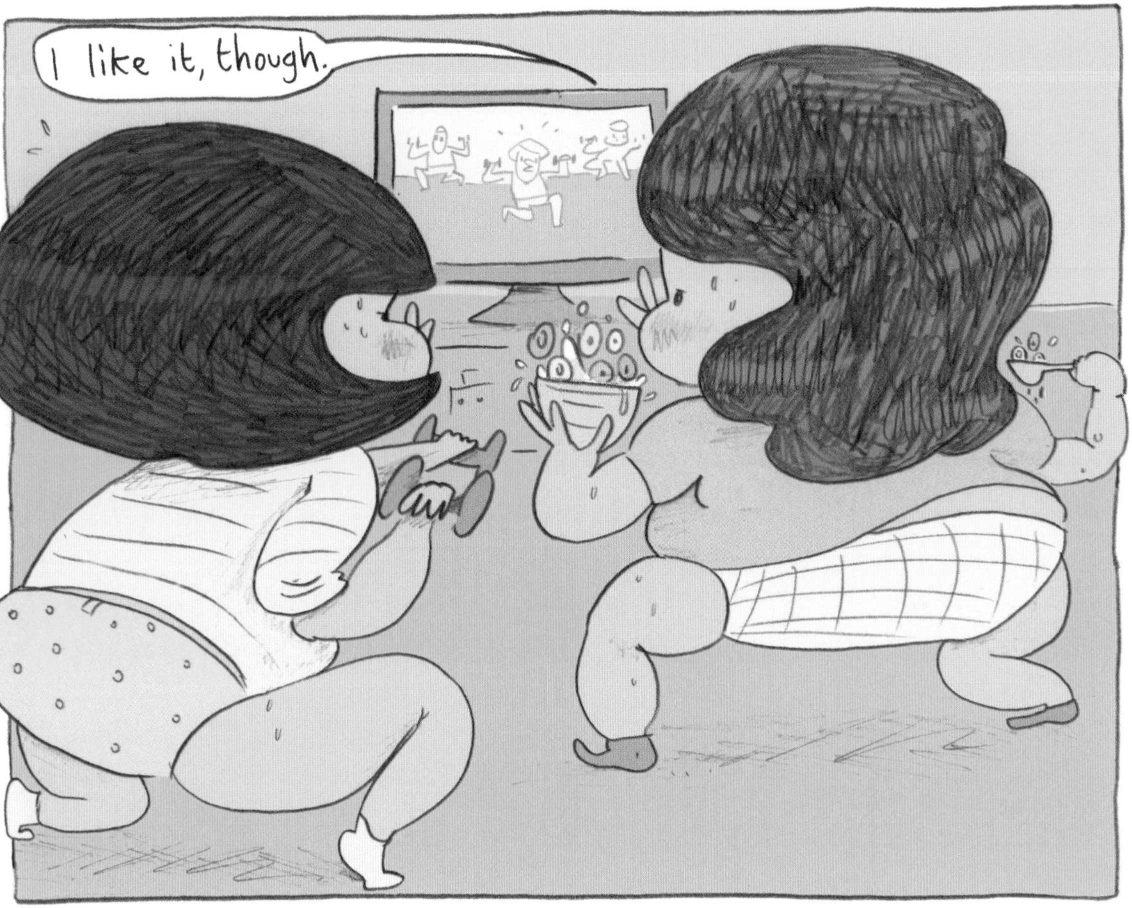
I like it, though.

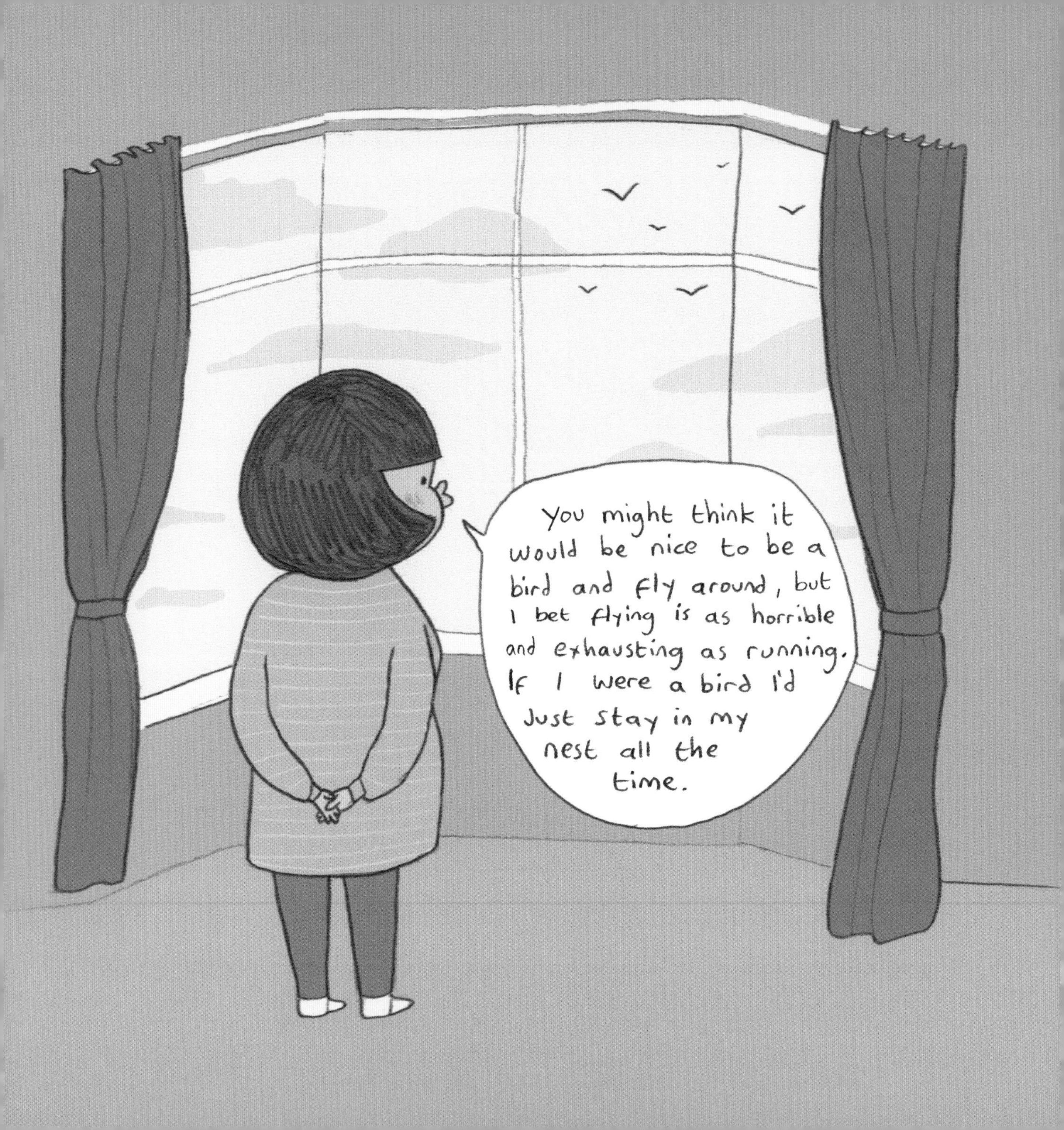
You might think it would be nice to be a bird and fly around, but I bet flying is as horrible and exhausting as running. If I were a bird I'd just stay in my nest all the time.

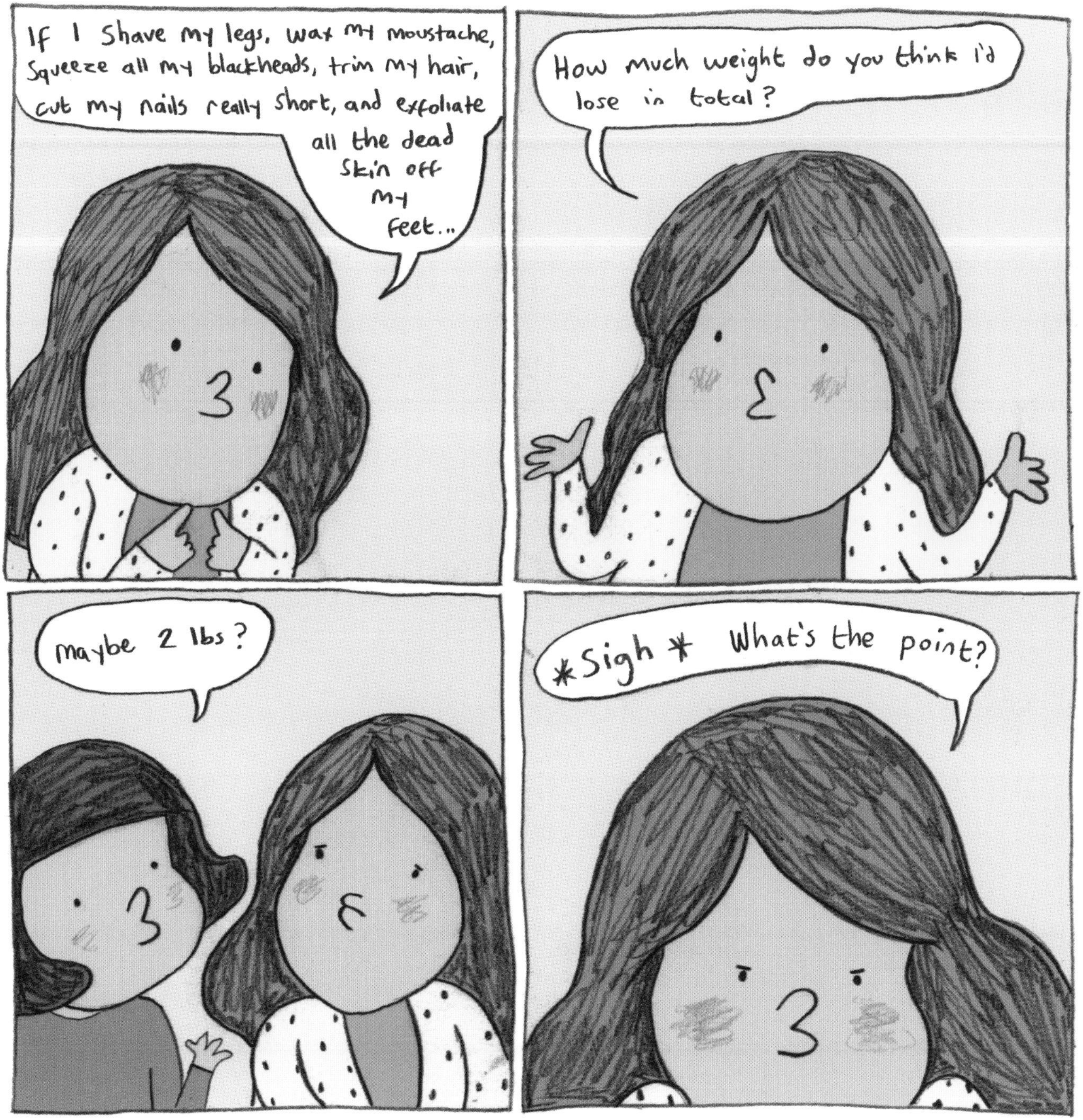
If I shave my legs, wax my moustache, squeeze all my blackheads, trim my hair, cut my nails really short, and exfoliate all the dead skin off my feet...
How much weight do you think I'd lose in total?
maybe 2 lbs?
Sigh What's the point?

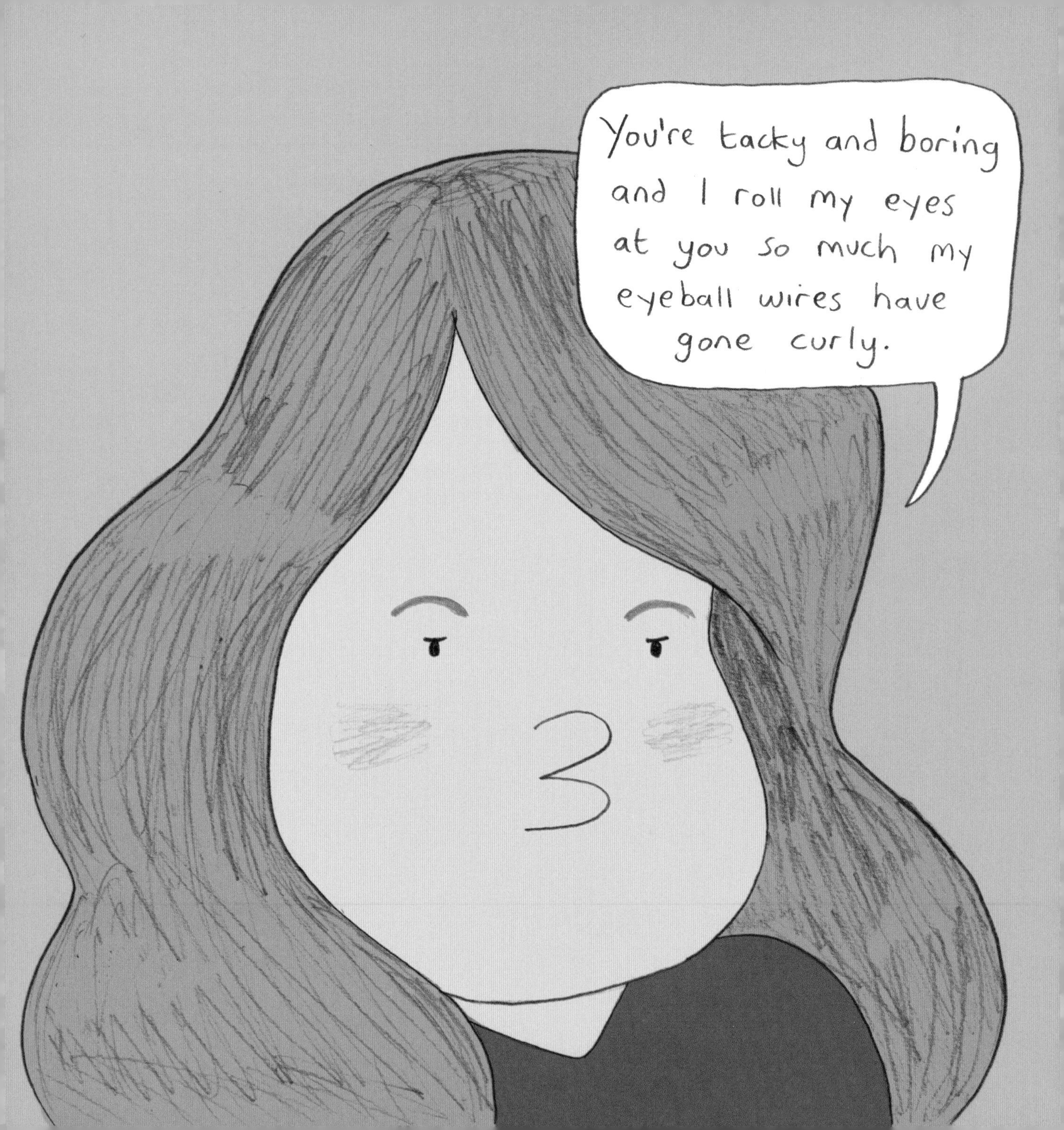
You're tacky and boring and I roll my eyes at you so much my eyeball wires have gone curly.

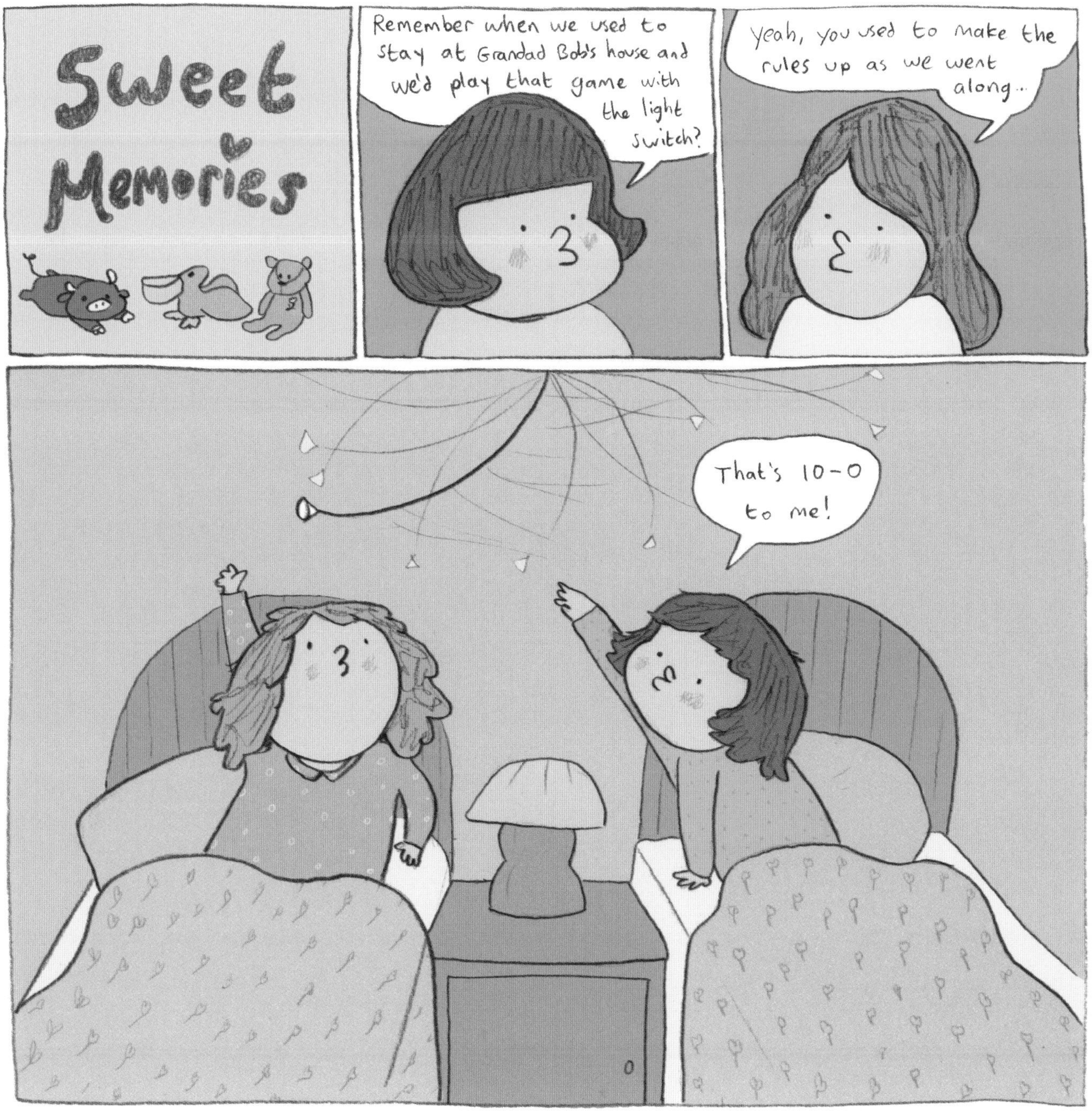
Sweet Memories
Remember when we used to stay at Grandad Bob's house and we'd play that game with the light switch?
Yeah, you used to make the rules up as we went along...
That's 10-0 to me!

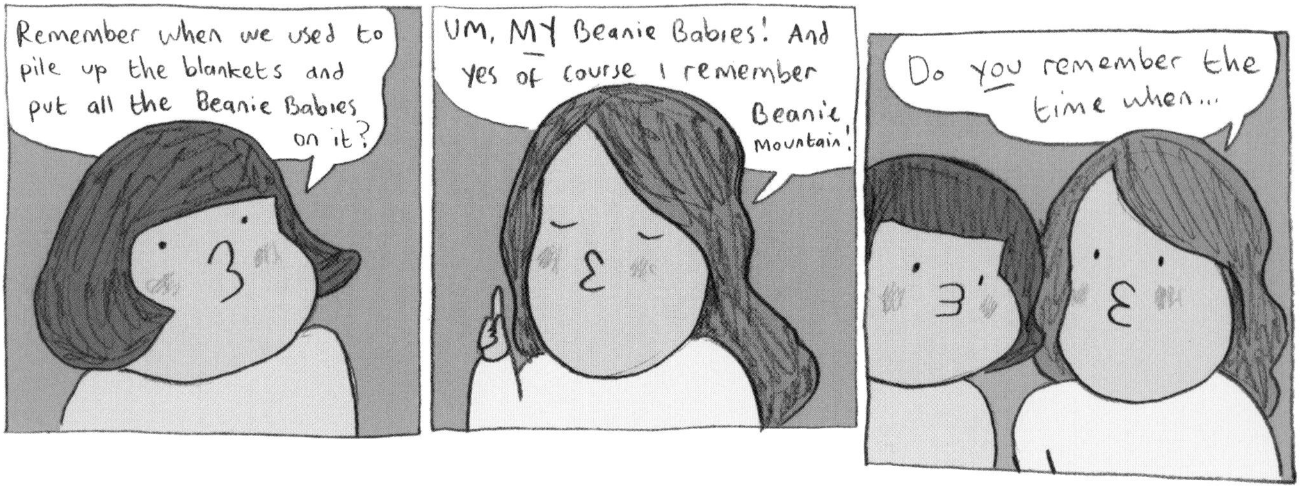
Remember when we used to pile up the blankets and put all the Beanie Babies on it?
UM, MY Beanie Babies! And yes of course I remember
Beanie Mountain!
Do YOU remember the time when...

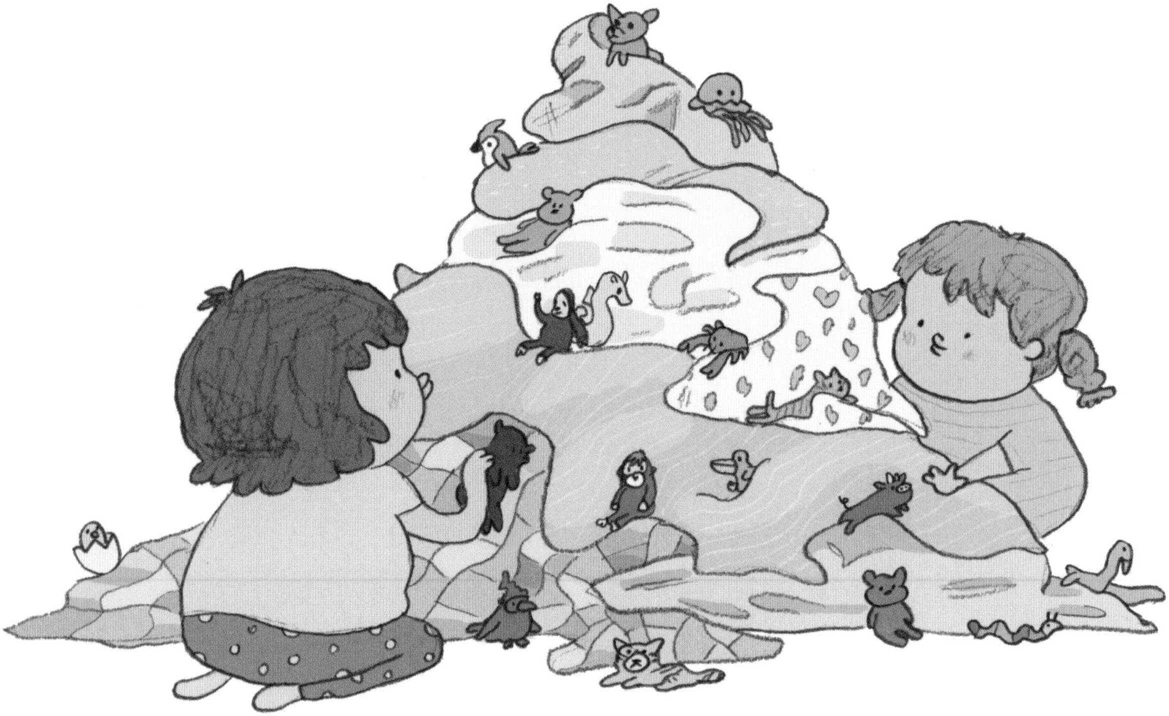

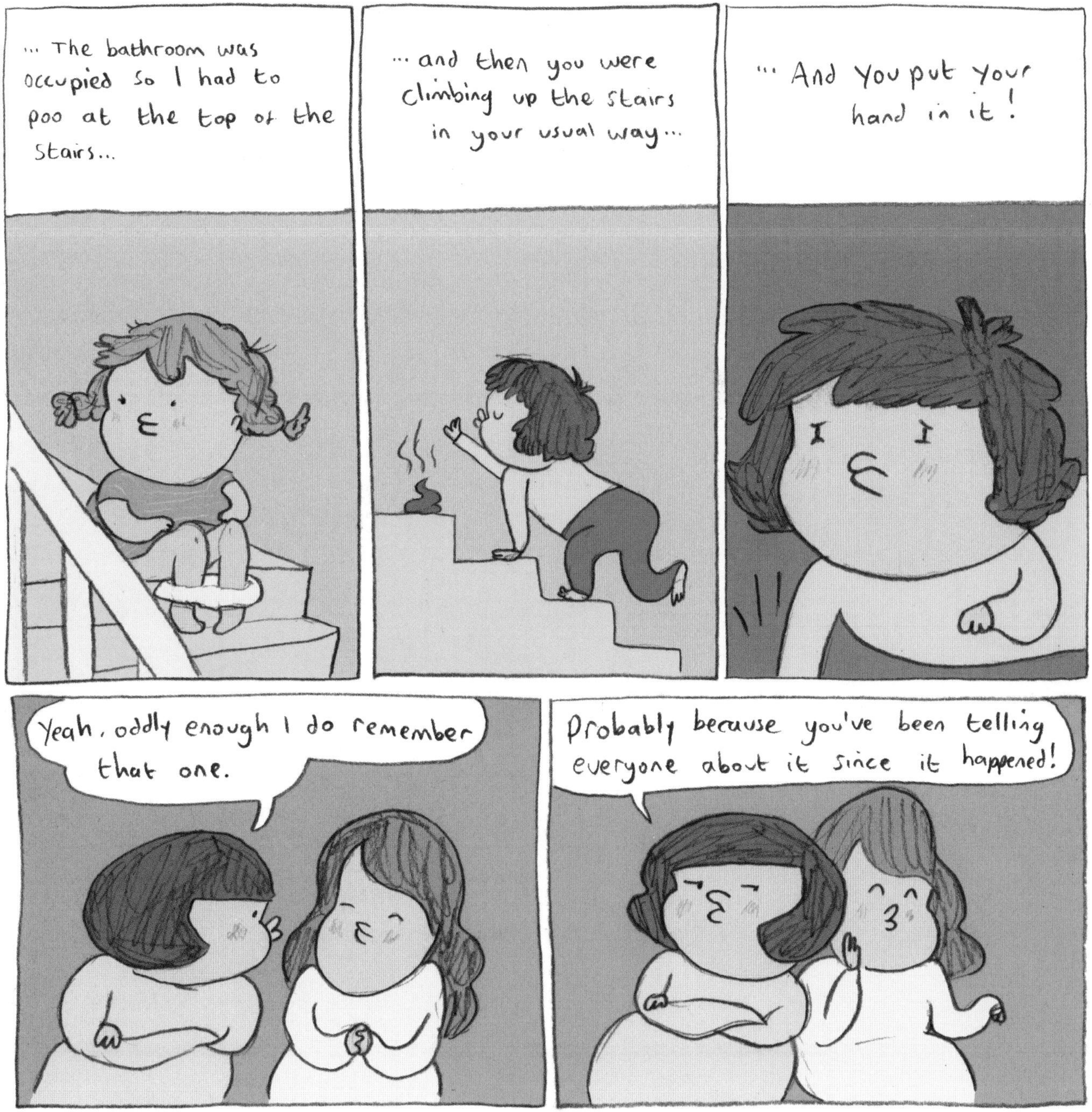
... The bathroom was occupied so I had to poo at the top of the stairs...
... and then you were climbing up the stairs in your usual way...
... And You put Your hand in it!
Yeah, oddly enough I do remember that one.
Probably because you've been telling everyone about it since it happened!

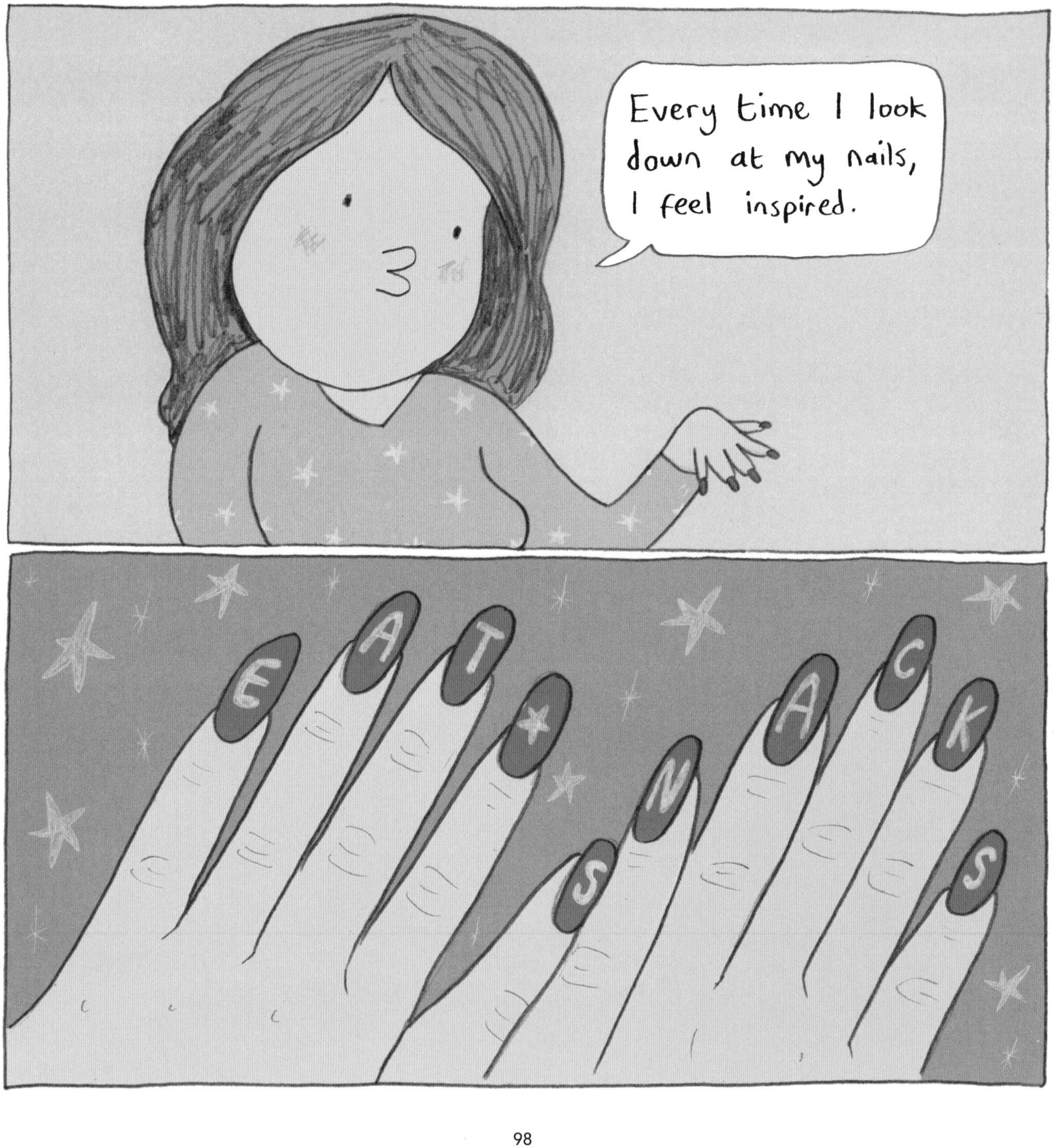
Every time I look down at my nails, I feel inspired.
EAT SNACKS

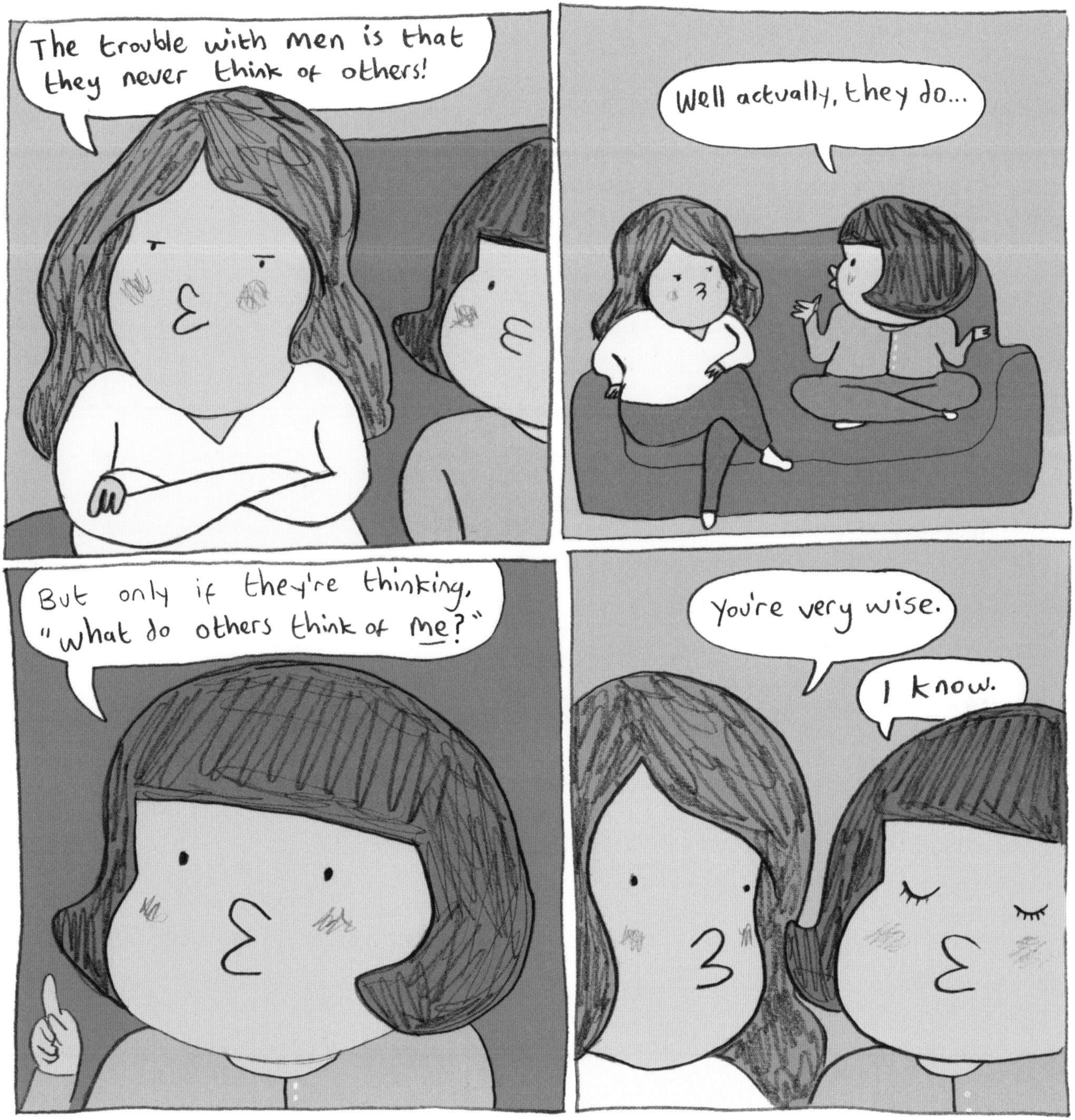
The trouble with men is that they never think of others!
Well actually, they do...
But only if they're thinking, "what do others think of me?"
You're very wise.
I know.

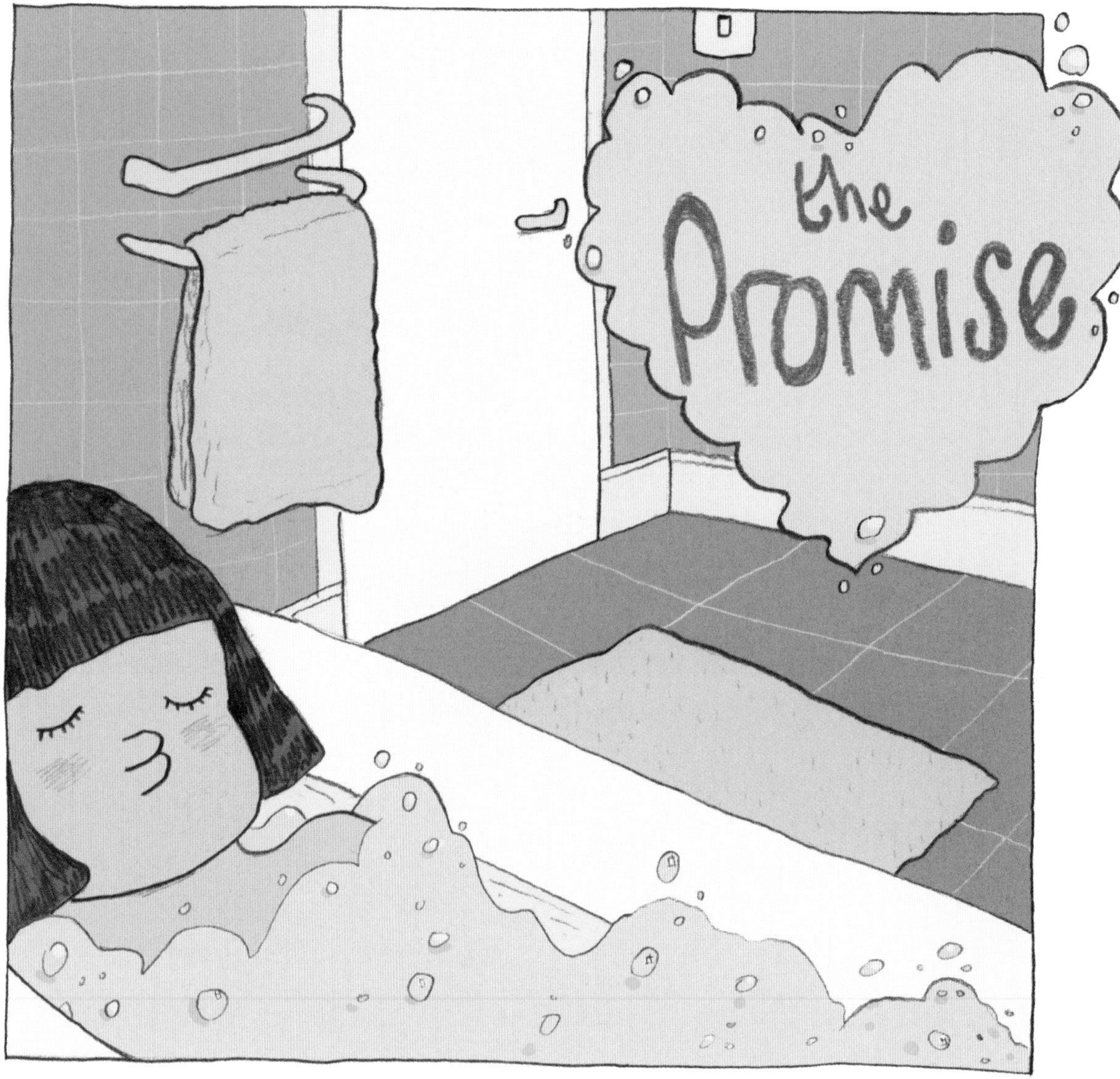
the Promise

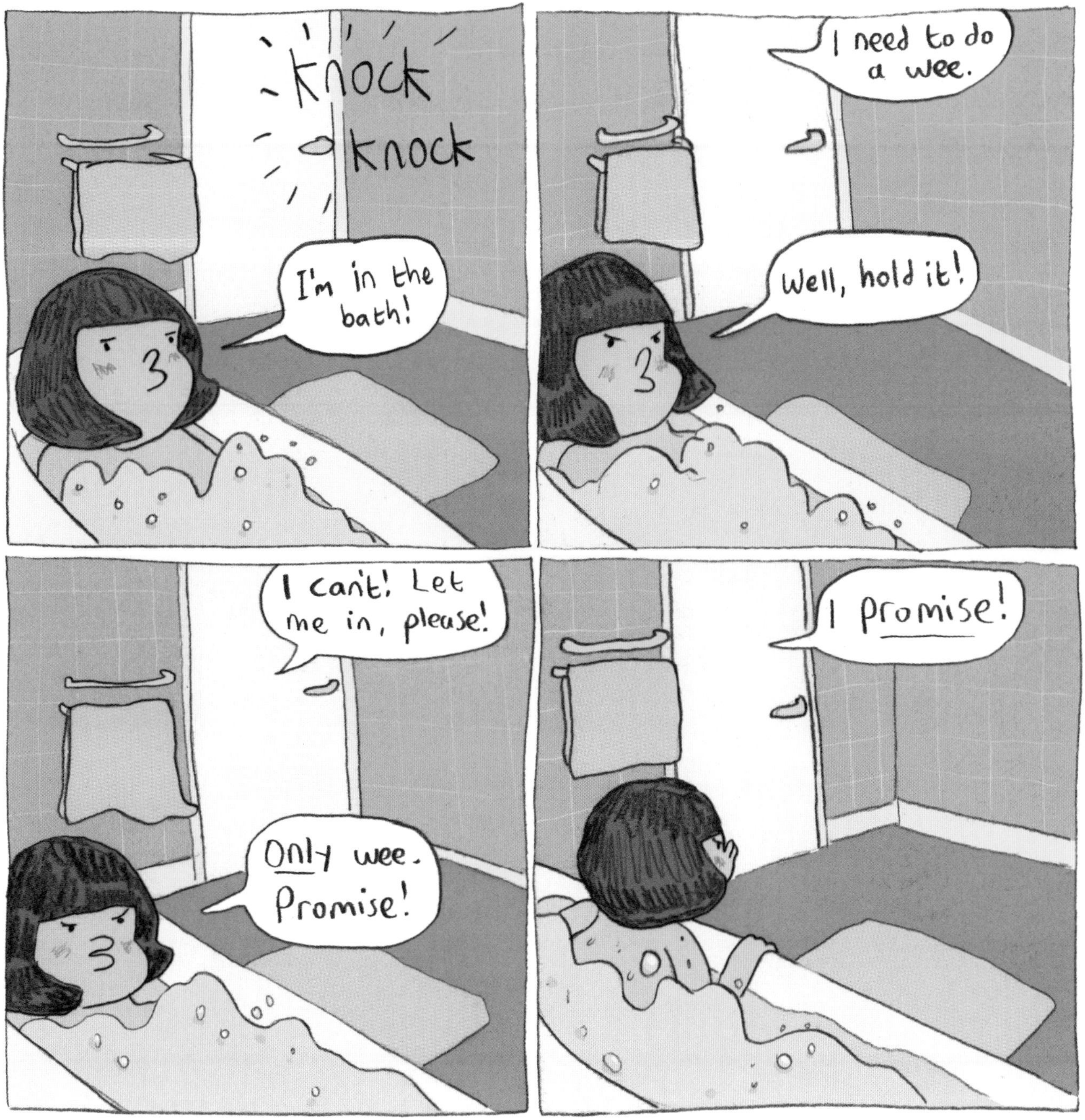
knock
knock
I'm in the bath!
I need to do a wee.
Well, hold it!
I can't! Let me in, please!
Only wee. Promise!
I promise!

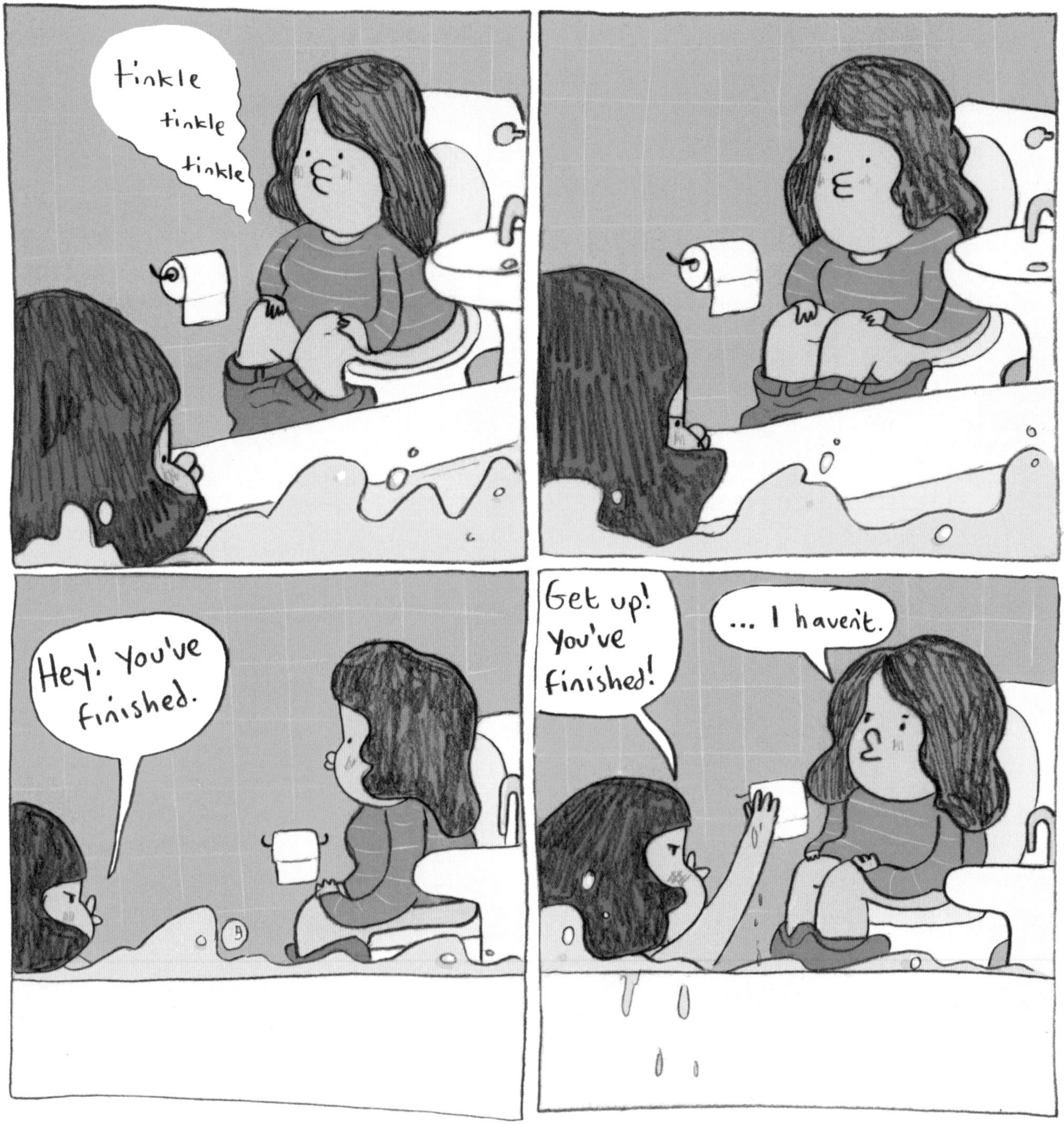
tinkle
tinkle
tinkle
Hey! You've finished.
Get up! You've finished!
... I haven't.

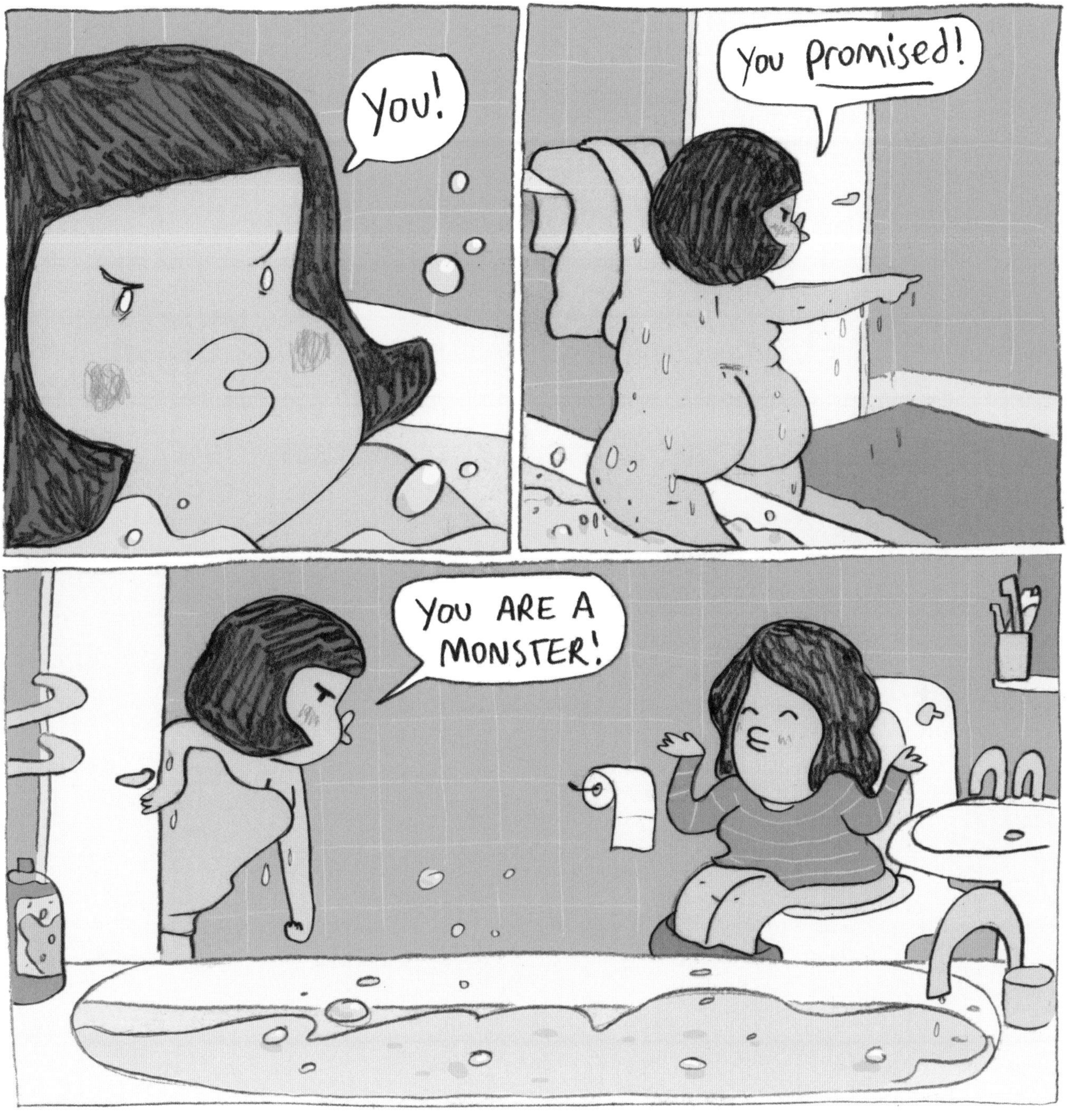
YOU!
YOU PROMISED!
YOU ARE A MONSTER!

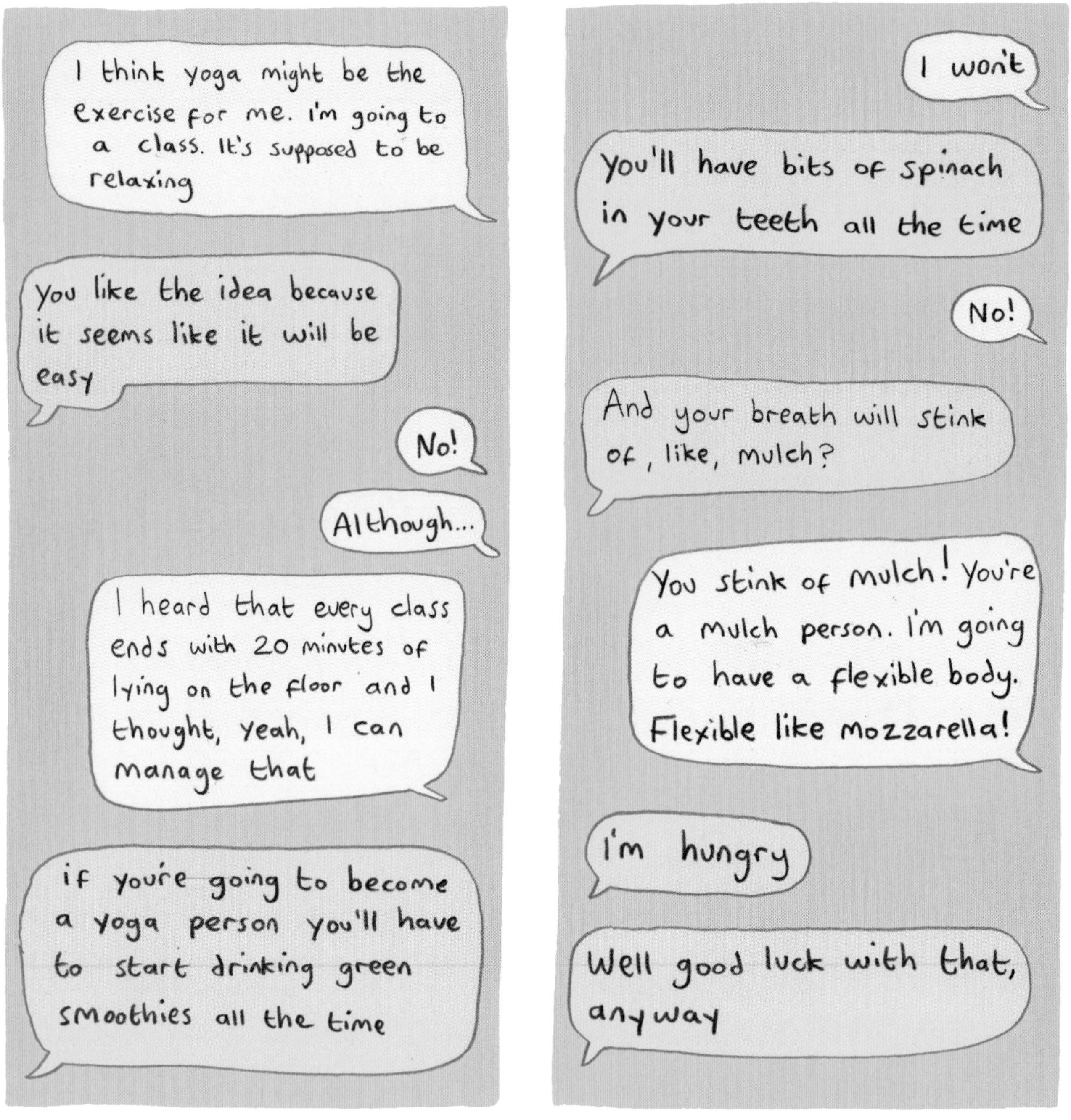
I think yoga might be the exercise for me. I'm going to a class. It's supposed to be relaxing
You like the idea because it seems like it will be easy
No!
Although...
I heard that every class ends with 20 minutes of lying on the floor and I thought, yeah, I can manage that
if you're going to become a yoga person you'll have to start drinking green smoothies all the time
I won't
You'll have bits of spinach in your teeth all the time
No!
And your breath will stink of, like, mulch?
You stink of mulch! You're a mulch person. I'm going to have a flexible body. Flexible like mozzarella!
I'm hungry
Well good luck with that, anyway

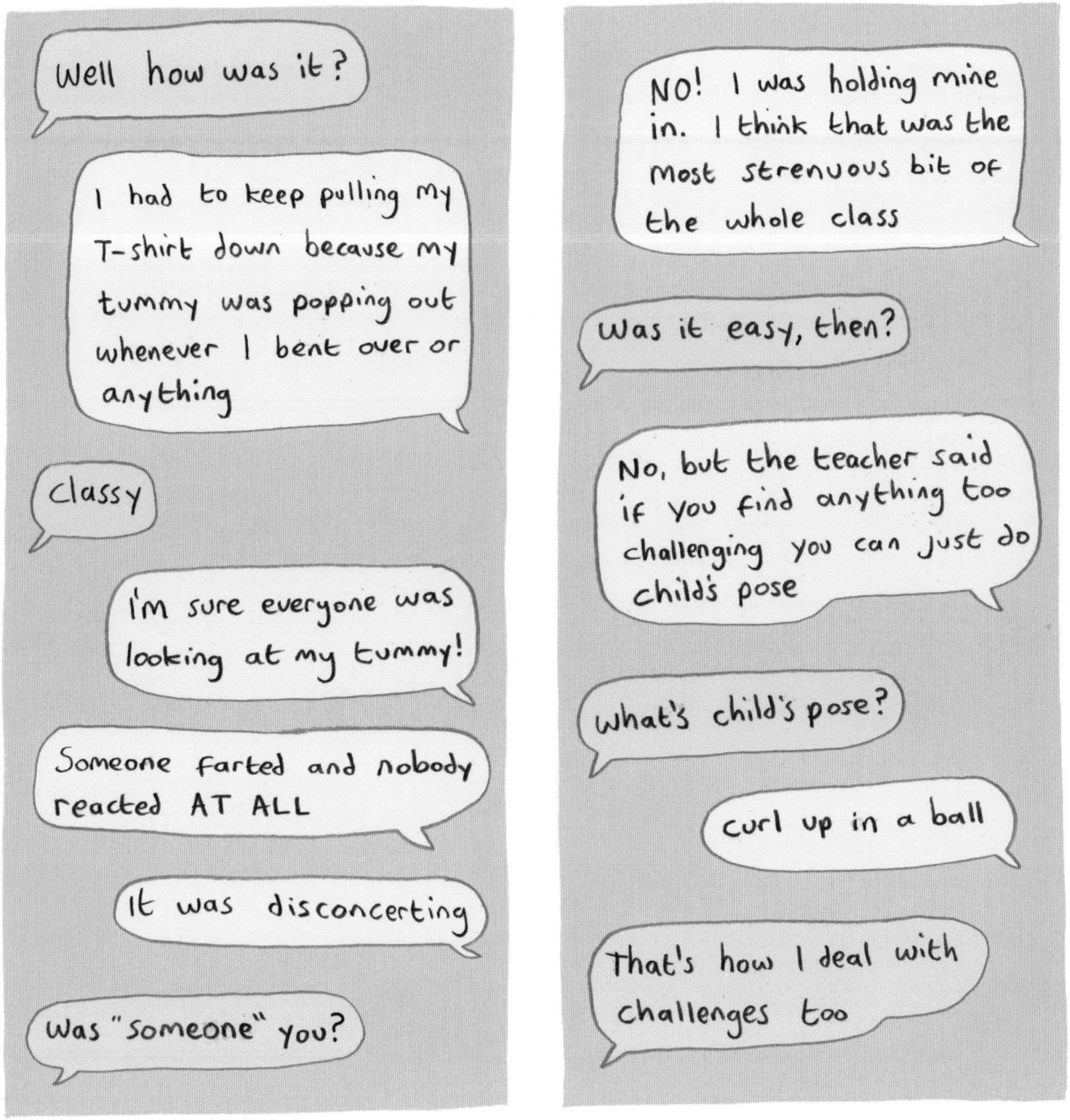
Well how was it?
I had to keep pulling my T-shirt down because my tummy was popping out whenever I bent over or anything
Classy
I'm sure everyone was looking at my tummy!
Someone farted and nobody reacted AT ALL
It was disconcerting
Was "someone" you?
NO! I was holding mine in. I think that was the most strenuous bit of the whole class
Was it easy, then?
No, but the teacher said if you find anything too challenging you can just do child's pose
What's child's pose?
curl up in a ball
That's how I deal with challenges too

Mood of the Day...

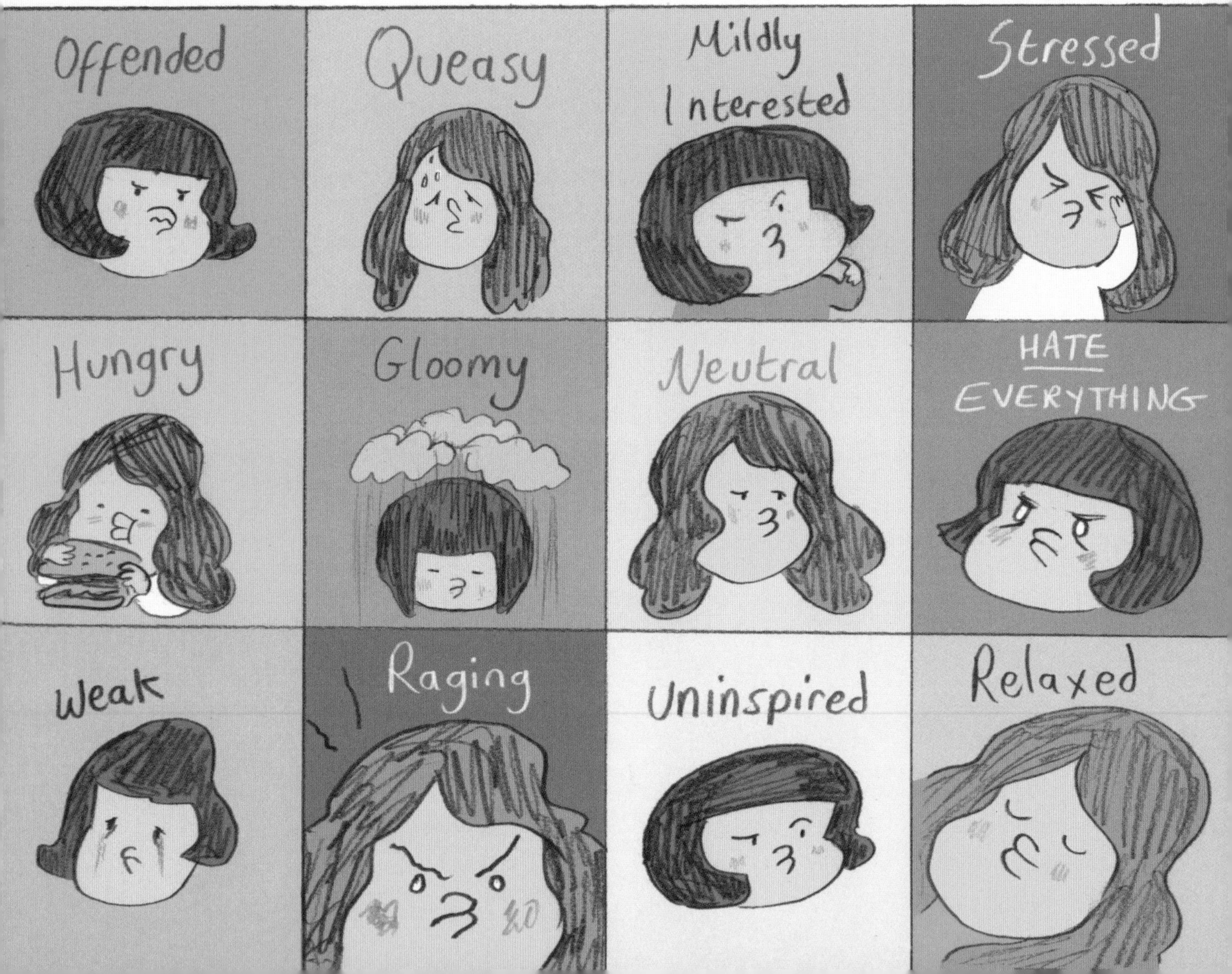
Offended
Queasy
Mildly Interested
Stressed
Hungry
Gloomy
Neutral
HATE EVERYTHING
Weak
Raging
Uninspired
Relaxed

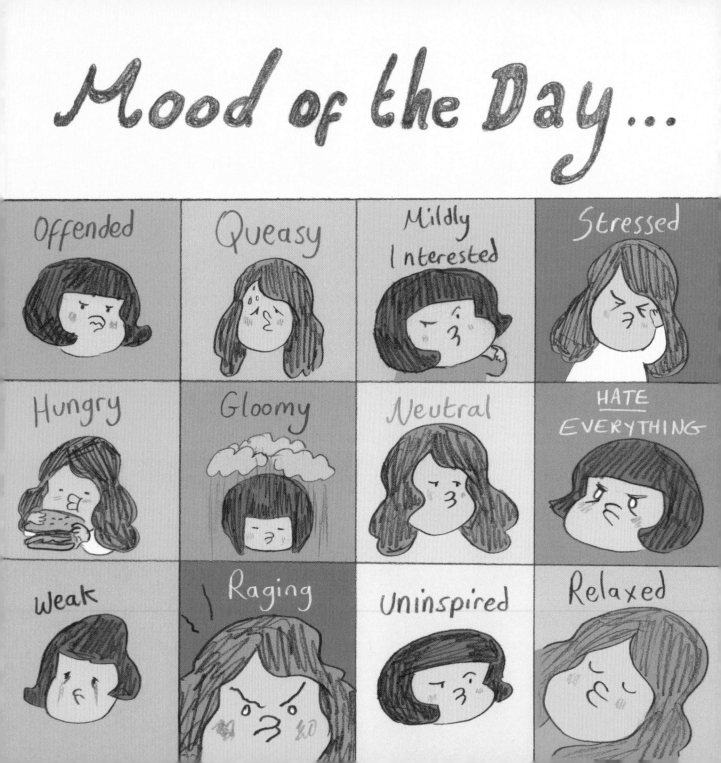

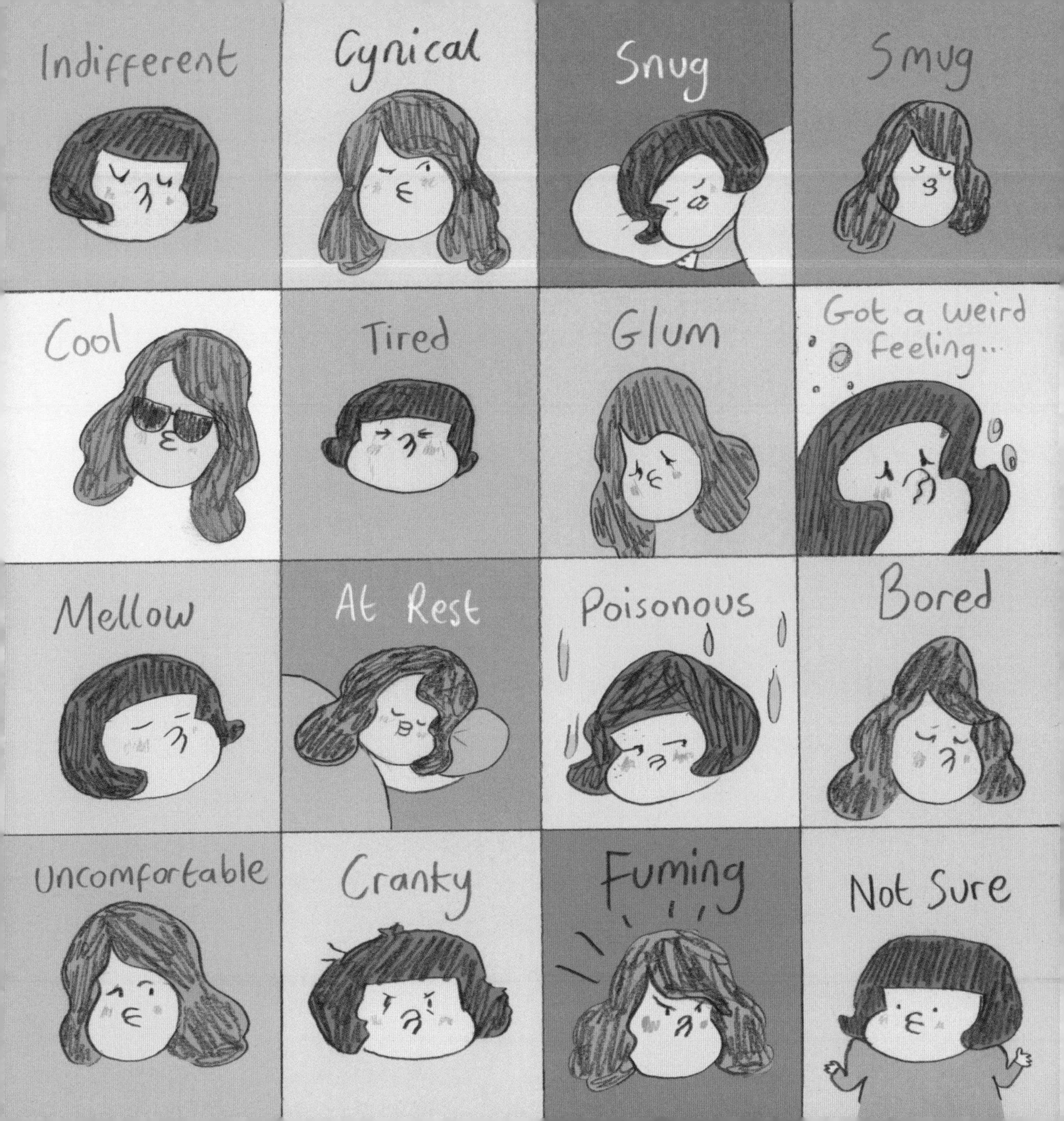
Indifferent
Cynical
Snug
Smug
Cool
Tired
Glum
Got a weird feeling...
Mellow
At Rest
Poisonous
Bored
Uncomfortable
Cranky
Fuming
Not Sure

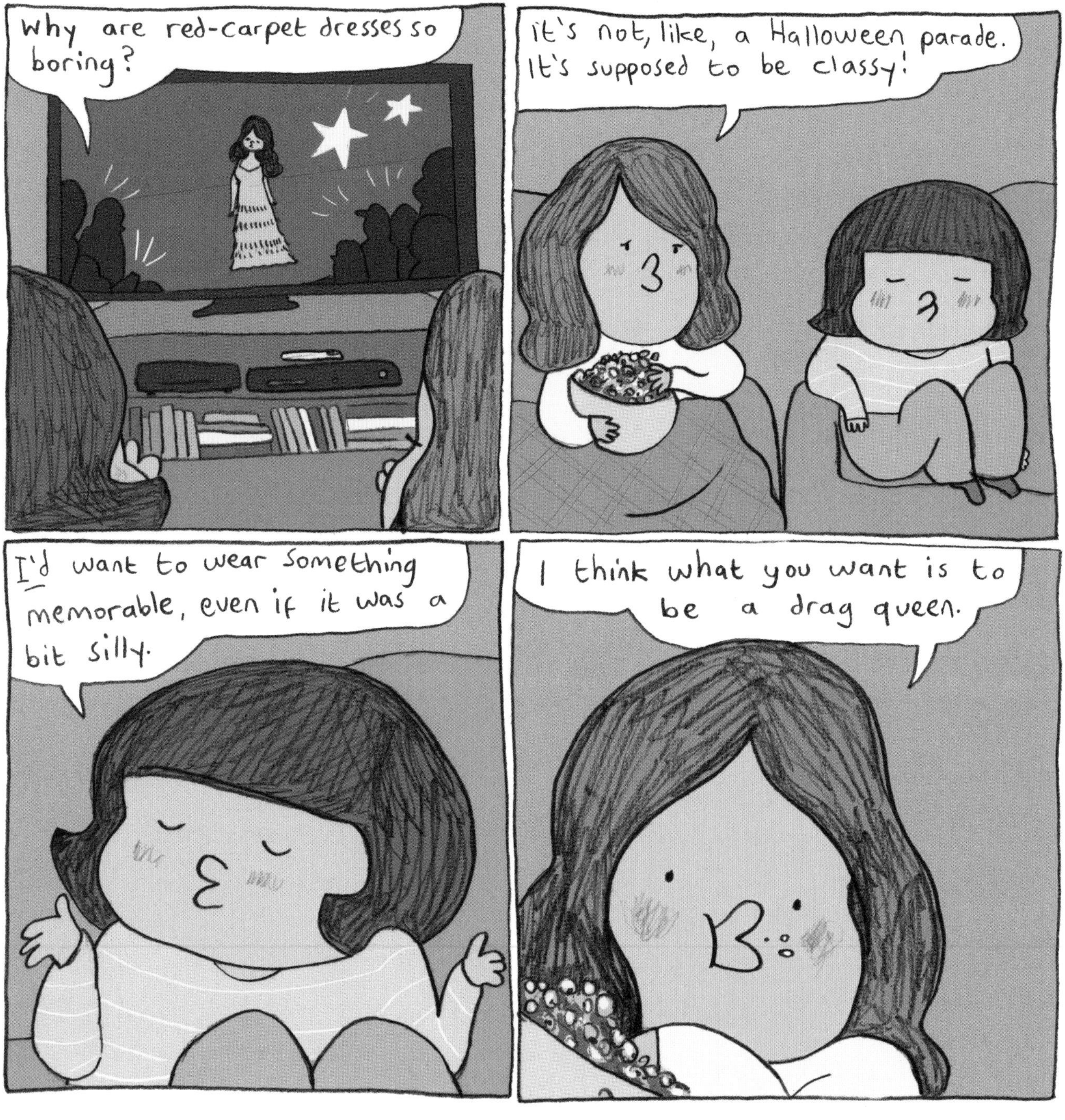
Why are red-carpet dresses so boring?
It's not, like, a Halloween parade. It's supposed to be classy!
I'd want to wear something memorable, even if it was a bit silly.
I think what you want is to be a drag queen.

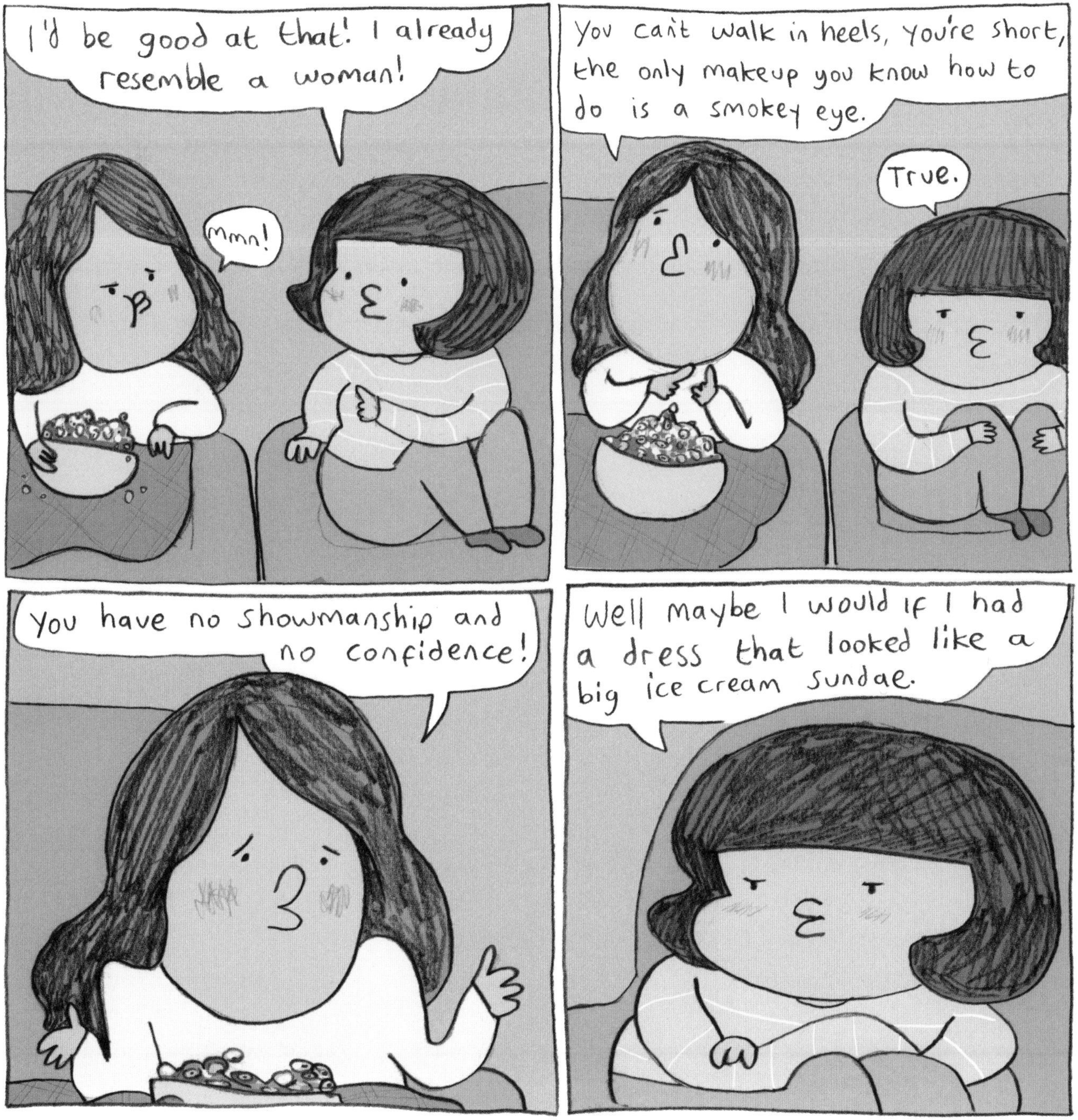
I'd be good at that! I already resemble a woman!
Mmn!
You can't walk in heels, you're short, the only makeup you know how to do is a smokey eye.
True.
You have no showmanship and no confidence!
Well maybe I would if I had a dress that looked like a big ice cream sundae.

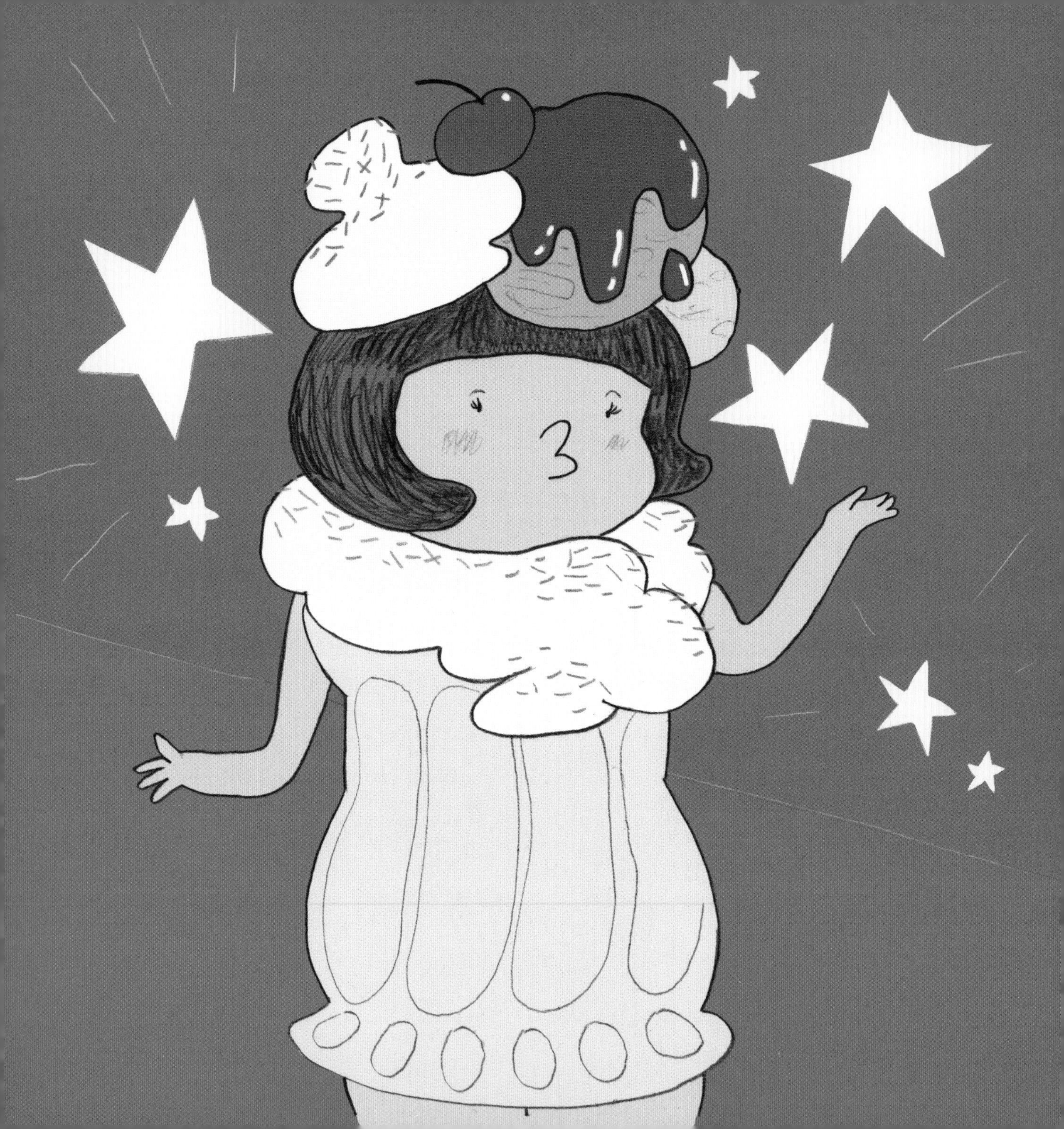

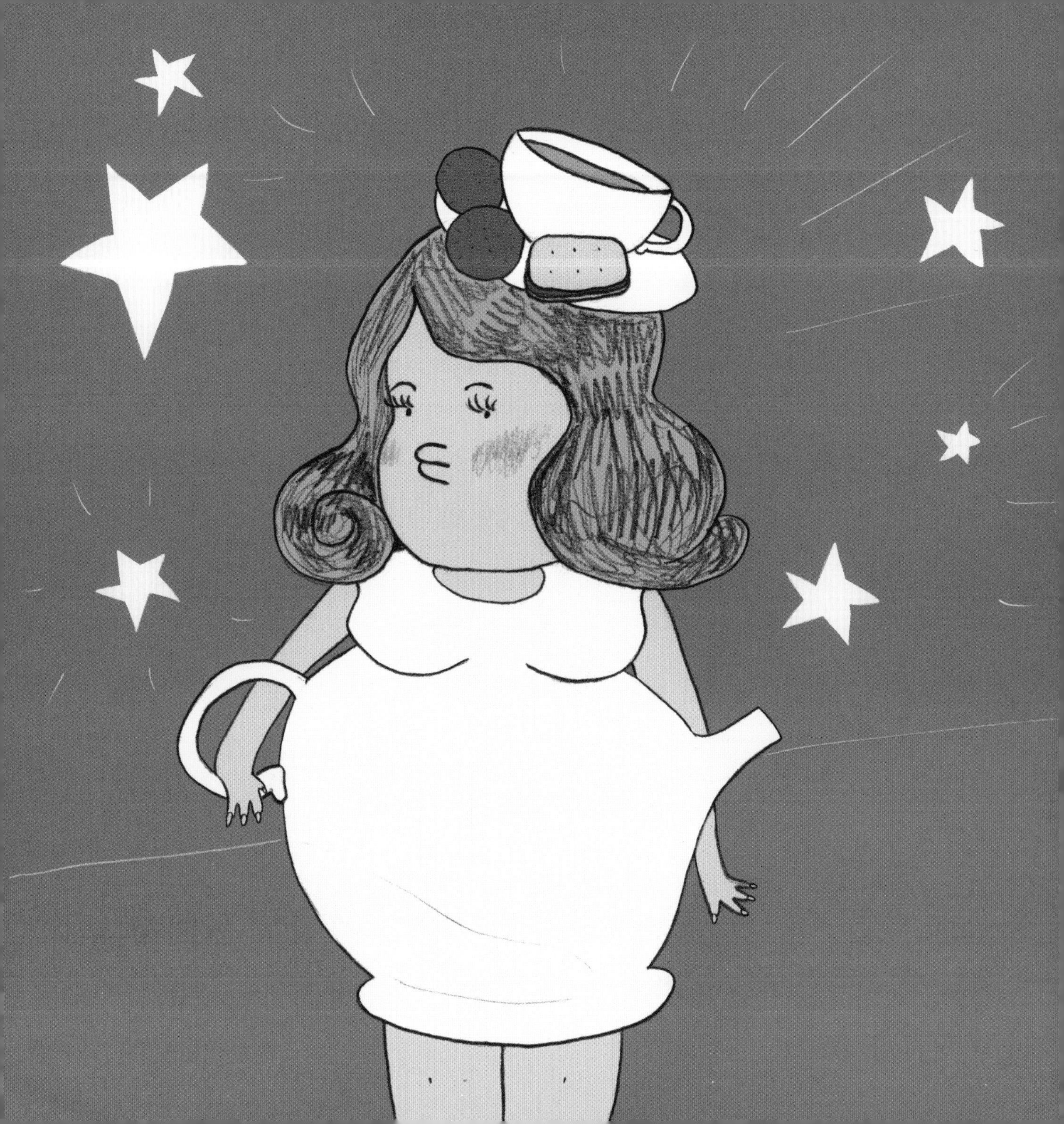

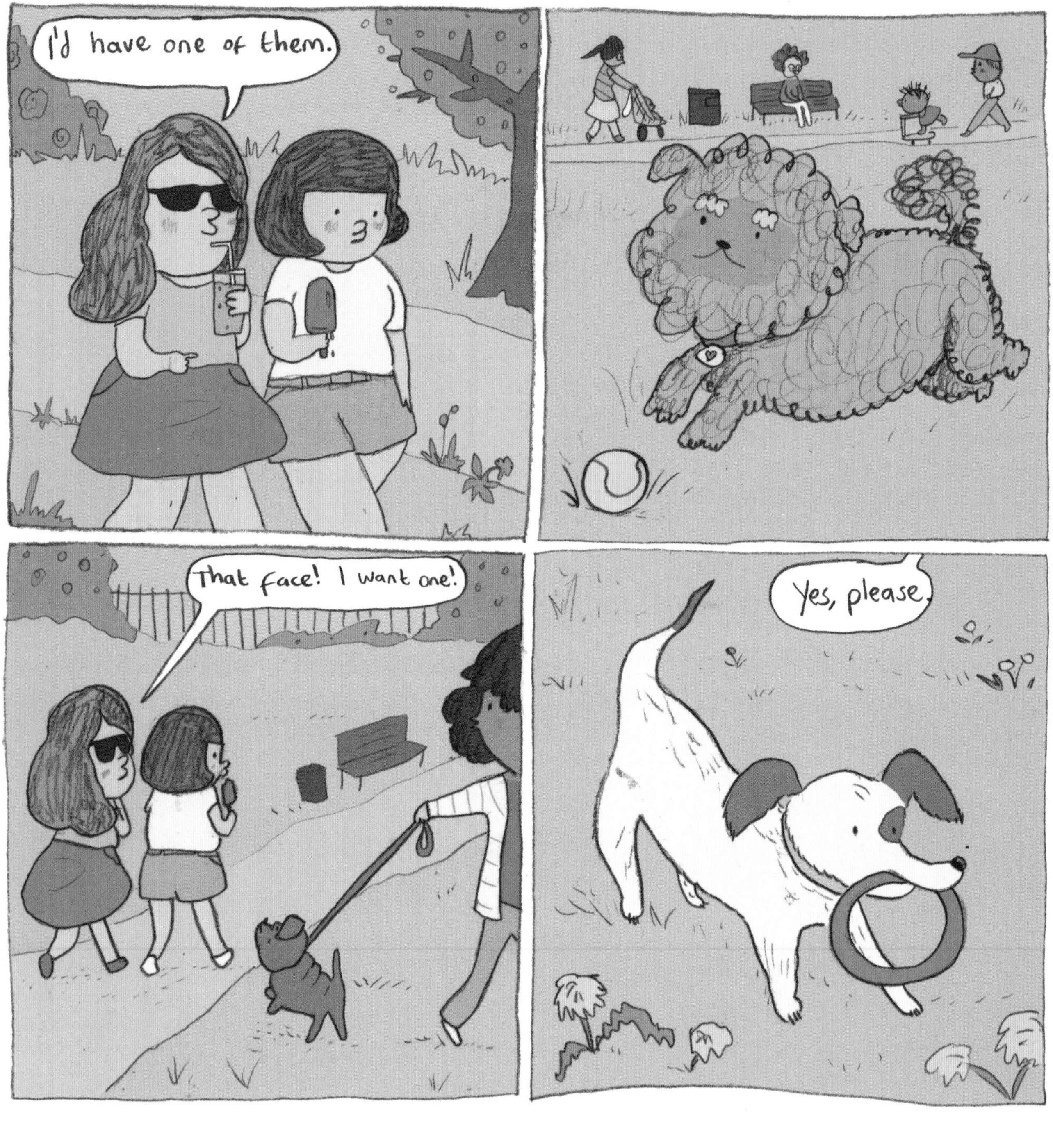
I'd have one of them.
That face! I want one!
Yes, please.

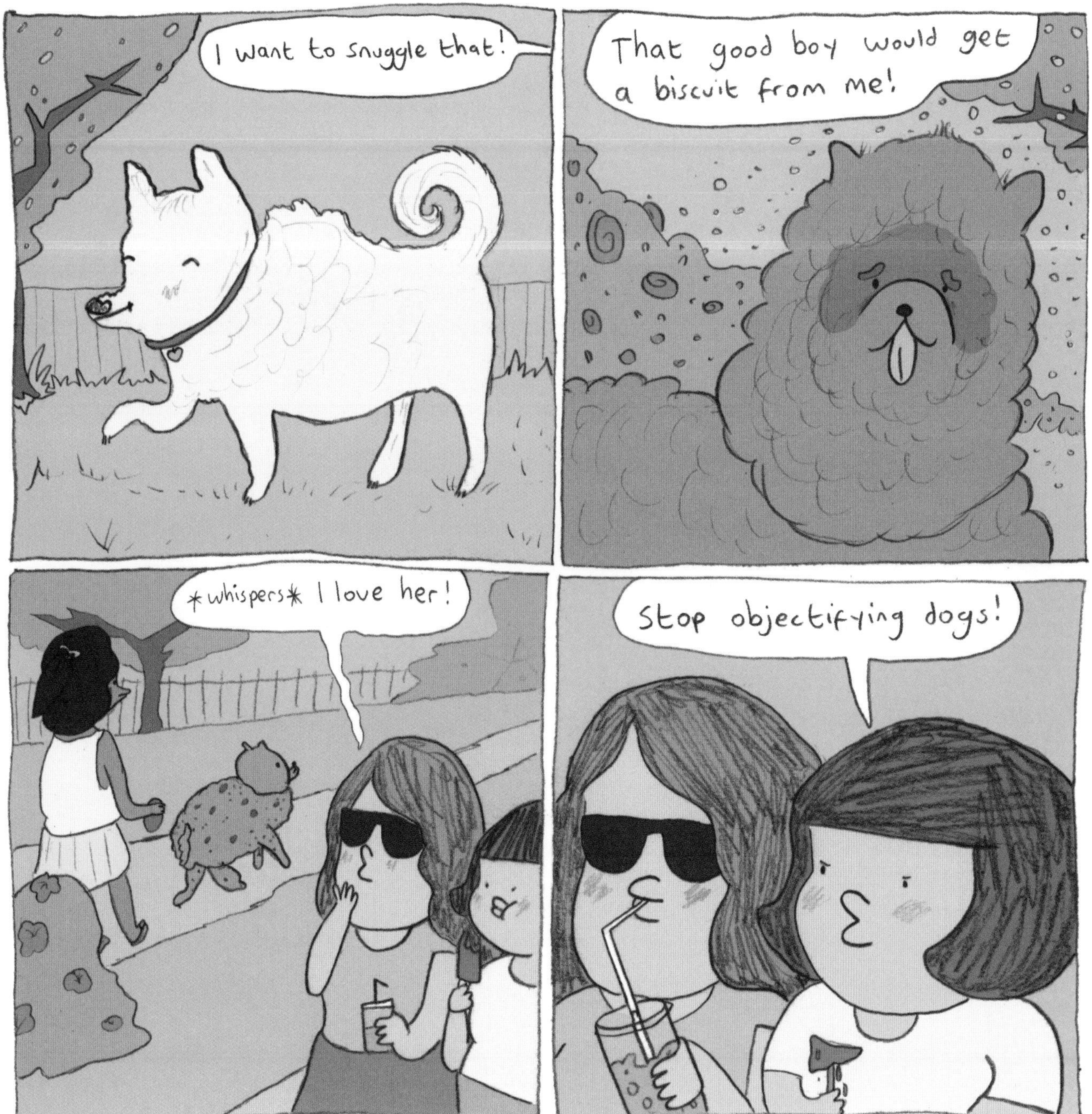
I want to snuggle that!
That good boy would get a biscuit from me!
whispers I love her!
Stop objectifying dogs!

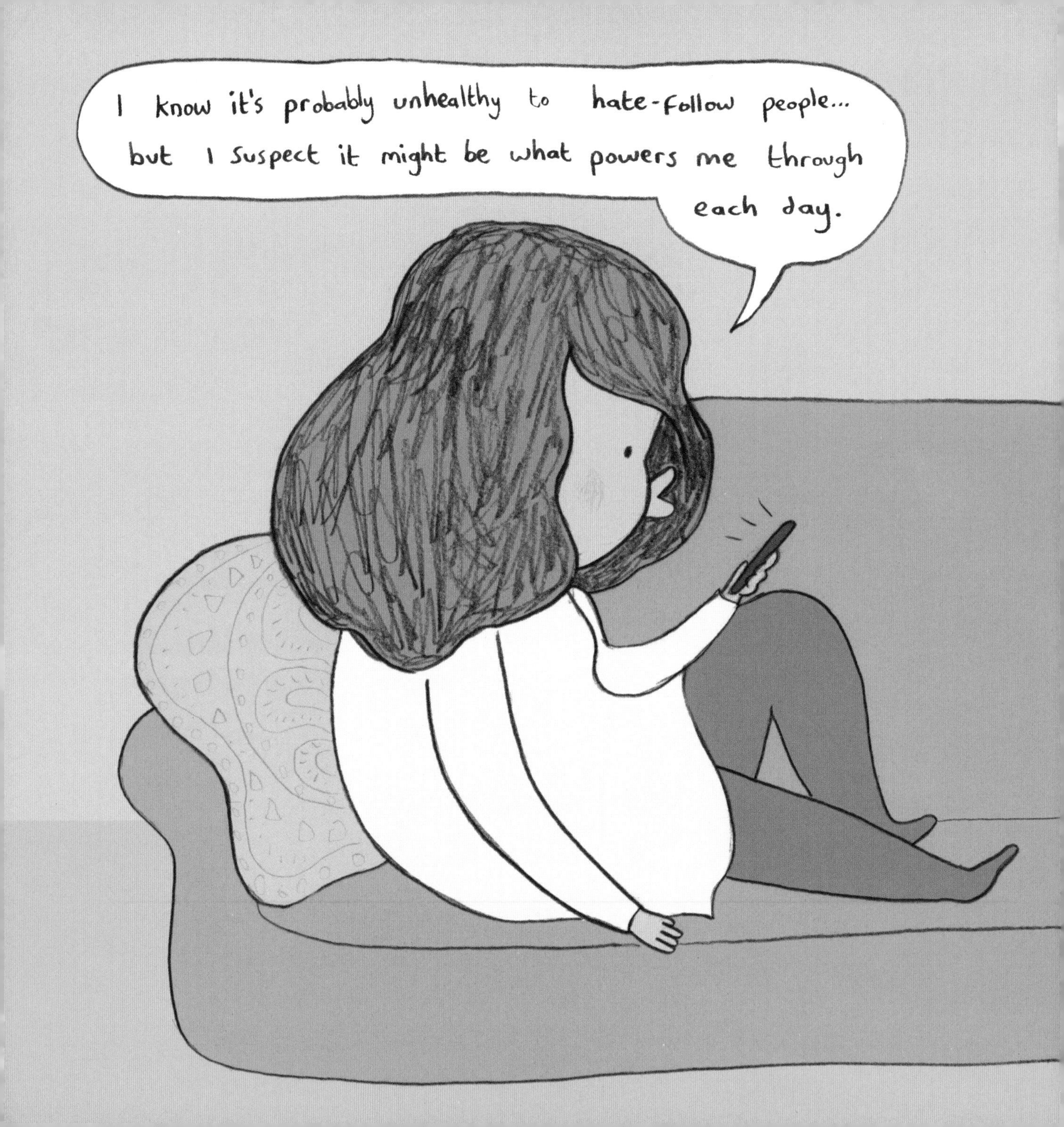
I know it's probably unhealthy to hate-follow people... but I suspect it might be what powers me through each day.

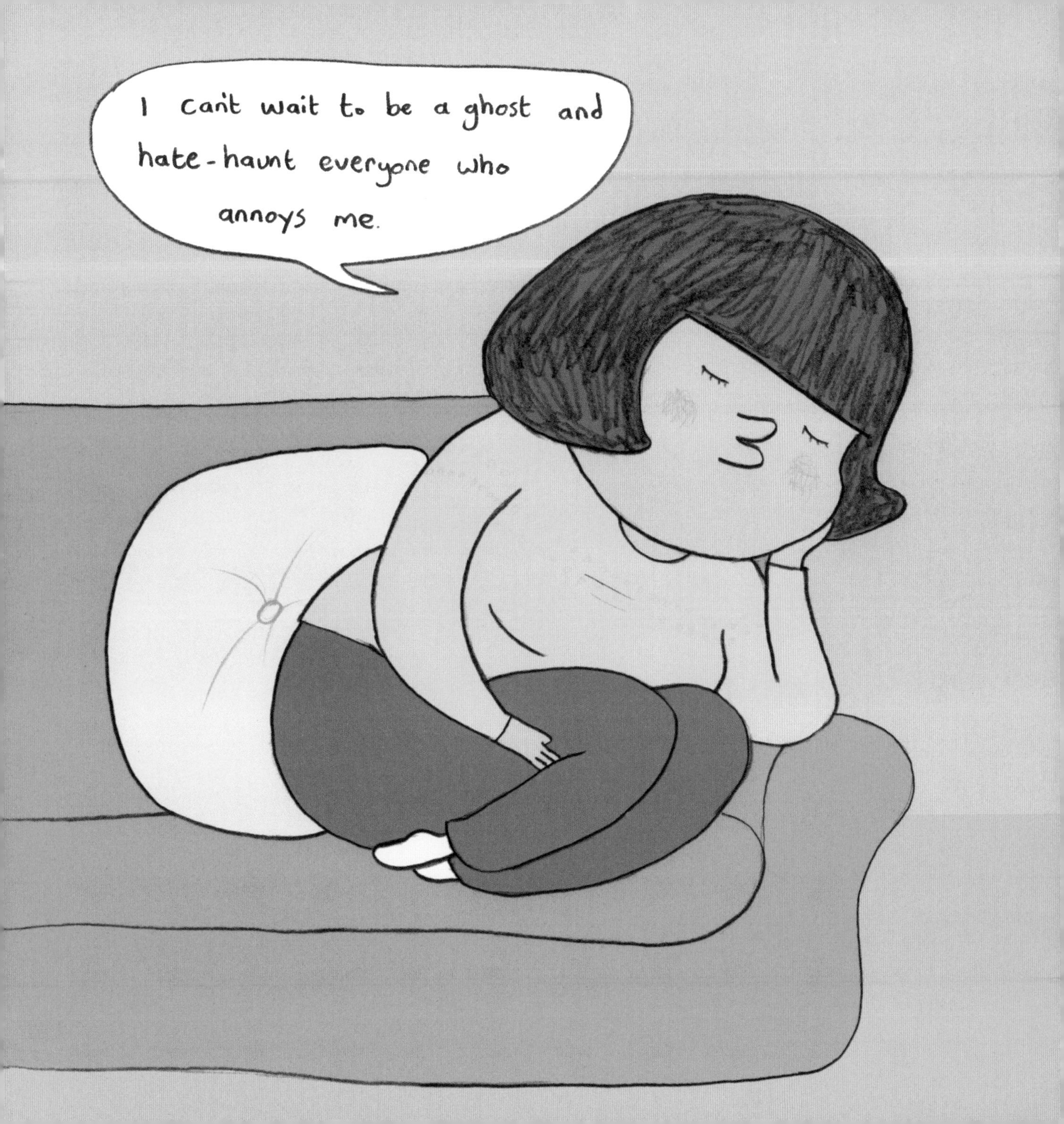
I can't wait to be a ghost and hate-haunt everyone who annoys me.

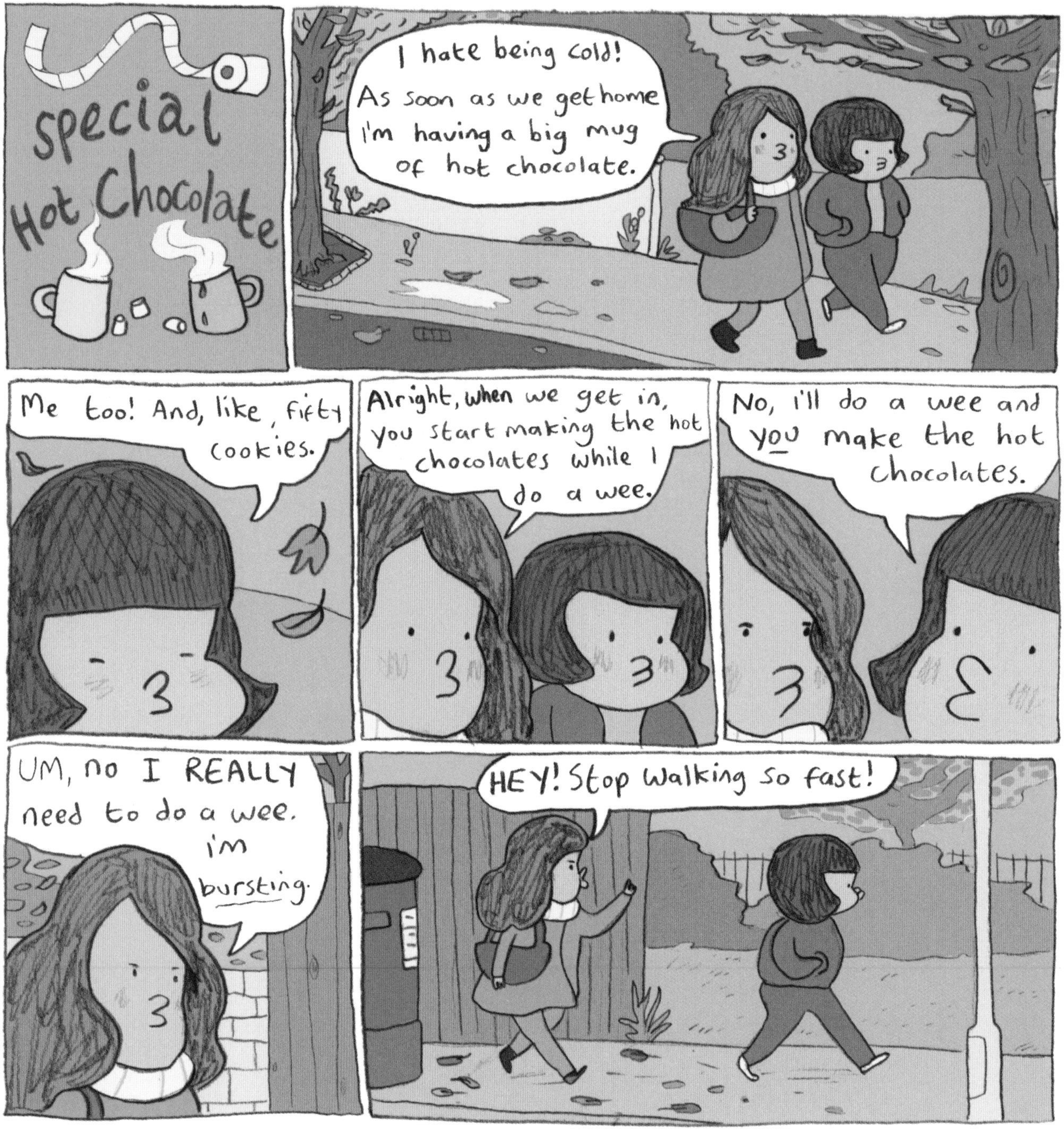
special Hot Chocolate
I hate being cold!
As soon as we get home I'm having a big mug of hot chocolate.
Me too! And, like, fifty cookies.
Alright, when we get in, you start making the hot chocolates while I do a wee.
No, I'll do a wee and you make the hot chocolates.
UM, no I REALLY need to do a wee. I'm bursting.
HEY! Stop Walking so fast!

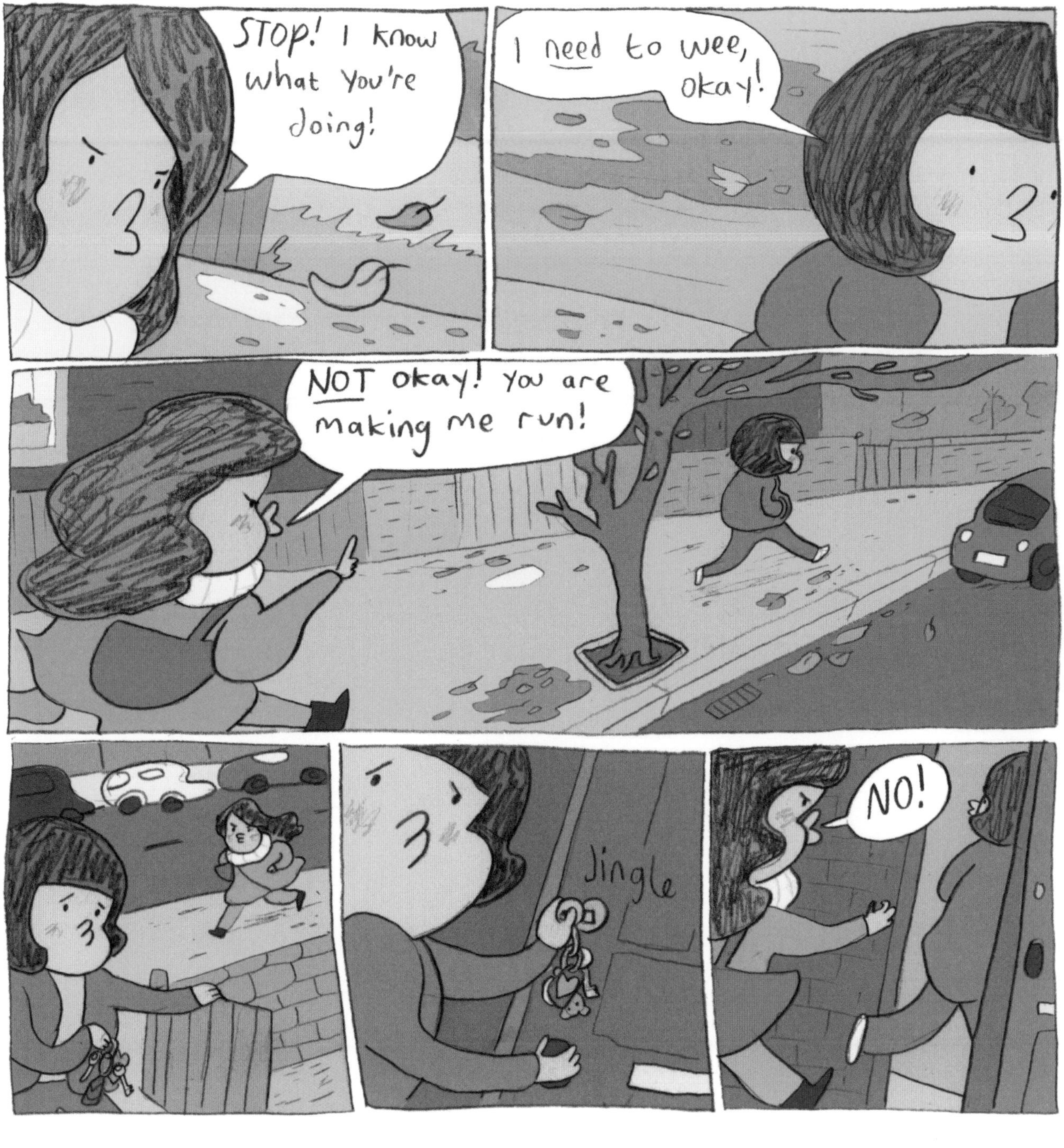
STOP! I know what you're doing!
I need to wee, okay!
NOT okay! You are making me run!
Jingle
NO!

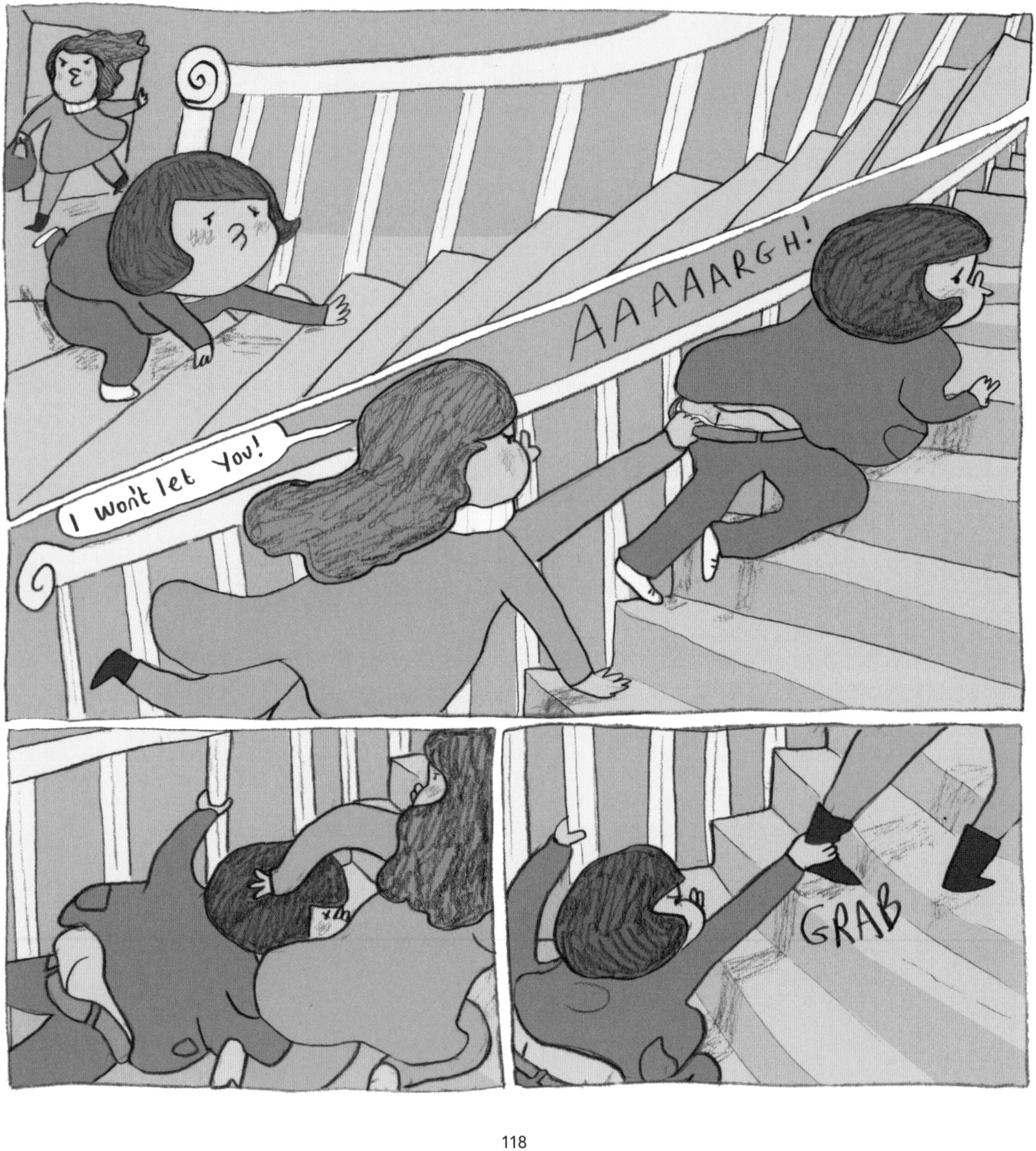
AAAAARGH!
I won't let You!
GRAB

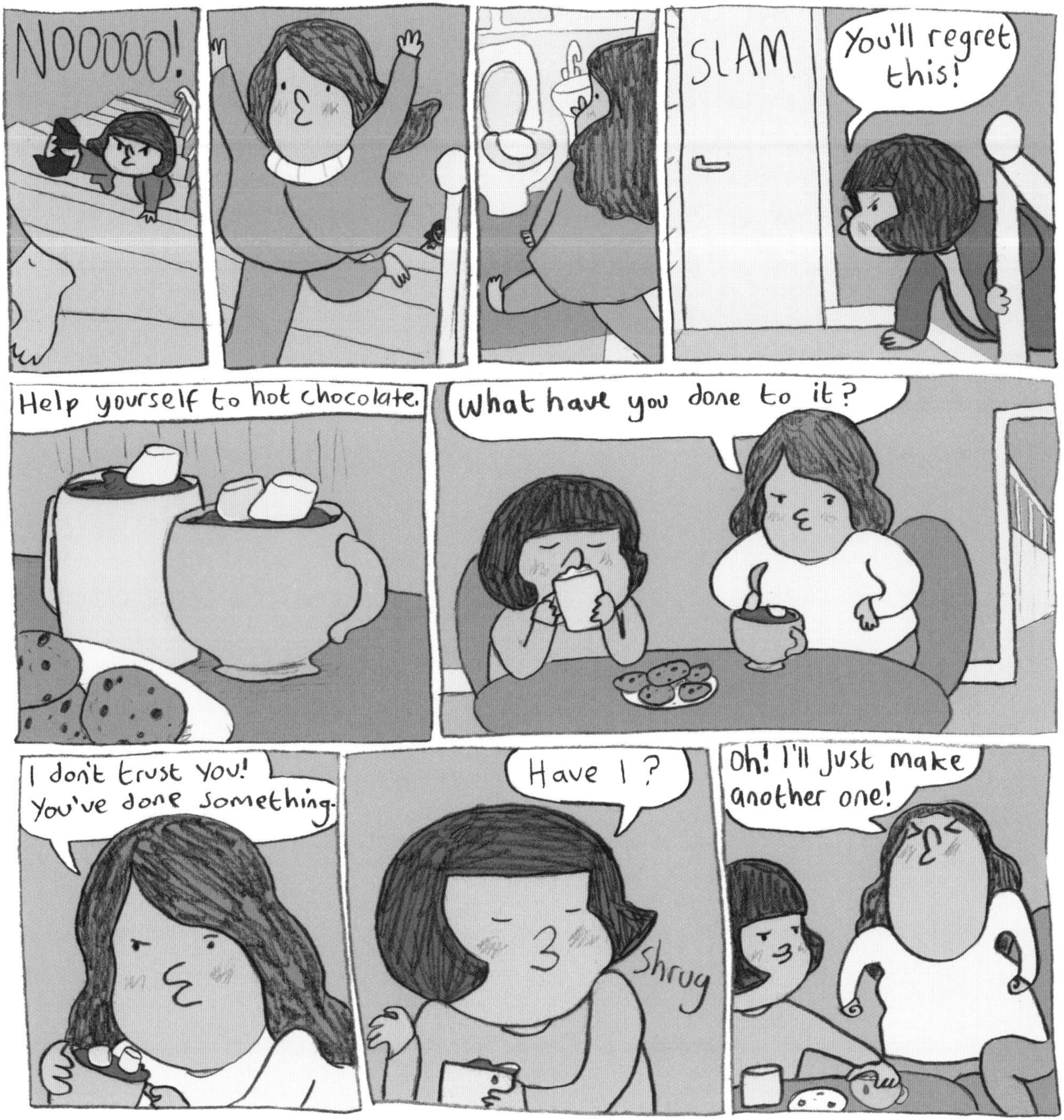
NOOOOO!
SLAM
You'll regret this!
Help yourself to hot chocolate.
What have you done to it?
I don't trust you! You've done something.
Have I?
Shrug
Oh! I'll just make another one!

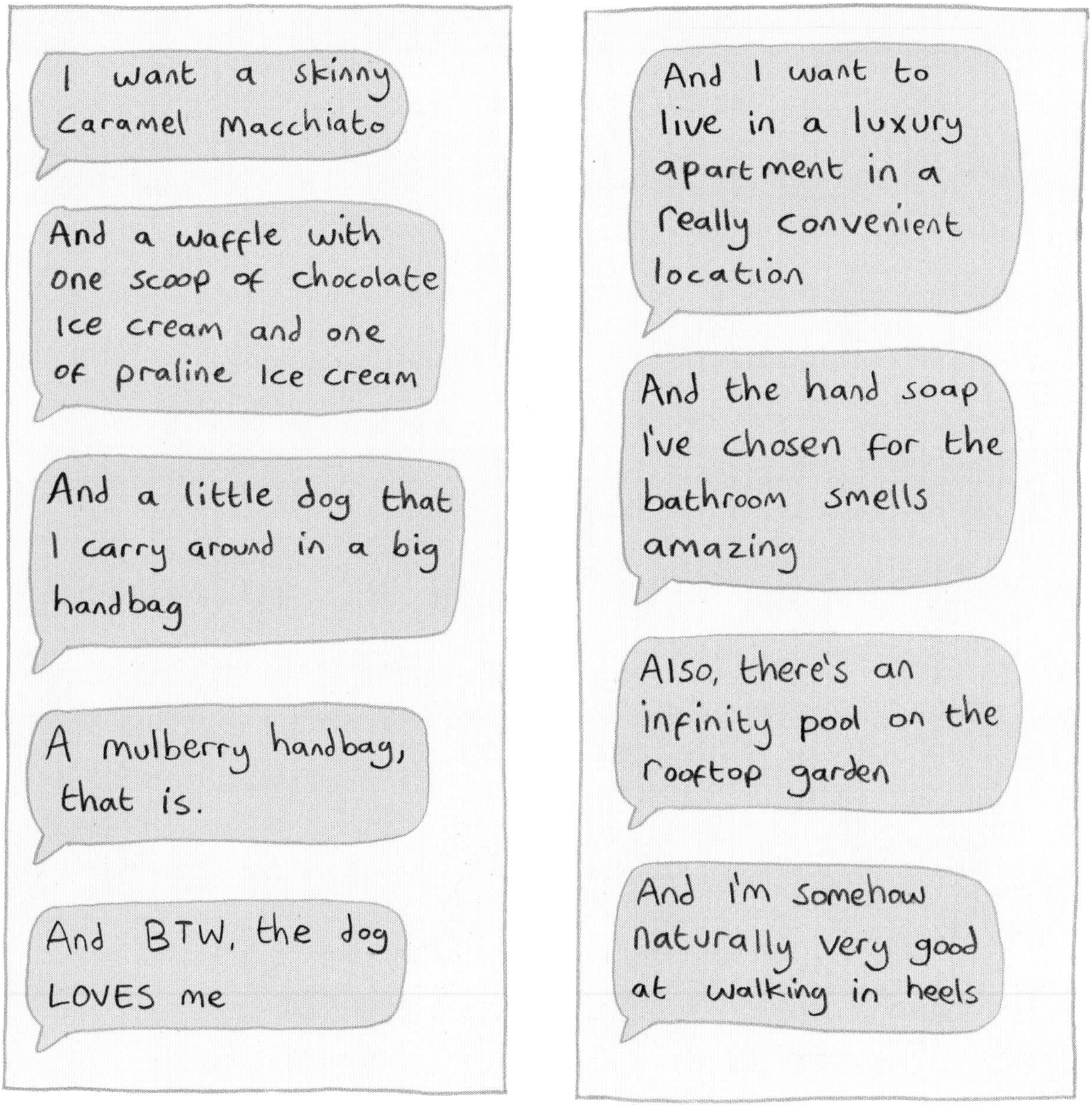
I want a skinny caramel macchiato
And a waffle with one scoop of chocolate ice cream and one of praline ice cream
And a little dog that I carry around in a big handbag
A mulberry handbag, that is.
And BTW, the dog LOVES me
And I want to live in a luxury apartment in a really convenient location
And the hand soap I've chosen for the bathroom smells amazing
Also, there's an infinity pool on the rooftop garden
And I'm somehow naturally very good at walking in heels

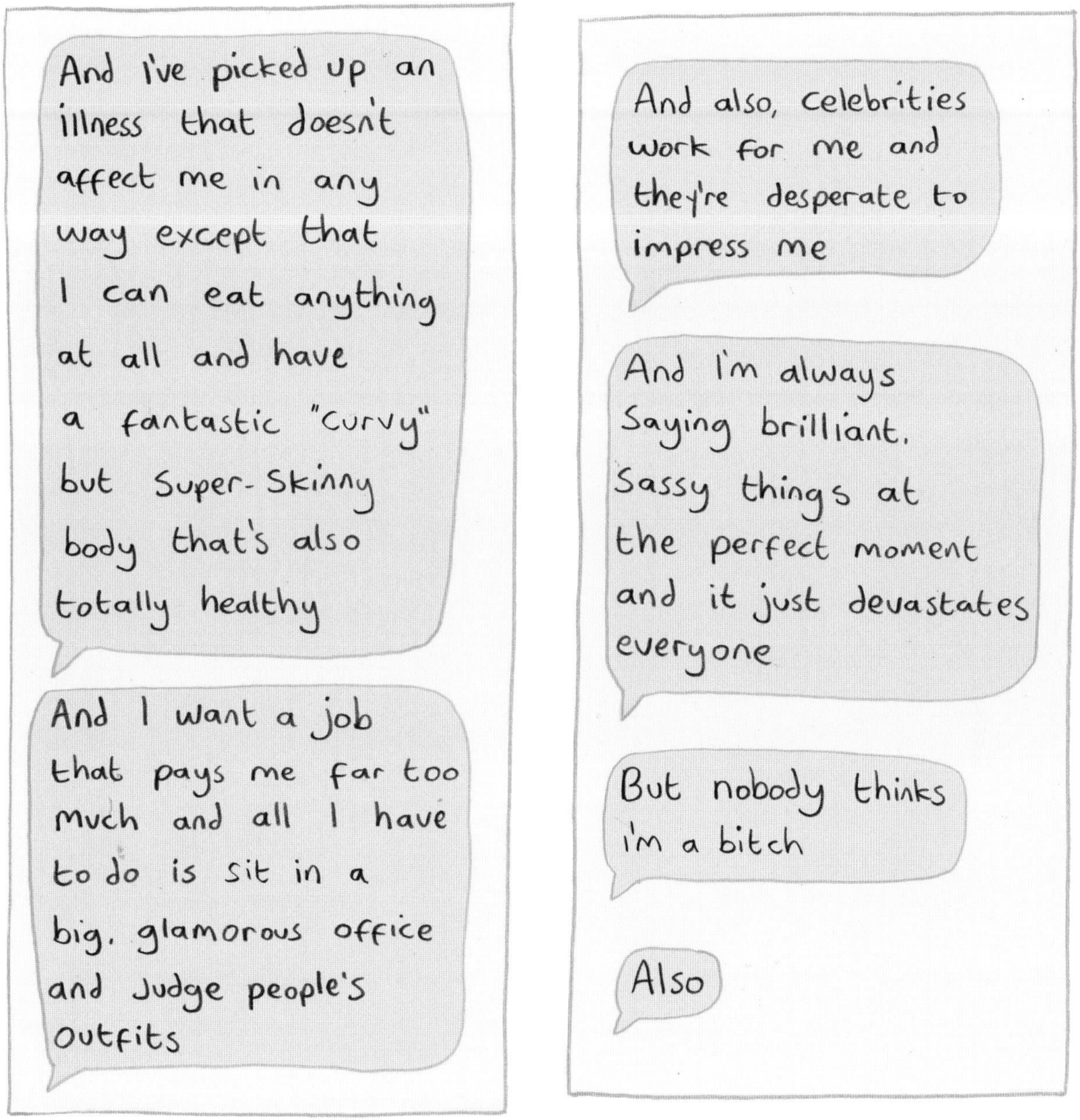
And I've picked up an illness that doesn't affect me in any way except that I can eat anything at all and have a fantastic "curvy" but super-skinny body that's also totally healthy
And I want a job that pays me far too much and all I have to do is sit in a big, glamorous office and judge people's outfits
And also, celebrities work for me and they're desperate to impress me
And I'm always saying brilliant, sassy things at the perfect moment and it just devastates everyone
But nobody thinks I'm a bitch
Also

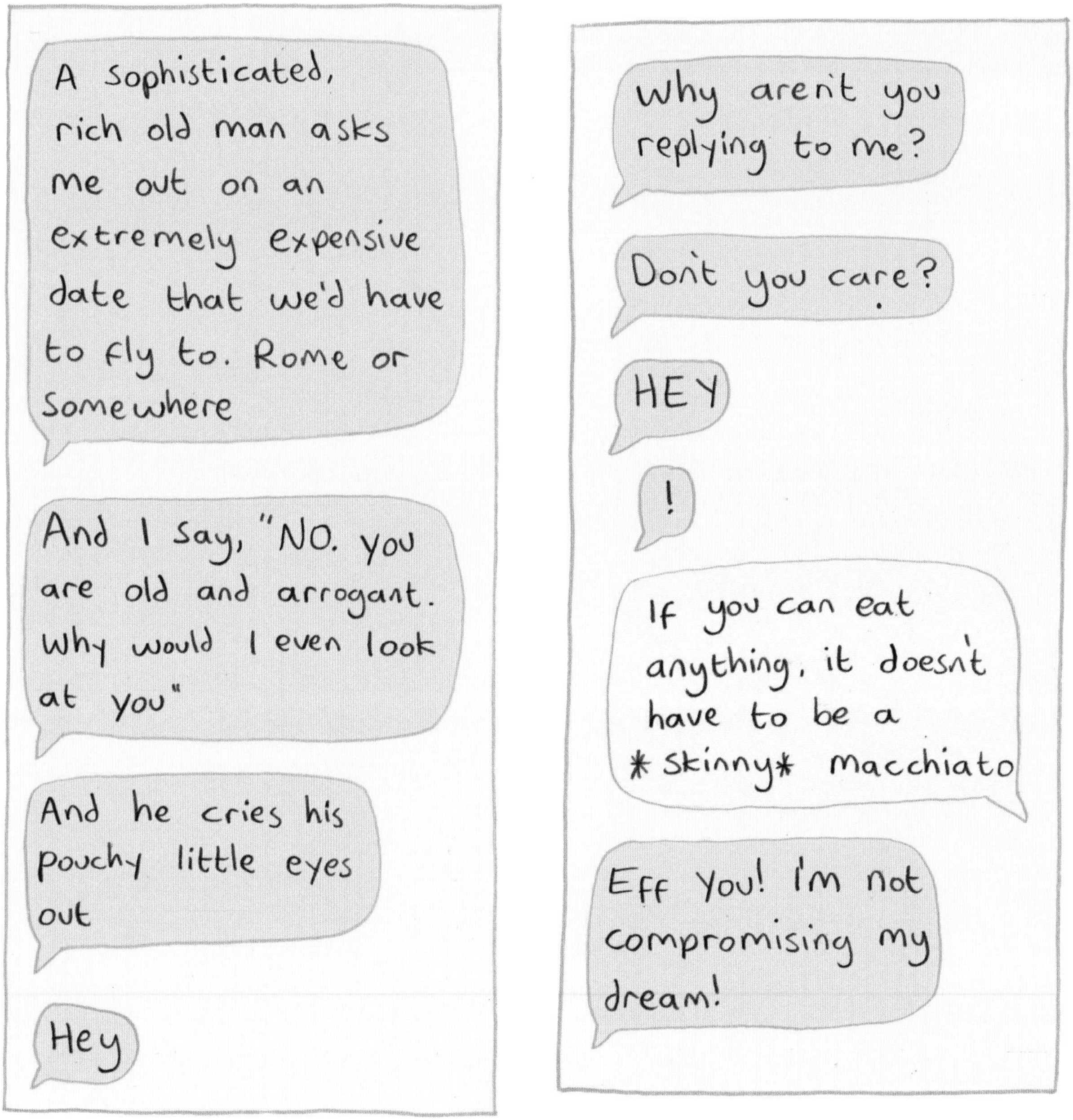
A sophisticated, rich old man asks me out on an extremely expensive date that we'd have to fly to. Rome or Somewhere
And I say, "NO. you are old and arrogant. Why would I even look at you"
And he cries his pouchy little eyes out
Hey
Why aren't you replying to me?
Don't you care?
HEY
!
If you can eat anything, it doesn't have to be a *skinny* macchiato
Eff You! I'm not compromising my dream!

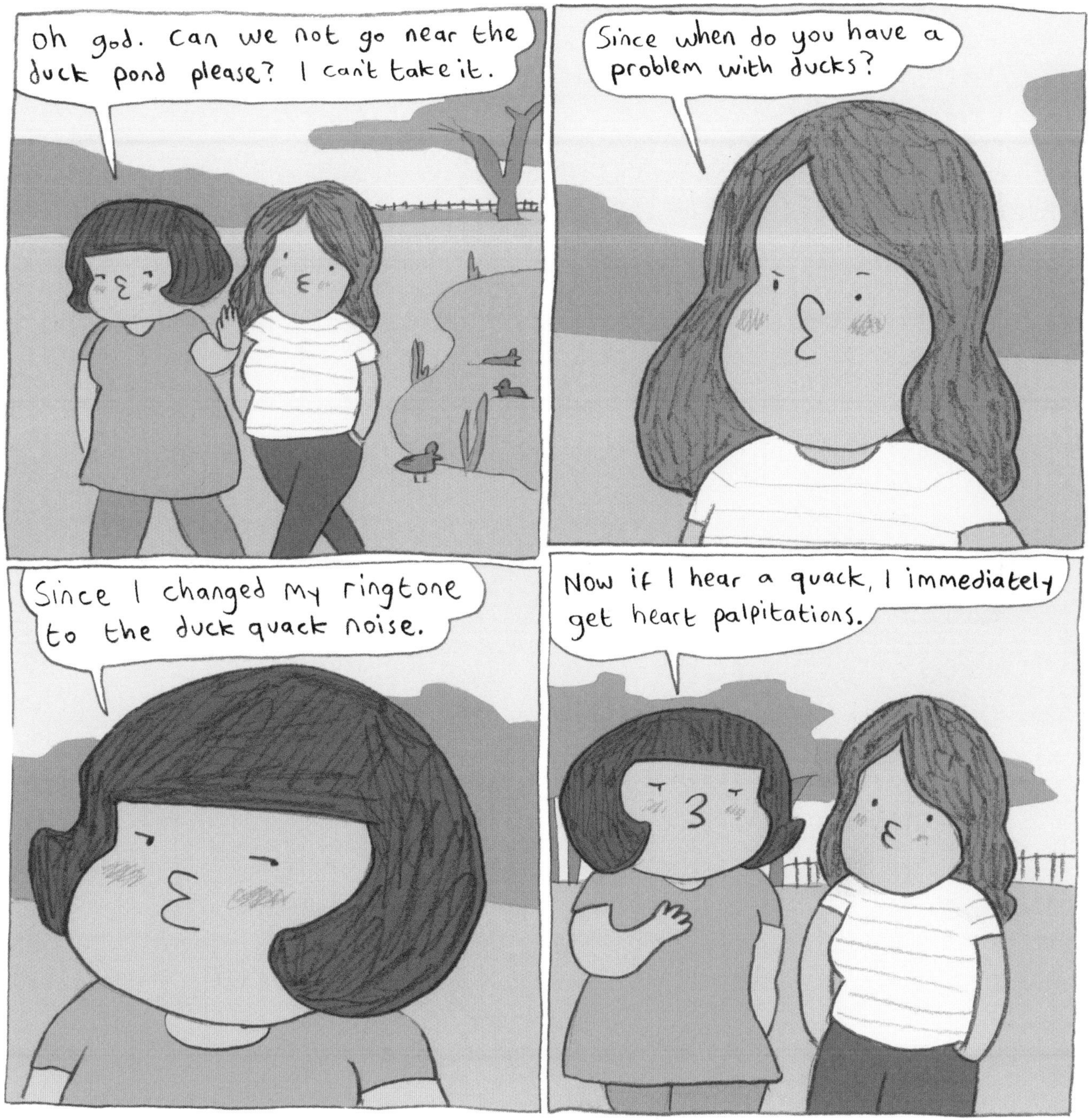
Oh god. Can we not go near the duck pond please? I can't take it.
Since when do you have a problem with ducks?
Since I changed my ringtone to the duck quack noise.
Now if I hear a quack, I immediately get heart palpitations.

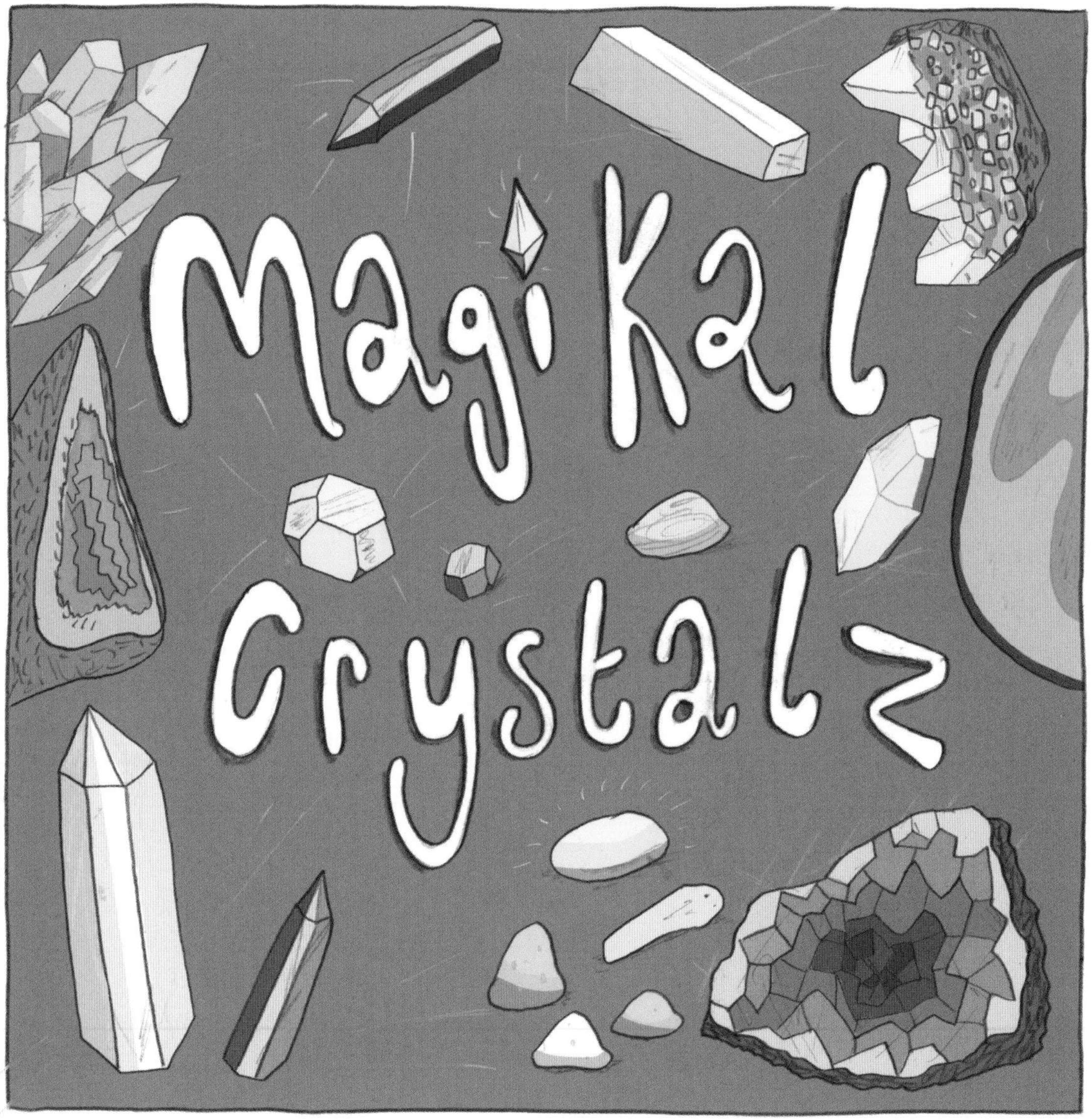
Magikal
Crystalz

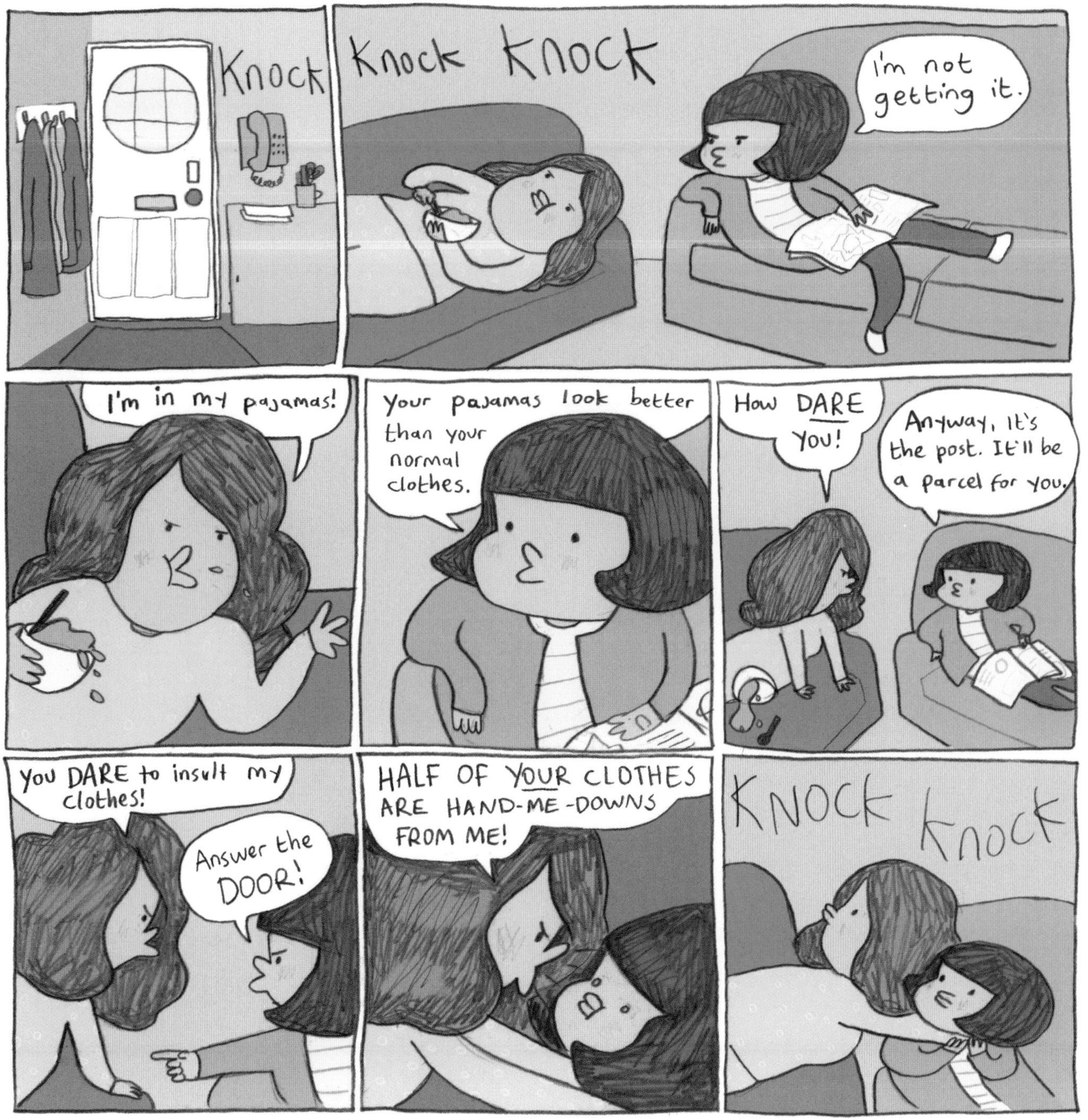
Knock
Knock Knock
I'm not getting it.
I'm in my pajamas!
Your pajamas look better than your normal clothes.
How DARE you!
Anyway, it's the post. It'll be a parcel for you.
You DARE to insult my clothes!
Answer the DOOR!
HALF OF YOUR CLOTHES ARE HAND-ME-DOWNS FROM ME!
KNOCK knock

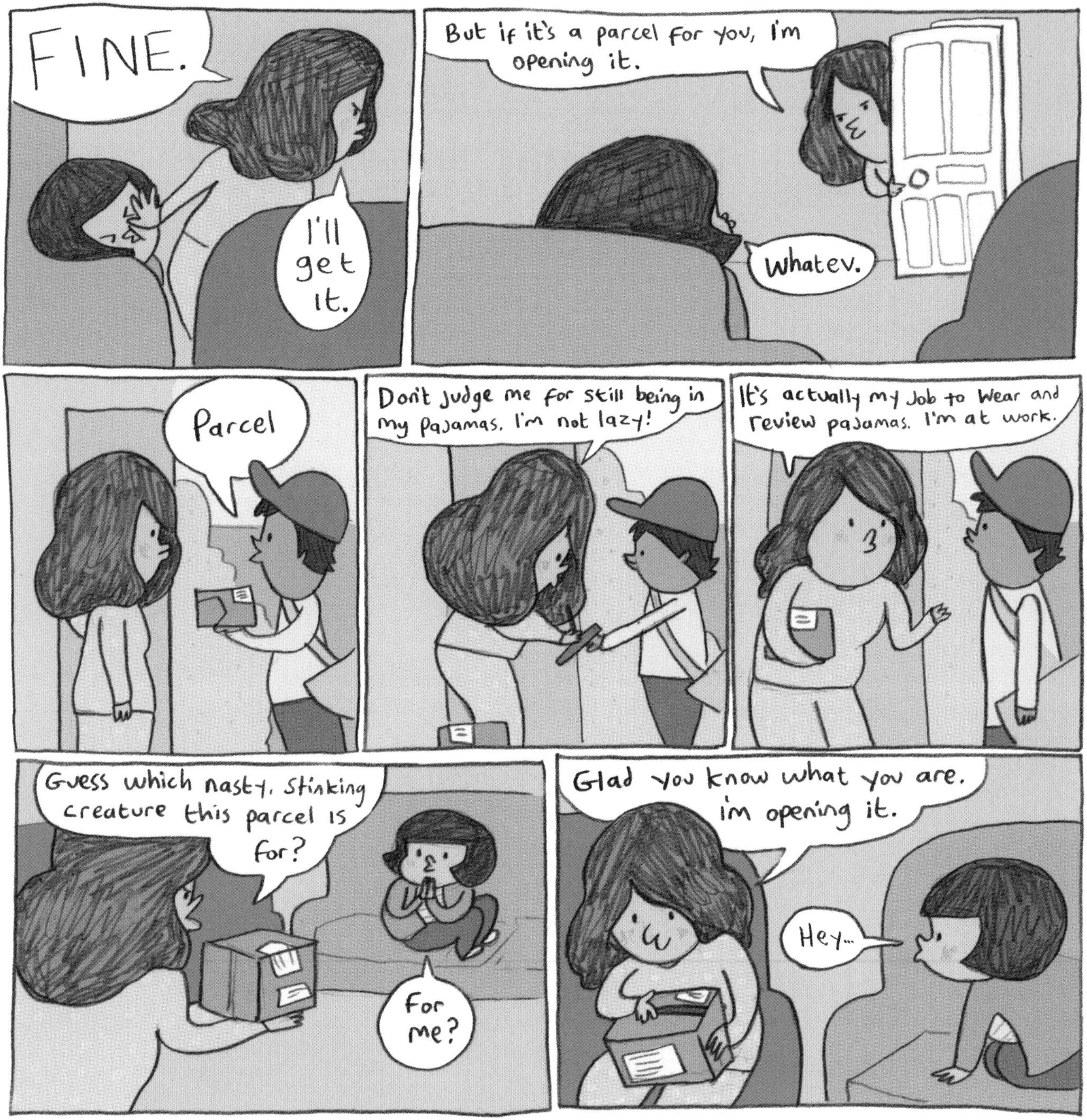
FINE.
I'll get it.
But if it's a parcel for you, I'm opening it.
Whatev.
Parcel
Don't judge me for still being in my pajamas. I'm not lazy!
It's actually my job to wear and review pajamas. I'm at work.
Guess which nasty, stinking creature this parcel is for?
For me?
Glad you know what you are. im opening it.
Hey...

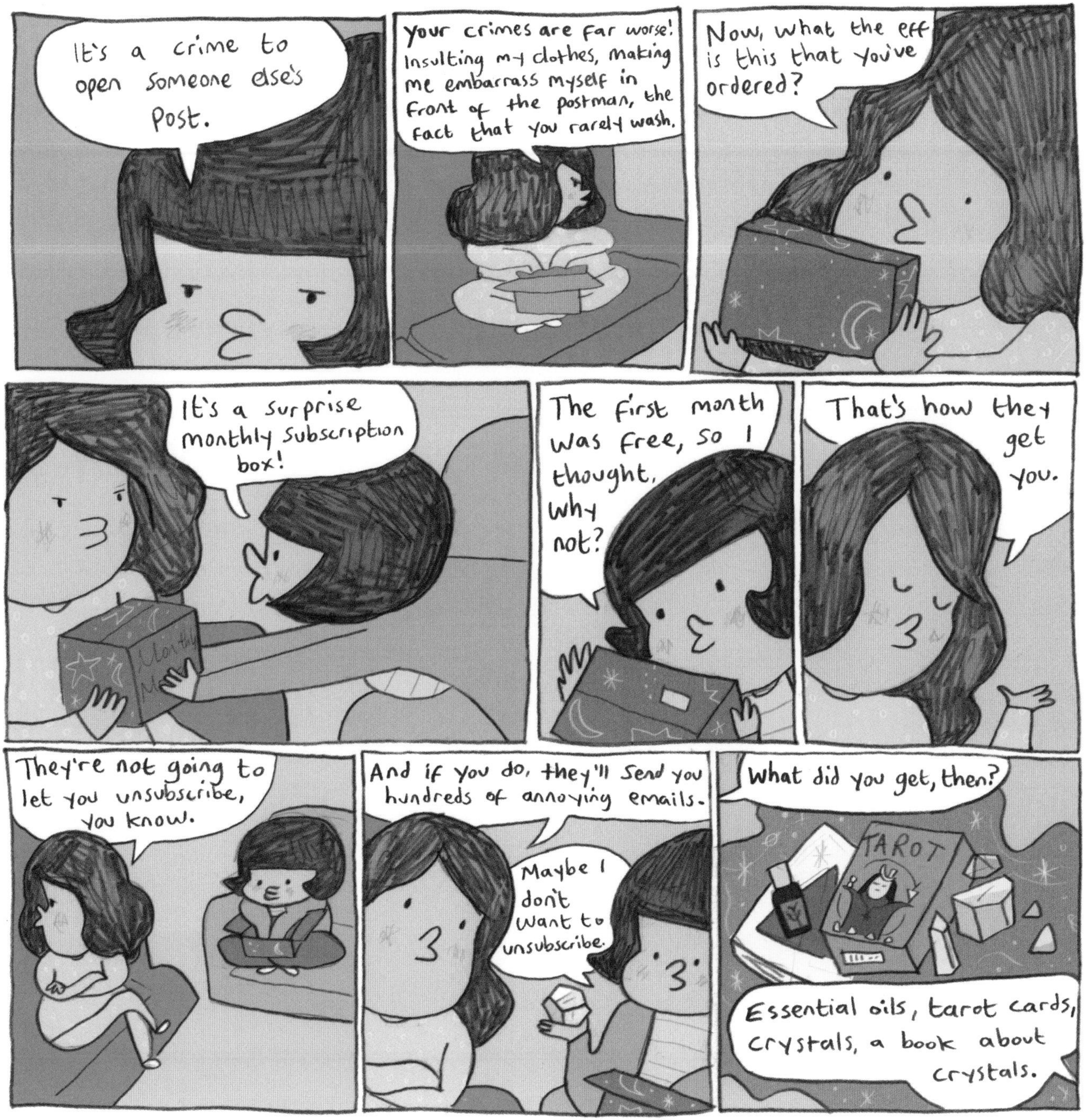
It's a crime to open someone else's post.
Your crimes are far worse! Insulting my clothes, making me embarrass myself in front of the postman, the fact that you rarely wash.
Now, what the eff is this that you've ordered?
It's a surprise monthly subscription box!
The first month was free, so I thought, why not?
That's how they get you.
They're not going to let you unsubscribe, you know.
And if you do, they'll send you hundreds of annoying emails.
Maybe I don't want to unsubscribe.
What did you get, then?
TAROT
Essential oils, tarot cards, crystals, a book about crystals.

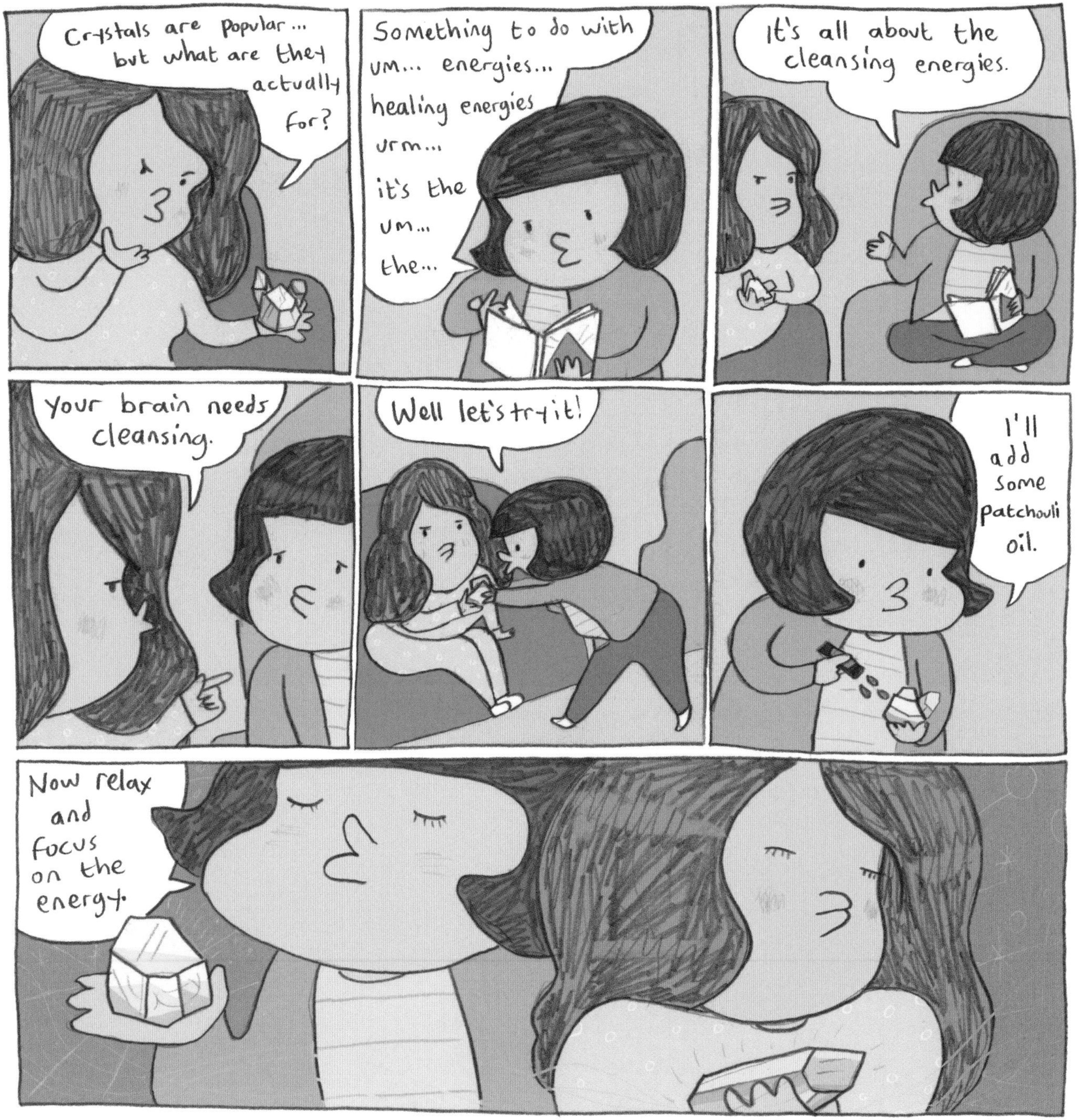
Crystals are popular... but what are they actually for?
Something to do with um... energies... healing energies urm... it's the um... the...
It's all about the cleansing energies.
Your brain needs cleansing.
Well let's try it!
I'll add some patchouli oil.
Now relax and focus on the energy.

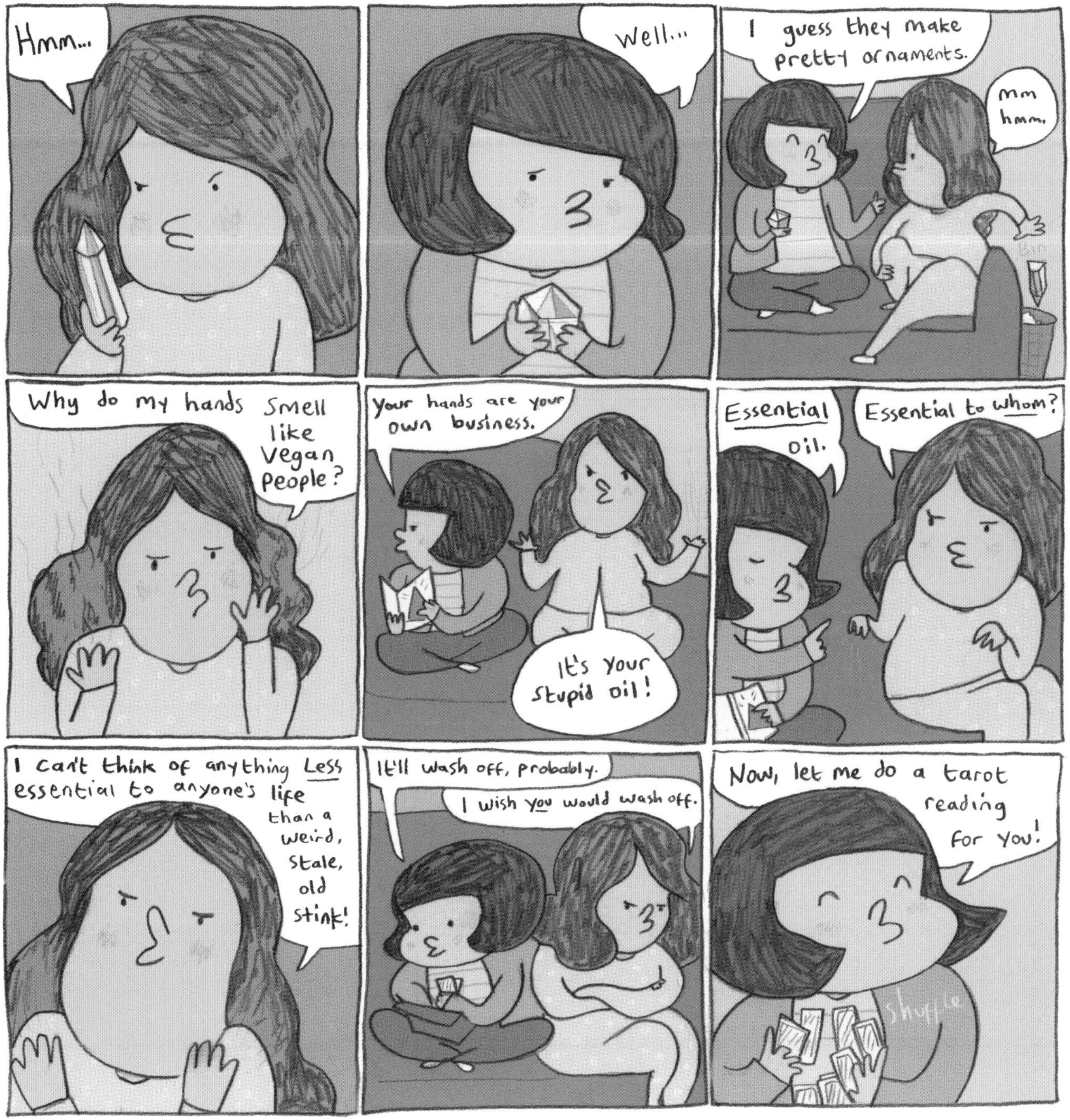
Hmm...
Well...
I guess they make pretty ornaments.
Mm hmm.
Why do my hands smell like vegan people?
Your hands are your own business.
It's your stupid oil!
Essential oil.
Essential to whom?
I can't think of anything less essential to anyone's life than a weird, stale, old stink!
It'll wash off, probably.
I wish you would wash off.
Now, let me do a tarot reading for you!
shuffle

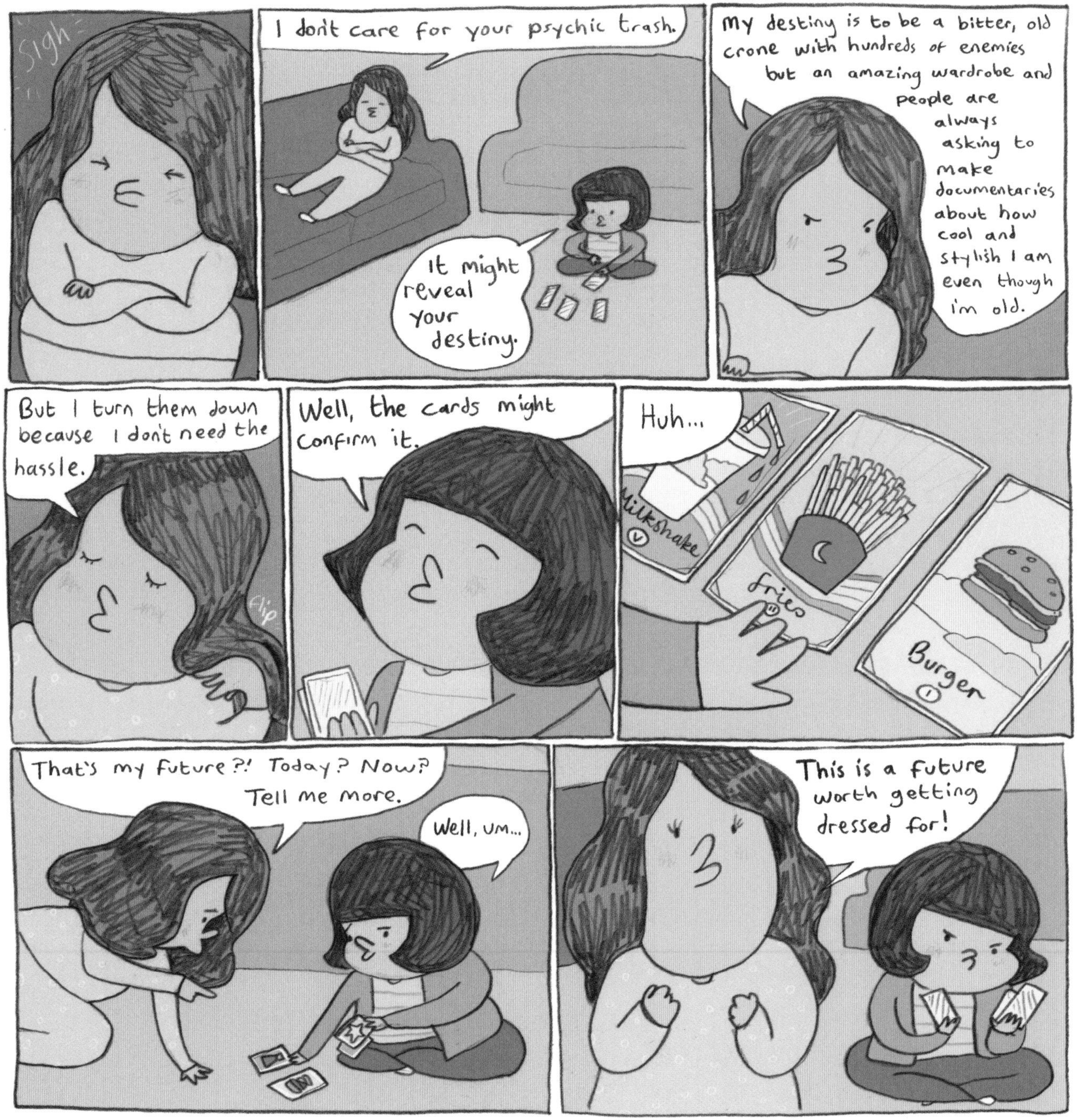
Sigh
I don't care for your psychic trash.
It might reveal your destiny.
My destiny is to be a bitter, old crone with hundreds of enemies but an amazing wardrobe and people are always asking to make documentaries about how cool and stylish I am even though I'm old.
But I turn them down because I don't need the hassle.
Flip
Well, the cards might confirm it.
Huh...
Milkshake
Fries
Burger
That's my future?! Today? Now? Tell me more.
Well, um...
This is a future worth getting dressed for!

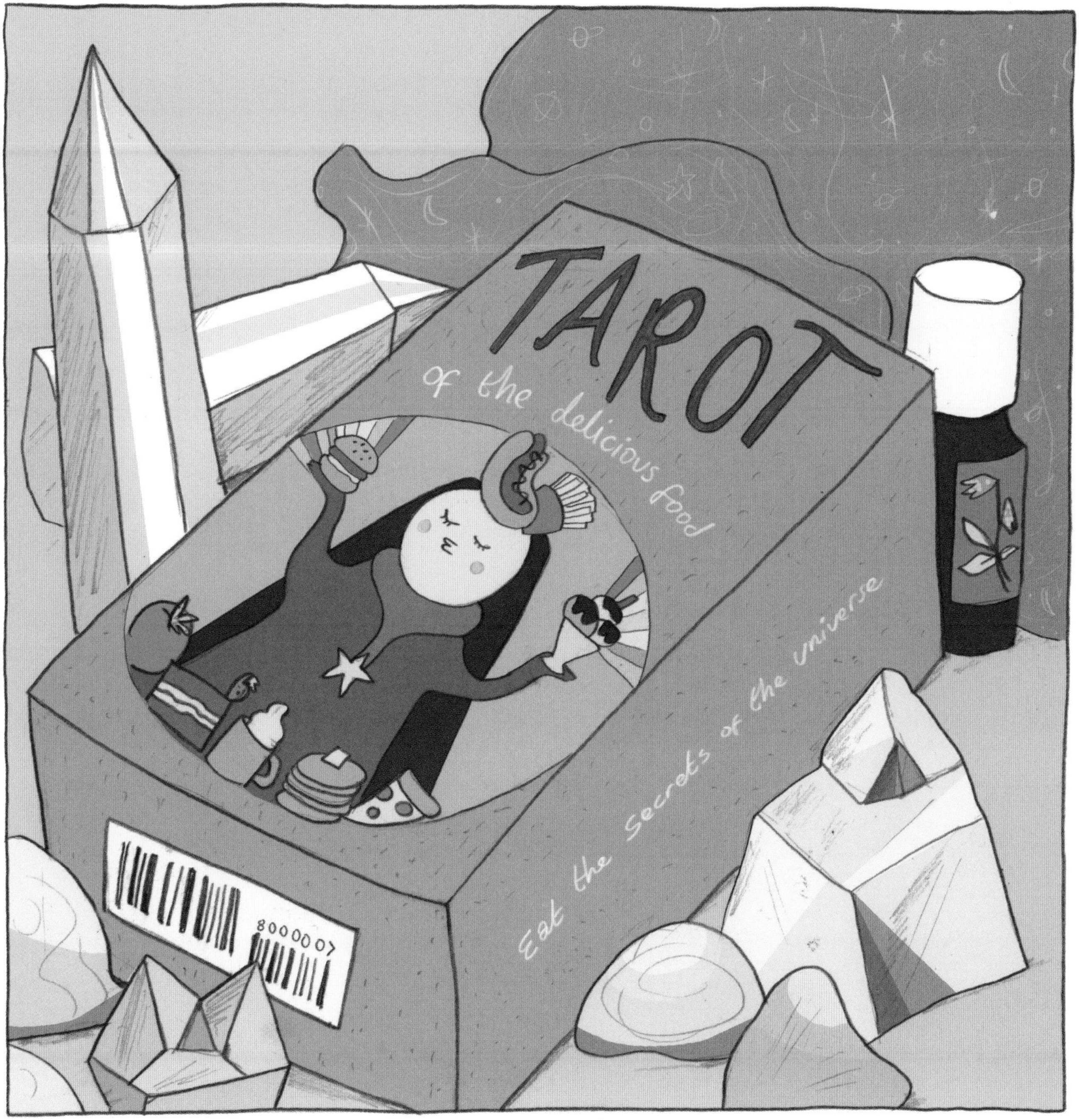
TAROT
of the delicious food
Eat the secrets of the universe
800000

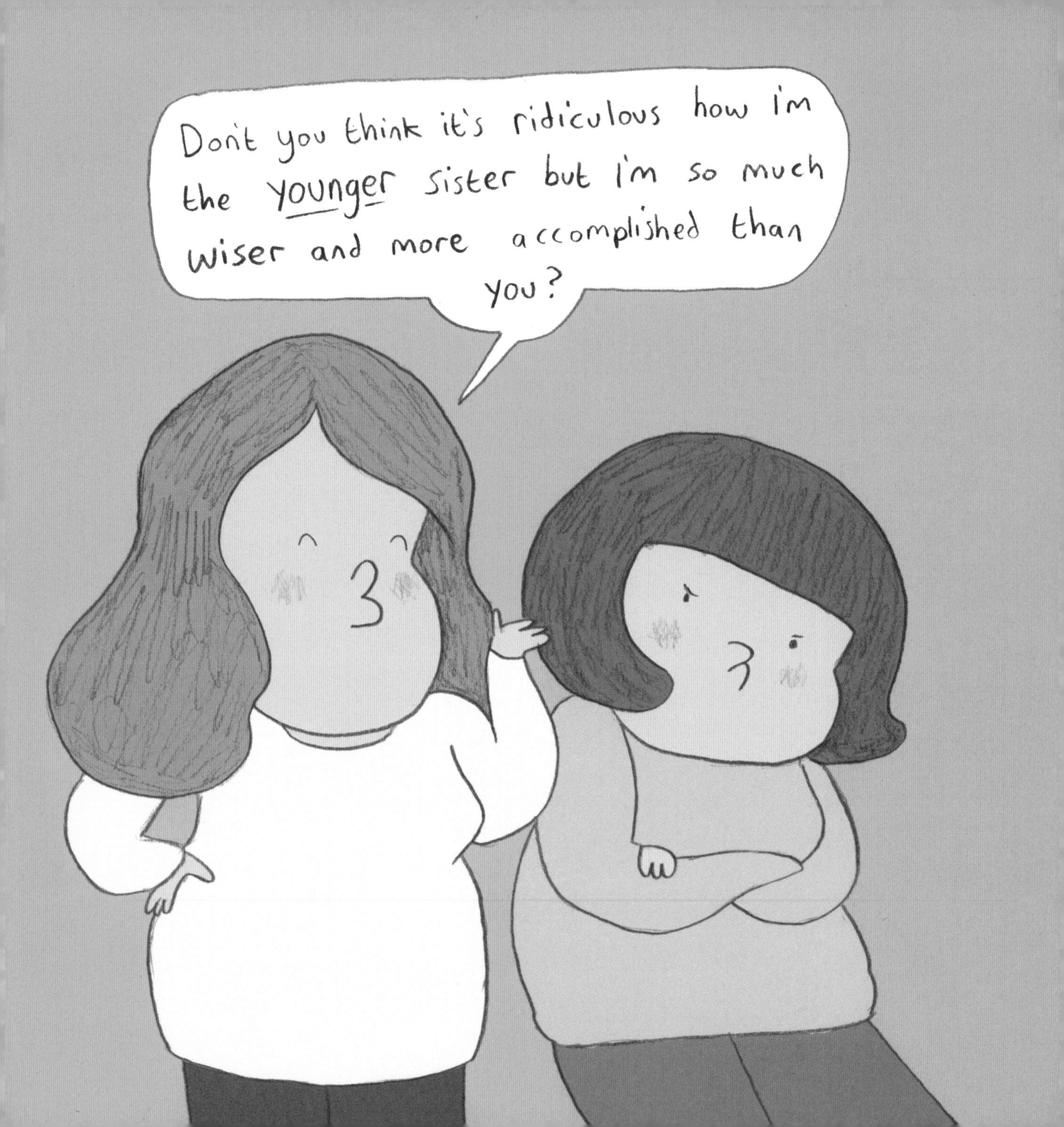
Don't you think it's ridiculous how I'm the YOUNGER sister but I'm so much wiser and more accomplished than you?

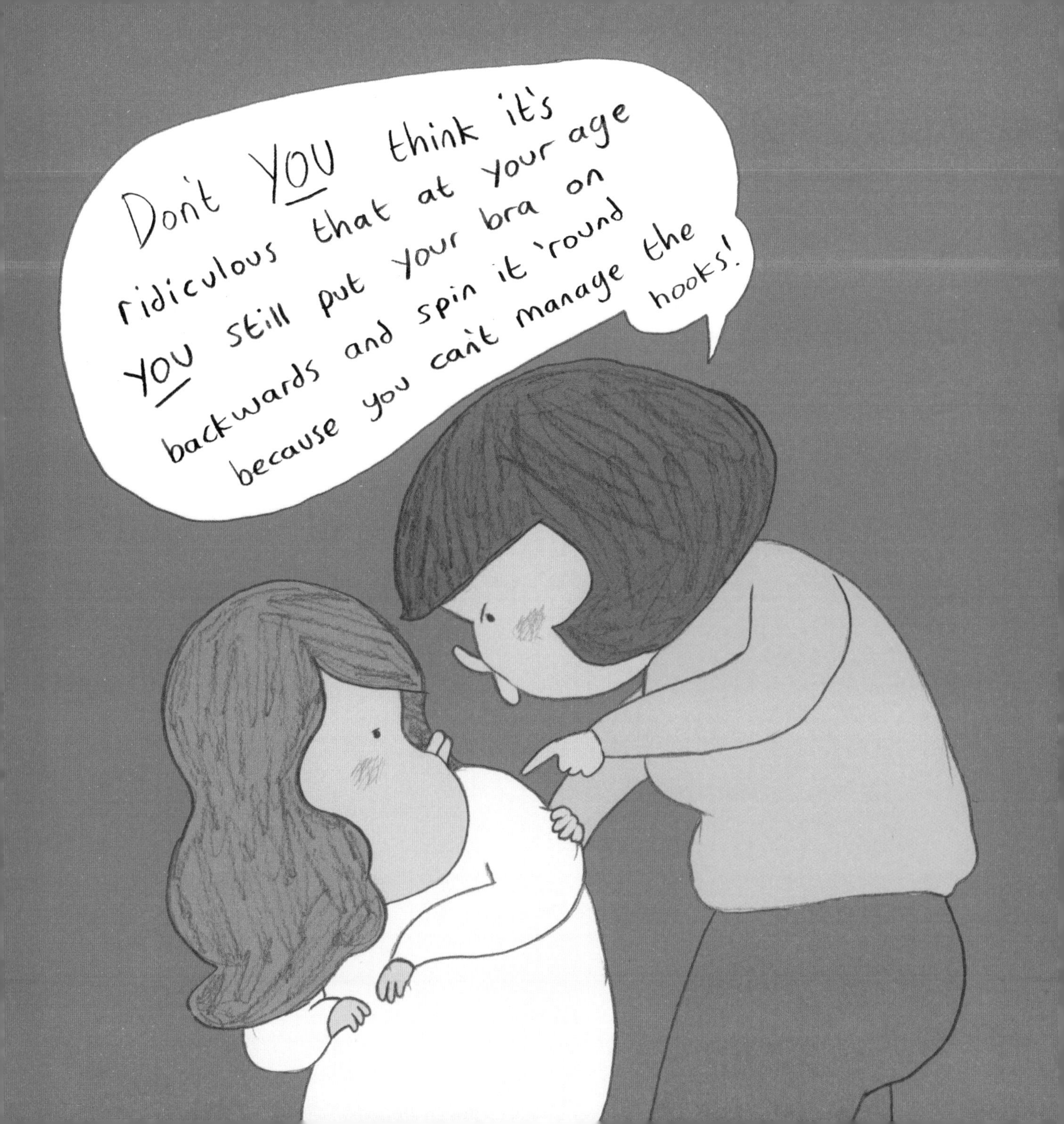
Don't YOU think it's ridiculous that at your age YOU still put your bra on backwards and spin it 'round because you can't manage the hooks!

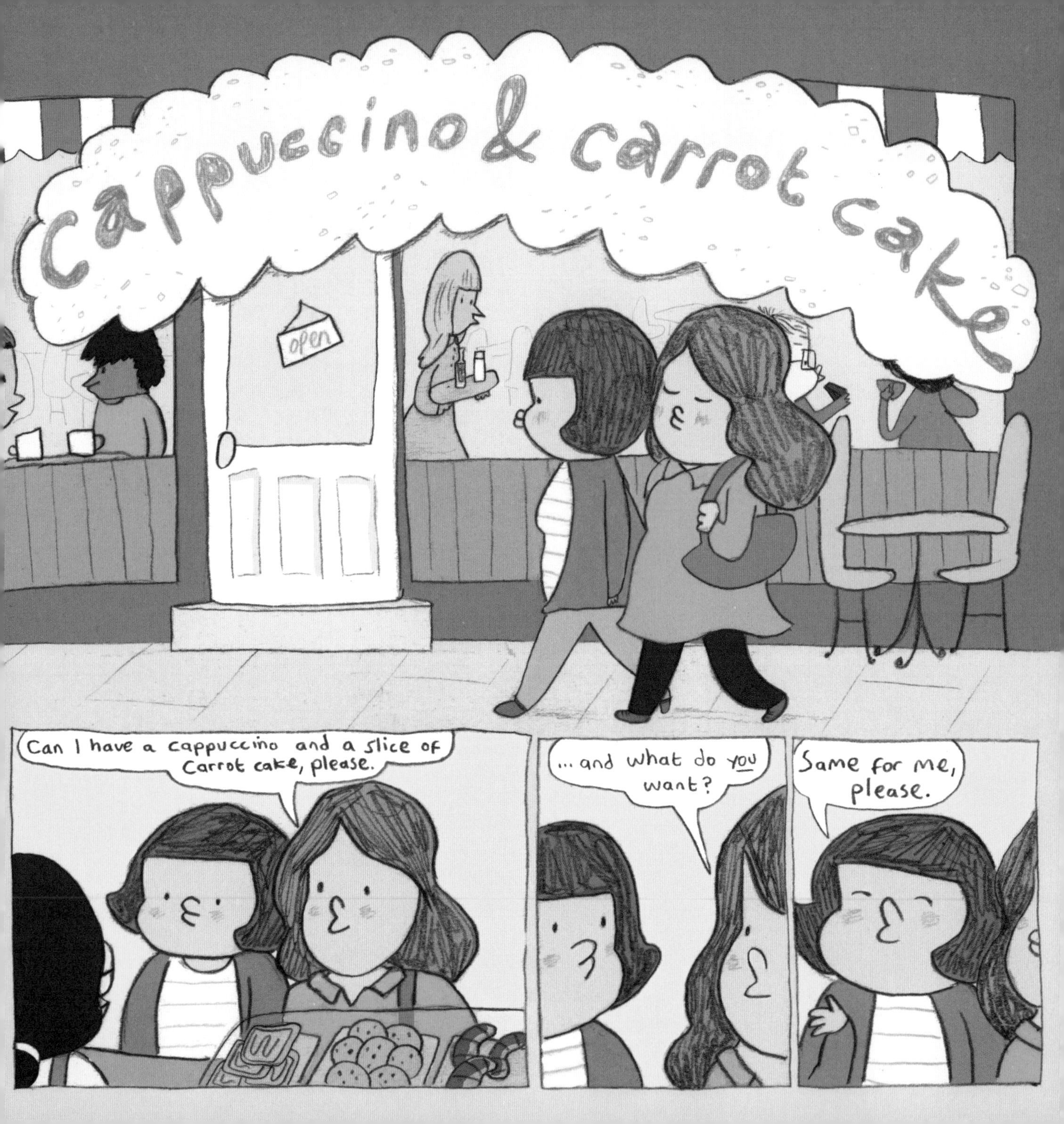
Cappuccino & carrot cake
open
Can I have a cappuccino and a slice of Carrot cake, please.
... and what do you want?
Same for me, please.

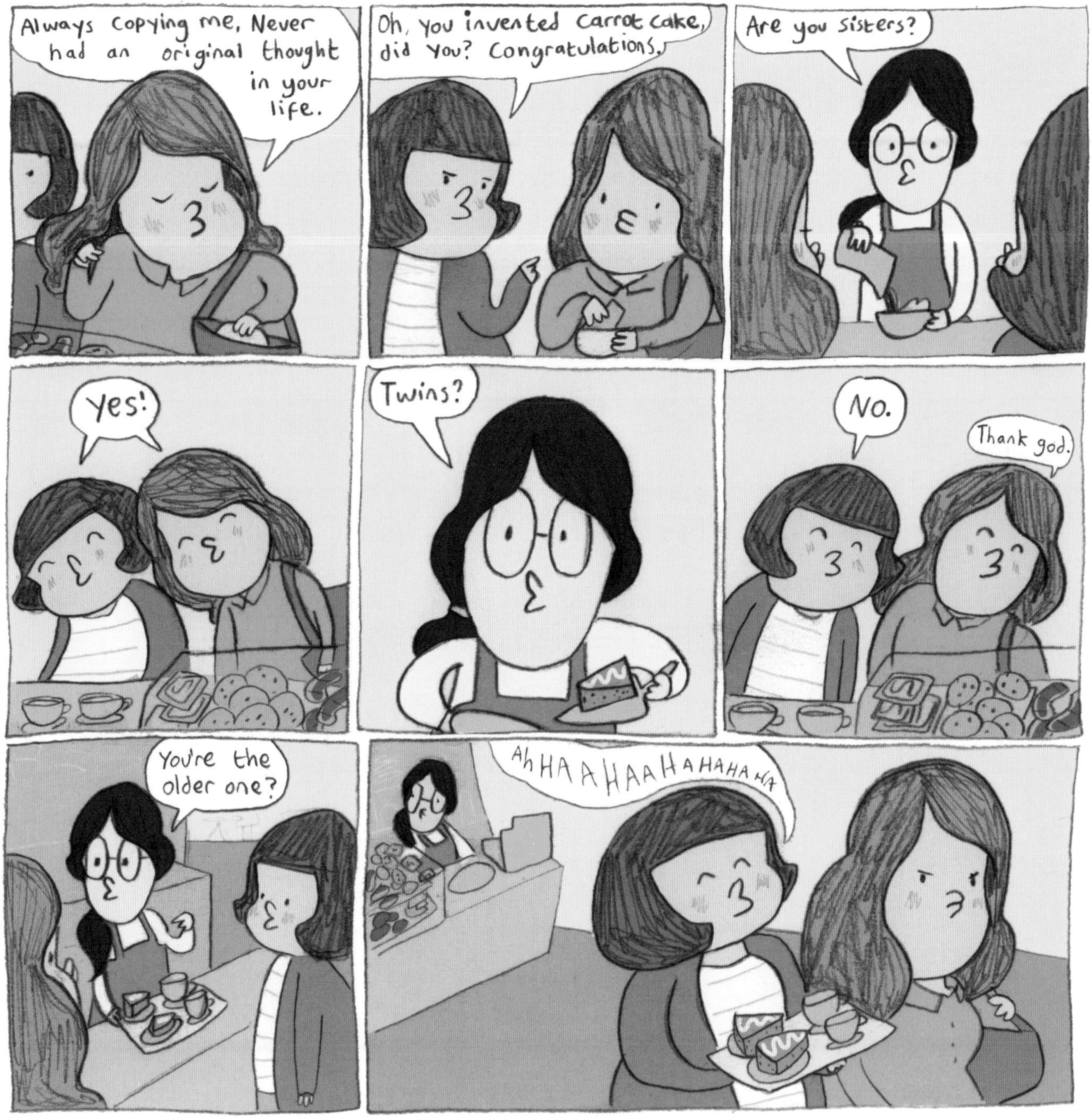
Always copying me, Never had an original thought in your life.
Oh, you invented carrot cake, did you? Congratulations.
Are you sisters?
yes!
Twins?
No.
Thank god.
You're the older one?
AhHAAHAAHAHAHAHA

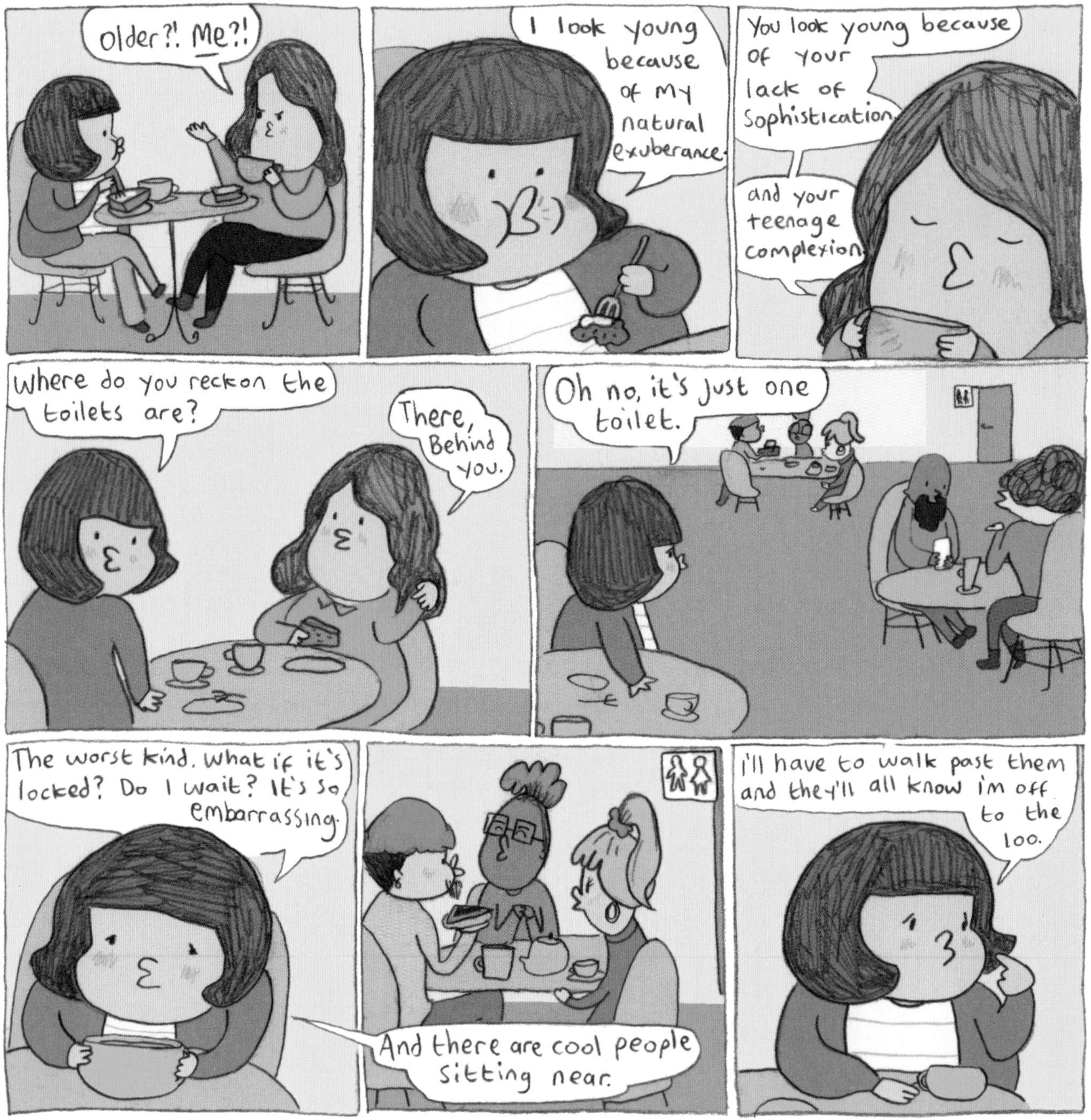
Older?! Me?!
I look young because of my natural exuberance.
You look young because of your lack of sophistication
and your teenage complexion.
Where do you reckon the toilets are?
There, Behind you.
Oh no, it's just one toilet.
The worst kind. What if it's locked? Do I wait? It's so embarrassing.
And there are cool people sitting near.
I'll have to walk past them and they'll all know I'm off to the loo.

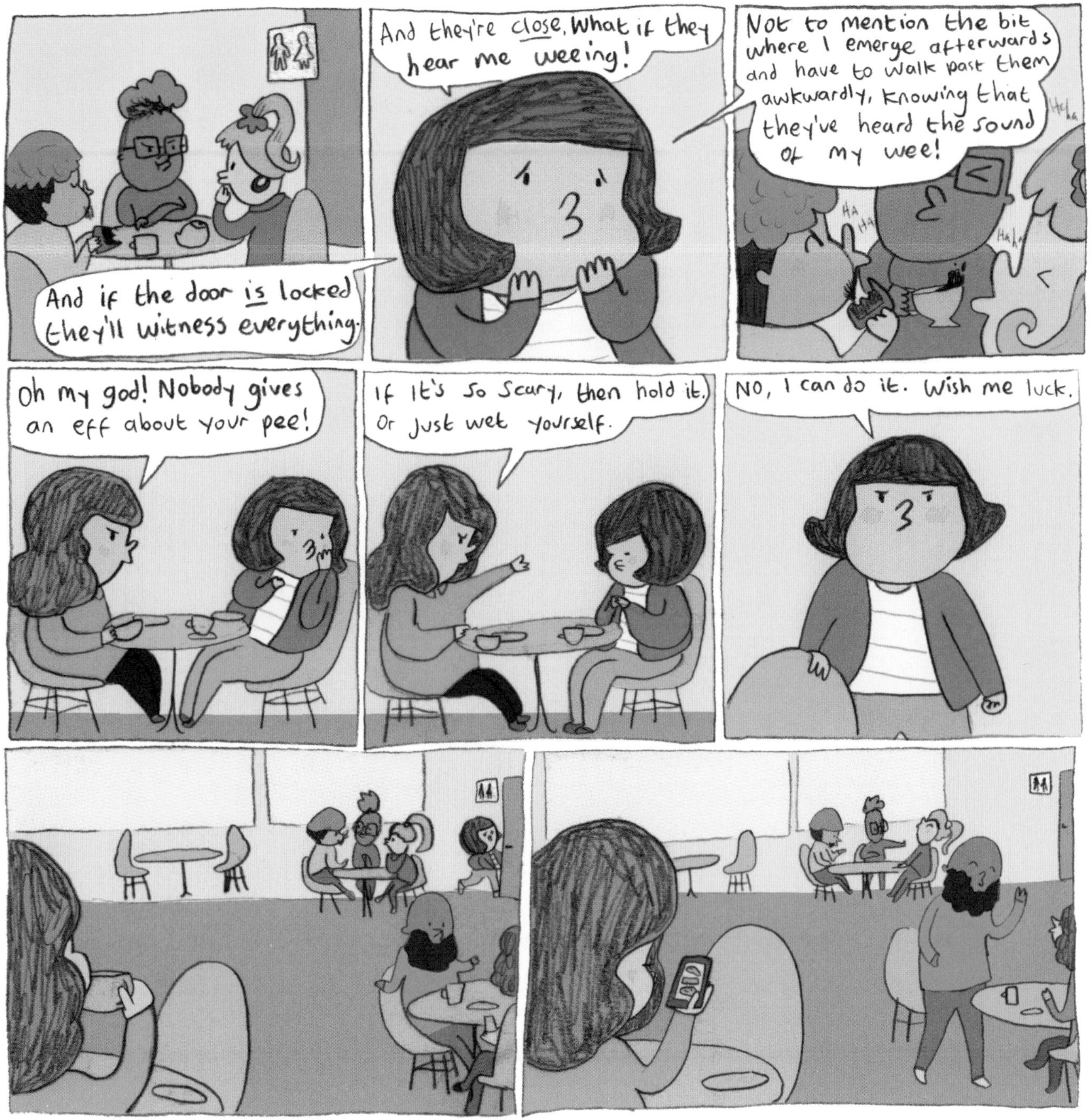
And if the door is locked they'll witness everything.
And they're close. What if they hear me weeing!
Not to mention the bit where I emerge afterwards and have to walk past them awkwardly, knowing that they've heard the sound of my wee!
HA HA
Ha ha
Oh my god! Nobody gives an eff about your pee!
If it's so scary, then hold it. Or just wet yourself.
No, I can do it. Wish me luck.

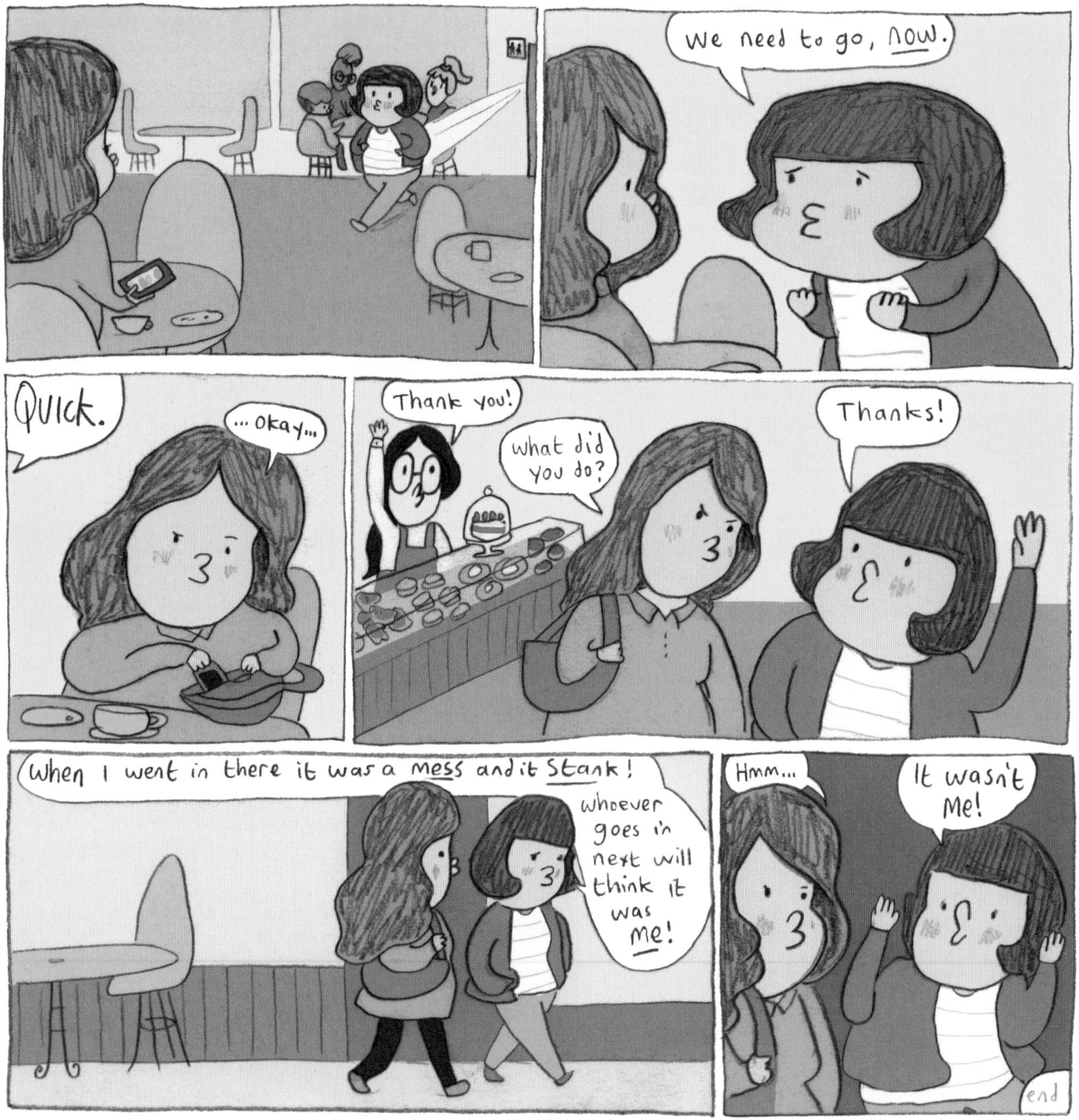
We need to go, NOW.
QUICK.
... okay...
Thank you!
what did you do?
Thanks!
When I went in there it was a mess and it stank!
whoever goes in next will think it was me!
Hmm...
It wasn't me!
end

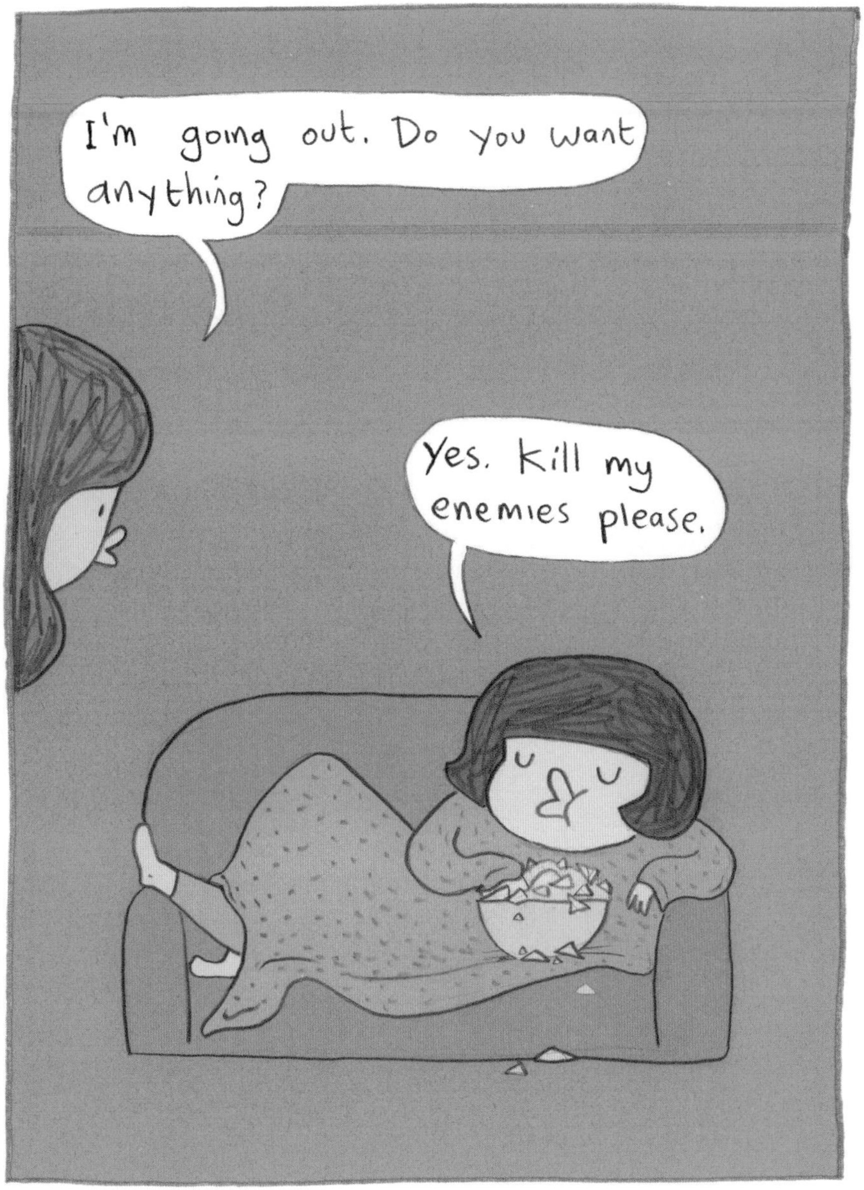
I'm going out. Do you want anything?
Yes. Kill my enemies please.

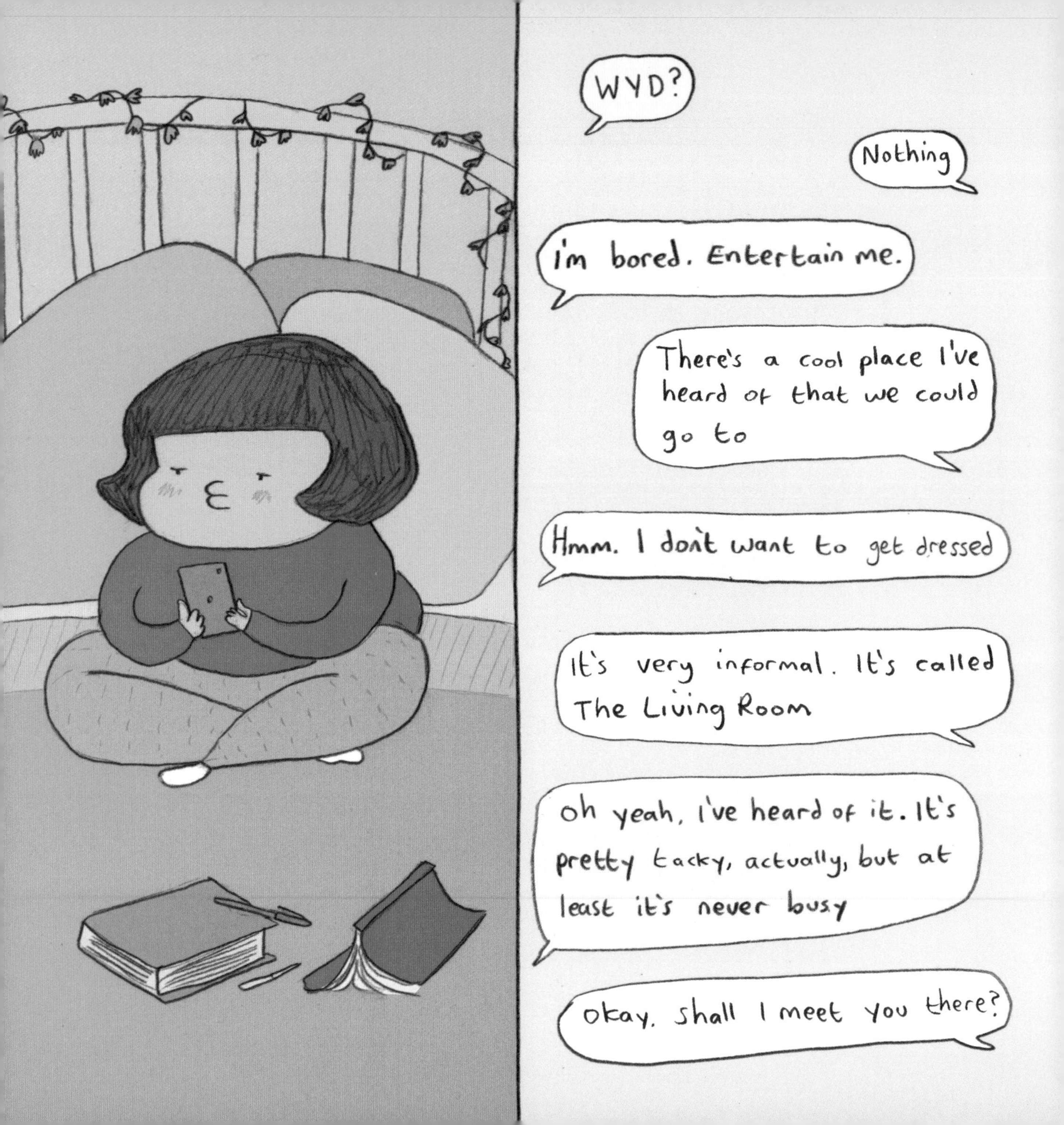
WYD?
Nothing
i'm bored. Entertain me.
There's a cool place I've heard of that we could go to
Hmm. I don't want to get dressed
It's very informal. It's called The Living Room
oh yeah, i've heard of it. It's pretty tacky, actually, but at least it's never busy
okay. Shall I meet you there?

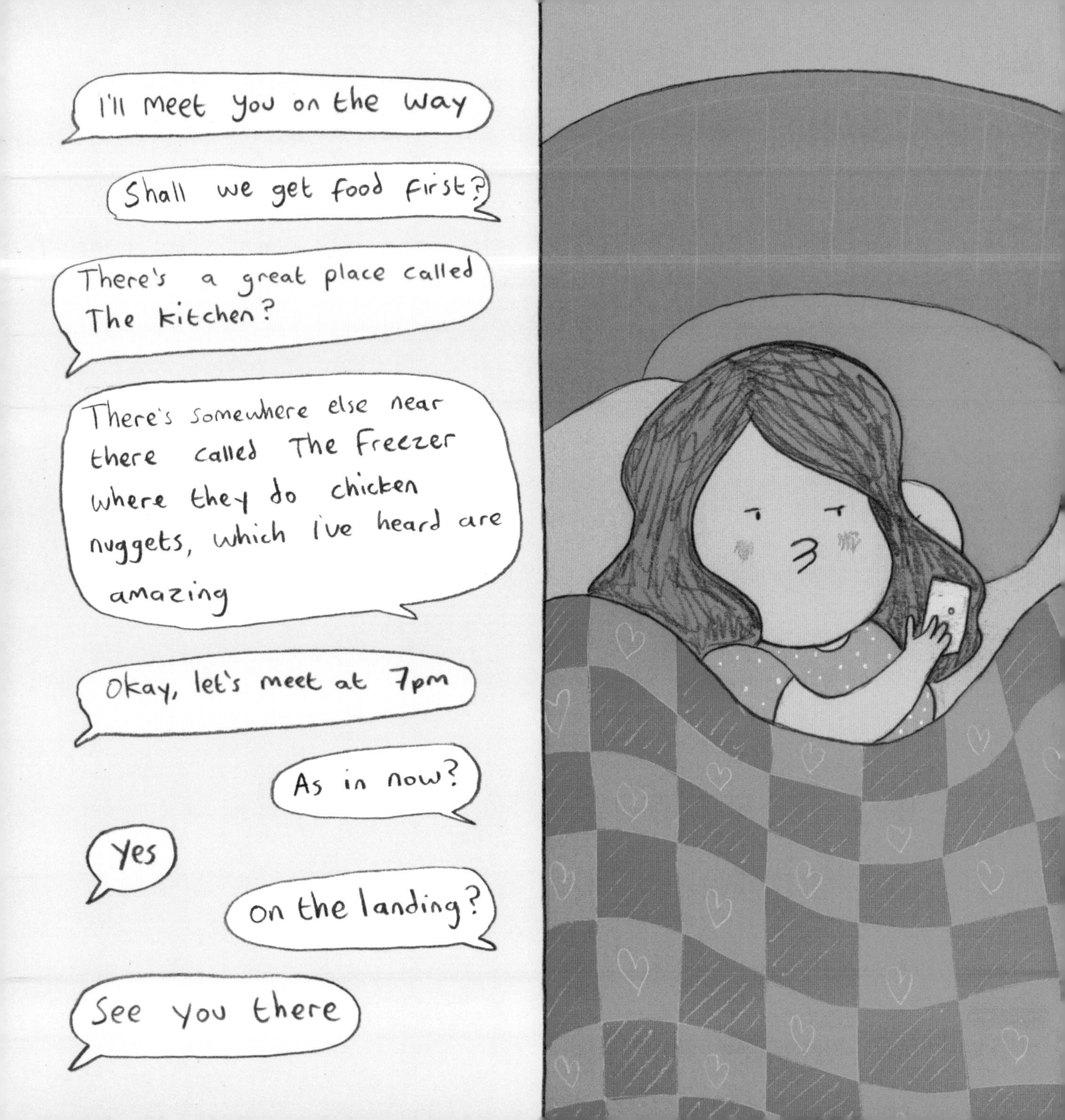
I'll meet you on the way
Shall we get food first?
There's a great place called The kitchen?
There's somewhere else near there called The Freezer where they do chicken nuggets, which I've heard are amazing
Okay, let's meet at 7pm
As in now?
Yes
on the landing?
See you there

Philippa Rice is a sassy, independent woman who makes comics, animations, and illustrations, including her autobiographical romantic book, SOPPY, stop-motion crochet characters, and webcomic, My Cardboard Life

Andrews McMeel Publishing
a division of Andrews McMeel Universal
1130 Walnut Street, Kansas City, Missouri 64106

www.andrewsmcmeel.com

18 19 20 21 22 SDB 10 9 8 7 6 5 4 3 2 1

ISBN: 978-1-4494-8935-9

Library of Congress Control Number: 2018933439

Editor: Patty Rice
Art Director: Holly Swayne
Production Editor: Elizabeth A. Garcia
Production Manager: Tamara Haus

ATTENTION: SCHOOLS AND BUSINESSES
Andrews McMeel books are available at quantity discounts with bulk purchase
for educational, business, or sales promotional use. For information,
please e-mail the Andrews McMeel Publishing Special Sales Department:
specialsales@amuniversal.com.

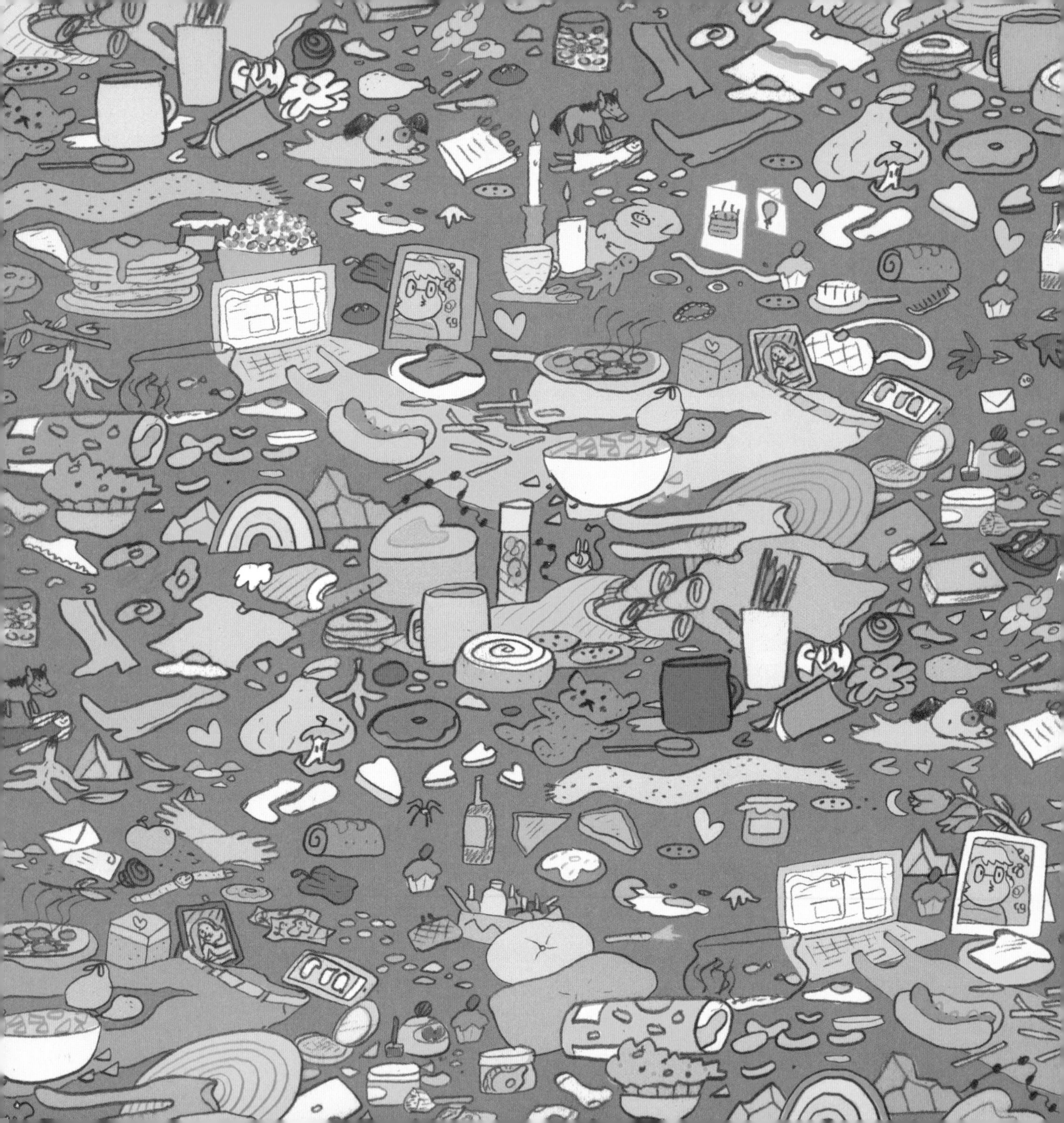